# THE MATHESON MONOGRAPHS

The principal objective of the Matheson Trust is to promote the study of comparative religion from the point of view of the underlying harmony of the great religious and philosophical traditions of the world. This objective is being pursued through such means as audio-visual media, the support and sponsorship of lecture series and conferences, the creation of a website, collaboration with film production companies and publishing companies as well as the Trust's own series of publications.

The Matheson Monographs will cover a wide range of themes within the field of comparative religion: scriptural exegesis in different religious traditions; the modalities of spiritual and contemplative life; in-depth mystical studies of particular religious traditions; broad comparative analyses taking in a series of religious forms; studies of traditional arts, crafts and cosmological science; and contemporary scholarly expositions of religious philosophy and metaphysics. The monographs will also comprise translations of both classical and contemporary texts, as well as transcriptions of lectures by, and interviews with, spiritual and scholarly authorities from different religious and philosophical traditions.

# LOUIS MASSIGNON

# LOUIS MASSIGNON

## The Vow and the Oath

## Patrick Laude

Translated from a revised and augmented version of
*Massignon intérieur* (Lausanne: L'Âge d'Homme, 2001)
by Edin Q. Lohja

THE MATHESON TRUST
For the Study of Comparative Religion

© The Matheson Trust, 2011

The Matheson Trust
PO Box 336
56 Gloucester Road
London SW7 4UB, UK
http://themathesontrust.org

ISBN: 978 1 908092 06 9 paper

British Library Cataloguing-in-Publication Data.
A catalogue record for this book is
available from the British Library

# CONTENTS

To Seyyed Hossein Nasr who gave the spark,
and Jacques Keryell, who fed the fire.

# INTRODUCTION

The life and work of Louis Massignon (1883-1962) are informed, oriented and determined by the sense of the Absolute. For him, the truth is always situated beyond the relativity of concepts and actions which might reduce one's relationship with the Absolute to a vain philosophy or a mere contract of good conduct with Heaven. This uncompromising sense of the Absolute constitutes without any doubt the major affinity connecting Massignon to Islam. The grammatical structure of the type *ce n'est pas ... c'est*[1]—so representative of Massignon's style —is akin to a spiritual sympathy at once profound and subtle: it echoes as a leitmotif the *nafy* (negation) and *ithbāt* (affirmation) of the *shahādah*, the profession of faith in Islam.[2] Thus everything is negated that could be erected or construed as an object of worship, in order to clear the ground for the witnessing of the One Reality. The Massignonian approach is therefore fundamentally oriented towards the inner truth of the soul and the ultimate Object of its love.

In a world where ideas and actions are often evaluated by standards of flat literality or in their relation with slogans and conventions which limit their meaning to easily marketable and

---

[1] Below, we quote a few typical examples gleaned from Massignon's work: "Man is not made for works of external mercy, but first of all to worship the divine Guest in his heart, in the present moment." "Time is therefore not a continuous duration, but a constellation of instants." "Understanding the Bible does not mean unifying as we please, by way of new theories, meanings which are parcelled out beforehand in contraposition, but rather to go back to the purest unity of intention that inspired it...."

[2] Let us recall that the first part of the testimony of faith in Islam, *lā ilāha illa 'Llāh* (no god but God), is based on a marked contrast between the negation (*nafy*) of idols and vanities, and the affirmation (*ithbāt*) of the Divine as the only Reality.

reassuring formulae, an unconditional pilgrim of the Absolute such as Massignon could not but run the risk of being misunderstood. From this point of view, Massignon may be deemed to be in spiritual consonance with the *khadiriyyah*[3] inspiration (to which he would devote a good number of pages), the gentle breeze of the solitary initiator—*al-Khidr* ("the Verdant"), in the sense of being quite often misunderstood and isolated, frequently considered as barely "orthodox" or even "scandalous", precisely because he strove to find his spiritual bearings in accordance with the heart and the divine *fiat*, according to the Spirit and not the letter. In the Church, he was like a "Muslim", misunderstood and feared by many, an "exalted" idealist who had no sense of the contingent social "realities", and little consideration for the European and North American "civilising genius" with which representatives of Western Christianity have so often and repeatedly compromised the message of the Gospel. He became a Melkite priest in order to remain faithful to the Abrahamic transcendence, one of the highest witnesses of which was, for him, the Arabic language. Thus he remained within the Church, as an "oriental Catholic", in a position of marginal, almost exiled, integration. In Islam, he was not infrequently considered a spy or a proselytiser, an ambiguous presence intent on subverting Islam in order to Christianise it from within. His spiritual marginality, founded as it was on the unconditional choice of the Absolute and of Justice, was also manifested in his affinity with spiritual figures, schools and movements of an atypical character, like Hallāj, Salmān al-Fārsī, extremist Shī'ites, French legitimists; it also manifested visibly in his mystical apology of women as martyrs of the Spirit; not that all of these tendencies were expressed by virtue of a certain complacent curiosity *vis-à-vis* his own idiosyncratic characteristics, but rather in accordance with an indelible inner mark.

This book is not a biography, nor even a spiritual portrait, of Louis Massignon. Experts and friends of Louis Massignon

---

[3] We are referring here to the universal initiator and mysterious spiritual guide al-Khidr (or al-Khadir), whom Sufism associates with the freedom of the Spirit "which bloweth where it listeth".

have had the great merit of providing us with comprehensive and insightful works of such a kind, such as Jean Moncelon and Christian Destremau's *Louis Massignon: Le "cheikh admirable"* (Le Capucin, 2005) and Jacques Keryell's *Louis Massignon: De Bagdad au jardin d'une parole extasiée* (Angers, 2008) in French, and Mary-Louise Gude's *Louis Massignon: The Crucible of Compassion* (University of Notre Dame Press, 1997) in English. Our purpose is different, albeit parallel in spirit: it aims at exploring the inner dimensions of Massignon's work and suggesting the spiritual coherence of its intricate landscape. In quest of this inward dimension of the Massignonian opus, our study is oriented by two axes and four poles. There is first of all a dimension which we propose to describe as the formal pole of Massignonian spirituality, his being rooted in the "mythological" and sacramental context of religion, a dimension which manifests itself most directly in the spiritual geography that "consecrates" his mystical point of view. Then there is another pole, which we would characterise as the informal space of inner femininity, that which Massignon himself called, with Thomas Merton, *le point vierge*, the virginal core of human consciousness. Herein lies the seat of a divine "piercing" or "springing up" that radically transcends all traditional "cartography" of the Spirit; it is also the domain *par excellence* of the freedom of the Spirit, and a plunging into the unadulterated purity of one's relationship with God. Finally, with respect to the world, the Massignonian perspective unfolds in two directions, one principally inclusive, and the other exclusive, the first integrating the diverse expressions of the Spirit on the universal horizon of religious truth—an intrinsic unity asymptotically espoused by a desire for God—and the second pitting its inner strength against the illusory idols of the modern world—on the "battlefield" of the crucifying outwardness constructed by the rejection of God. This Massignonian combat is not a superficially conservative or reactionary rejection of the present, but an uncompromising reminder that modernity is most often understood and built as a pretentious substitute for reality, a delighted island of Promethean promises always at the point of being swallowed into the abyss that keeps it in existence *for the moment*. The four chapters of this book are thus conceived as complementary critical explorations of these diverse orientations, in a sort of mystical "cross" which may be deemed to embrace the essentials of the inner landscape of the great French islamicist. In tracing this "cross", our intention is to unfold some of the richest and most profound implications of the two faces of Massignon's life and work, his spiritual secret and his active destiny, the inner sanctity of his "vow" and the outer witnessing of his "oath".

1

# SPIRITUAL SPACE AND AXIAL VOCATION

The importance of the high places of the Spirit in the life and work of Massignon has often been noted. Thus, his whole personal sacred geography retraces the steps of an itinerary that is profoundly one and diverse at the same time. This geography is both objective and subjective—it is based upon the collective data of religious mythology and theurgic imprints of the sacred, while being situated and interpreted in terms of a personal set of spiritual issues. Massignon has sometimes been reproached for speaking basically just about Louis Massignon, finding the reflected image of his own spiritual reality in the mirror of places and beings.[1] What this kind of criticism actually affirms, in spite of itself as it were, is that every exceptional spiritual personality necessarily sheds light on the phenomena which it considers from the vantage point of a personal archetype that manifests in an all the more coherent and all-embracing mode as its "secret" is lived more profoundly. Among the great spiritual figures of the twentieth century, perhaps none has emphasised in such a marked and continuous way as Massignon the spiritual meaning and impact of sacred space, which he conceived as a divine

---

[1] Denis Gril, in his study of the role of spiritual space, stresses the fundamentally idiosyncratic character of Massignon's approach and conclusions in the following words: "In order to display his astonishing personality, he needed all the space of his opus, and to recognise himself [he needed] witnesses reflecting back the image of his passion. His reader remains condemned to perplexity; between him and his research he will find Louis Massignon." "Espace sacré et spiritualité, trois approches: Massignon, Corbin, Guénon," in *D'un Orient l'autre*, Vol. II—Identifications, Paris: CNRS, 1991.

1

"opening" out and above the at once thickened and fragile space of earthly experience. So it is first of all because spiritual space is so to speak "constituted" by sacred hospitality and the recognition of the Other inherent to it. The encounter with the divine or human Other crystallised by the salutation (*al-salām*) opens a symbolical space which is the *templum* of transcendence. During this encounter, language itself reveals its nature of "pilgrimage" as a way of going out of oneself in order to converge with another in the presence of the Divine Absentee.[2] In this sense, the homogeneity of the egoic and "endogamic" space is totally disrupted by a "visitation from the Stranger". This visitation from the Divine by and through a human intermediary is formalised by liturgies and proverbs through a set of gestures and consecrated words.[3] A true meeting is not simply an exchange of formalities, it is a blessing and a prayer. This is what modern expeditiousness fails to understand, when mocking the slow, ceremonial, interminable greetings and "*as-salam 'alaykum*" of traditional people.

It is already intimated that, with Massignon, the mystical concept of a "composition of place"—inherited from Ignatian meditation—takes on a meaning that goes beyond a mere technique of mental meditation. It is not just a matter of conditioning the soul through an imaginary configuration that would provide an adequate psychic framework for formal meditation. In the case of Massignon, the composition of place is rather a way of setting oneself to listen to the spiritual vibrations of a geographical hierophany, so that our own inner voice may converge with that of others whose desire for truth is likewise magnetised by a common place of grace and revelation. In this sense, pil-

---

[2] "For language is both a 'pilgrimage' and a 'spiritual displacement', since a language is not elaborated but to get out of oneself in the direction of another: in order to evoke with him an Absentee, the third person ... the Unknown." "Valeur de la parole humaine en tant que témoignage," (1951), *Opera Minora II*, Paris: Presses Universitaires de France, 1969, p. 581.

[3] "The Salutation is an exodus of pilgrims seeking to conclude a pact of spiritual hospitality, which necessarily associates (since there is no carnal kinship) the liturgy of the rite to invisible presences." "L'involution sémantique du symbole," (1960), *OM II*, p. 627.

grimage is a communion with the "simple hearts" who are unaware of the mental substitutes for the actual visit of sacred sites,
those mental journeys "without the need to get up from one's
chair".[4] Hence, for Massignon, pilgrimage is the only genuine
means of collective sanctification: it is the support *par excellence* of a kind of communal meditation in action. The opening
words *Je reviens de ... où je* ... "I have just come back from ... where
I ...", so typically Massignonian, and reoccurring throughout all
of his works like an obsessively reiterated testimony, expresses
the immediate and concrete hallmark of a spirituality that un-
ceasingly relates to the "incarnating" localisation of the Spirit,
as well as to the dynamics of suffering among faithful masses.
Symptomatically, Massignon likes to draw a contrast between
the two spiritual attitudes that he conceives, in this respect, as
respectively "abstract" and "concrete"; thus, his emphasis upon
the abyss separating the decadent imagination of a Huysmans[5]
before his conversion—the literary and cerebral "carnal" musing
about a place anticipated by a craving for sensual experiences,
as in the novel *Against the Grain*, where the city of London is
experienced by the main protagonist, Des Esseintes, in the very
midst of Paris at the Bodega—from the tactile materiality of Father Foucauld's relationship with the holy Site.[6] The decadent
"lives", through an imaginary projection, the place of his purely

---

[4] "Le Pélerinage," (1949), *OM III*, p. 818.

[5] The nineteenth-century French writer Joris-Karl Huysmans, one of the
inspirations and "intercessors" of Massignon, converted to Catholicism following a complex itinerary that took him through aestheticist and "deca-
dentist" experiments, as in his novel *À Rebours (Against the Grain)*, in which
the central character, Des Esseintes, epitomises the end-of-century excesses
of artistic refinement and hyper civilised hedonism.

[6] "Thus, a sceptical Huysmans organised a short trip to London, without
leaving his table at the 'Bodega.' In contrast, let us recall the gesture of
Foucauld writing in the little notebook which he used to hold on his heart
when on pilgrimage, and he was a perpetual pilgrim, a 'universal brother':
touching the stone of such and such a holy place, where he had managed to
kneel with great pain and difficulty, knocking his hard forehead against the
blessed slab which he had kissed." "Le pélerinage," (1949), *OM III*, p. 818.

cerebral dreams, whereas the saint touches the very texture of the sacred earth or the theurgic object.

This emphasis on the materiality of physical contact is linked, we believe, to the two fundamental elements of the Christian spiritual economy: the sense of the Incarnation of the divine Presence, and the participation in the sufferings of the Passion. The site of pilgrimage places us in the direct presence of God: it also invites us to transcend ourselves in the sacrifice of our journey towards the beacon of hope. In stressing this sacrificial dimension, Massignon's intention is no doubt to take it out on the easiness and comforts of a lukewarm and abstract Christianity; symbolically speaking, such a spiritual deficiency also implies a gradual distancing, on the part of too many Christians, from the Oriental cradle of Christianity, and therefore *vis-à-vis* the authentically Semitic inspiration which would keep Christendom from civilisationist and "cultural" idolatry. Notwithstanding the incontestable pertinence of his concern for the need to remain faithful to the geographic "incarnation" of the Spirit, Massignon—in spite of the Hallājian inspiration permeating his work—may have sometimes under-emphasised the capacity of genuinely mystical forms and sensibilities to take stock of the ubiquity of the divine Presence in order to point to, and sometimes to realise in a fully consequential way, an inner experience of "displacement" towards the Centre. The circumambulation of Hallāj around the Kaaba of his heart provides, in this sense, a complementary counterpart to the physical hardships of external pilgrimage.

Be that as it may, the vocation of Massignon leads him to reach for high places of the Spirit where the prayers of the faithful masses converge in adoration and hope. In such places, personal vocation and collective destiny meet and intertwine— Massignon having always sought to remain, in conformity to his vow, a vigilant and compassionate witness of human crowds in spiritual migration. To him, a dynamic and collective understanding of pilgrimage may be deemed to be the most powerful antidote to the deadly, static structures of the "concentration camps" of the urban masses—prisoners of the feverish prodigies

4

of technology. These "concentrationary termite mounds",[7] hallu-
cinating creations of the Promethean world of industrial modernity, are polluted sources of vain atomisation and mortal hardening; they swarm with the anonymous masses of dehumanised
men who find themselves moved in all directions with a hopeless
lack of meaningful orientation. The sole legitimacy of these cities, which are barely true cities any longer, might be to remain
the passive repositories of a few quasi-deserted sanctuaries, or
what is more likely, the precincts of occult, inner sanctuaries of
perhaps forty or four hundred righteous ones, a sodality of forgotten, unrecognised souls who are probably even unaware of
their own being like pillars of light.

\*

\*  \*

It seems appropriate, as a way to preface what develops, to analyse the modes and significance of the spiritual and scholarly
emphasis on space in Massignon's understanding of Islam. It
is a known fact that a large segment of his studies in Muslim
sociology focuses on the religious and social use of space. The
"initiatic" study of the castle of Al-Okhaider (1909), the mediaeval topography of Baghdad (1911), the two major articles
devoted to the Muslim *awqāf* (1951) and the City of the Dead
in Cairo (1958), as well as commentaries on the plans of Kufa
(1935) and Basra (1954), are milestones in this spatial apprehension of Islam. In them Massignon reveals the sharpness of his
traveller's eye, his cartographer's flair, and his qualities as attentive observer of folkish mores. His scholarly observations amaze
readers by their immense scope and the diversity of their modes
of expression. Thus, a text on Basra can include considerations
on the development of local theological schools together with a
detailed list of building dates and types of ships. Precise topographical analyses join lists of personal fiefs as well as abruptly
juxtaposed mystical insights. As has been rightly suggested,
there is something "illegible" in these abounding and "nervous"

---

[7] "Le pèlerinage", p. 817.

texts filled with notes taken in haste, or with neat observations springing forth from brilliant intuitions, but this "illegibility" also suggests a seething life with all the richness of the spiritual encounters and social interactions shaping a town's identity. In addition, the choice of the objects of study is not without significance. Indeed, Massignon is primarily interested in the institutions of *awqāf* or religious endowments, in the cemeteries and the tombs of saints, which amounts to saying that archaeological research opens up very promptly onto spiritual considerations. As Denis Gril has pointed out, "in reality, in Massignon's analysis of the urban landscape another dimension is quickly included; archaeological traces remain for him a testimony of the saints of Islam."[8] In other cases—and we are referring especially to *The Passion of al-Hallāj*—it is, conversely, the mystical phenomenology that leads Massignon to lay the "topographical" foundations of the personal experience. Hence the first volume of *The Passion* develops a sociological contextualisation which allows us to better grasp the multiple ramifications of the mystical path of Hallāj in the socio-cultural framework of Abbasid Baghdad.

The discovery of the tombs of saints strikes one as a central element of Massignon's archaeological itinerary. In Baghdad, for example, the mystical archaeologist points out a topographical error made by Le Strange, a late nineteenth-century historian of Abbasid Baghdad, who had conjectured that the location of Junayd's tomb was "three miles" away from that of Maʿrūf al-Kharkī. Massignon underlines that this type of scholarly error results from the absence of a concrete study on location: historical abstraction lacks a sense of concrete and committed testimony, a lack that is also the fundamental flaw of the bourgeois religion criticised by Massignon. Correcting the error of Le Strange, Massignon locates Junayd's tomb "870 steps" away from that of al-Kharkī, and one is certainly tempted to read into these "steps" all the living reality of the scholarly pilgrim's hours of walking through the most obscure sites and streets of Baghdad. In contrast, a mere topographical error which could have

---

[8] Denis Gril, "Espace sacré et spiritualité, trois approches: Massignon, Corbin, Guénon," in *D'un Orient l'autre*, p. 50.

been ignored as a detail without any religious significance is in fact for Massignon both the mark and the cause of an incapacity to "orientate" the spiritual totality of Baghdad. The "cosmos" of Abbasid Baghdad is thereby left completely shattered: "... and its whole plan has been transformed by this single rectification."[9] The tomb of the saint does indeed evoke a spiritual geography which "magnetises" and "distributes" the fragrances of the *barakah*. The spiritual truth is "shrouded" and "dissimulated", and it requires the archaeologist's attention as much as it demands the mystic's loving intuition.

In the same register, at once topographical and mystical, Massignon discovers in Damietta—important ground for the spiritual geography associated with the ordeal of St. Francis[10]— the tomb of the thirteenth-century Sufi Shushtarī, thanks to the directions of local members of the Shādhiliyyah order. Now, Shushtarī also occupies an important place in what may be called Massignon's "Christic" archaeology of Sufism. Indeed, the literary output of this Andalusian Sufi is characterised by a kind of spiritual transmutation of the crude and popular expressions of love, including "a symbolic transposition of the profession of the prostitutes by singing it in the souqs."[11] In the context of the spiritual geography of the city, Shushtarī also represents the concrete presence of sanctity among the common people, and its

---

[9] "Le Strange reckons it to be ... three miles away from the well-known tomb of Ma'rouf al Kharkî (d. 200/816), without suspecting that Junayd's tomb still exists, almost buried, at the heart of a hillock, under the successive alluviums of the graves of his devotees, only 870 steps from the tomb of Ma'rouf al-Kharkî: this whole plan has been transformed by this single rectification." "Bagdad et sa topographie au Moyen Age: deux sources nouvelles," (1911), *OM III*, p. 88.

[10] "In Damietta, where St. Francis of Assisi offered himself to the trial of the Fire in 1219 in order to touch the heart of a single Muslim, the Sultan al-Mālik al-Kāmil. God then enabled him to know that He had set him aside for another martyrdom, namely that of stigmatisation and of the Throwing of the Spear of Love, which he would receive two years later, on Alverne, *nel crudo sasso*." "Cinquième mystère douloureux," (1957), *OM III*, 844.

[11] "Recherches sur Shushtarī, poète andalou enterré à Damiette," (1950), *OM II*, p. 406.

power to alchemically transmute the most lowly or ambiguous human manifestations:

> A shaykh from the country of Meknes
> Walks through the souqs singing:
> "What claim do these men have against me,
> And what claim do I have against them?"…
>
> Nothing is worth his word, when he goes all the way down
>     the souqs;
> Behold the shopkeepers bothering him,
> His begging bowl on his neck, his crutches, and his rebel
>     streaks.
> Ah! It is a *shaykh* built on a rock, like every edifice
> God Himself builds.[12]

The final reference to what "God Himself builds" seems particularly pertinent in the context of this urban spirituality; every justified "building" is a shrine, and there is no better shrine than a saint's body in which the divine Presence resides. From this perspective the city would appear as a dynamic place of spiritual testimonies which cross over and fertilise each other through the intertwining of the most diverse levels of traditional reality: work, trade, songs and dances, teaching, worship and religious preaching, not to mention the eccentric allusions of the hoaxer, and the existential riddles of the fool in God.[13]

---

[12] "Trois mystiques musulmans: Shoshtari, Ahmed Ghazali et Niyazi Misri," (1925), *OM II*, p. 367.

[13] "A city of Islam, as I have tried to show in the case of Baghdad … is first of all a place of gathering, not so much a gathering of monuments making up a fossil museum, but one of knots of streets where the oral testimonies of witnesses, *shuhūd*, circulate; be it for *dallāl* prescriptions for shouting out the sale of wares in the souqs, or making jokes pertaining to jurists in the mosques, schools and tribunals, or proverbs dear to peasants and caravan members, or spiritual sayings and 'city-street' songs heard in reception halls and baths, or else theophoric locutions conceived by solitaries in the wasteland of cemeteries," "La Cité des morts au Caire," (1958), *OM III*, p. 235.

In this context, the institution of *waqf*, too, has gained Massignon's attention in a very particular way. The *awqāf* are religious public properties, "mortmain estates", whose revenues are allocated to the financial support of the religious foundations, the *waqfiyāt*. The *waqf* is conceived by the believer as a sort of *zakāt* (alms) that is established in perpetuity. It is the conjunction of this dimension of perpetuity and the universal scope of the religious community it involves that gives the *waqf* its foremost spiritual value. Actually Massignon conceived of the principle of *waqf* (be it the case of sacred places, tombs, pilgrimage sites, Qur'anic schools or others) as "the maximal extension of the *Hijra*" both in space and in time.[14] The "exiles" of Islam, pilgrims, refugees or seekers of truth, are thus received everywhere in the maternal bosom of the *ummah*, in a kind of universal hospitality that echoes the Prophet's hospitality towards the *Ashāb as-Suffāh*, the People of the Bench in Medina. In addition, by giving to God, the donor makes it possible to reaffirm the religious cohesion of the community, which is strengthened by the establishment of a place of spiritual convergence. This is why the *waqf* may be considered as one of the most important juridical institutions of Islam: in it, the highest spiritual finality of religion is wedded to economic and social realities that are most fundamental for the very survival of the community. This important point demonstrates that Massignon's profound interest in the *waqf* is ultimately connected to the capacity of this institution to crystallise and co-ordinate a spiritual geography of collective sanctification.

Besides the *waqf*, the urban and spiritual geography of Massignon finds in the Muslim cemetery the testimony of an intricate tangle of individual sanctity and collective piety. If modern Western cemeteries are characterised by an utter absence of

---

[14] "(The essential role of the *awqāf* is to) perpetuate the community in time and space, since they allow the maximal extension of the Hijra, from the hegira of the voluntarily expatriated, of those displaced for religious reasons, to places where the science of their common faith can be renewed: *fi sabīl Allāh*," "Documents sur plusieurs waqfs musulmans," (1951), *OM III*, p. 181.

spiritual expression, an artificial and sterile separation from the world of the living and an individualistic gentrification of more or less dubious taste, the traditional Muslim cemetery is, on the contrary, a veritable centre of contact with the "hereafter" and an eschatological composition of space.[15] In this spiritual framework, Massignon strongly emphasises the role of women, their presence and piety being a determining factor in the spiritual vibrancy and secret inspiration of the "city of the dead". Women, inasmuch as they give life and perpetuate the "genealogical" line of believers (paradise "lies at the feet of mothers"), are also those who come to pray for the dead on Fridays, weaving thereby a quasi-mystical link between the elect of the hereafter and the believers of the here below. According to the Christian vision of Massignon, such a function arises from a dimension of "substitution", since, just like the *waqfa* of Arafāt—the standing before God at the Mount of Mercy—it implies a "participation in a common honour of workers",[16] which evokes the idea of a mystical body of believers, an inner solidarity of all members of the community in a reciprocal intercession and "substitutive love" of all for all. The cemetery is thus a place of privileged and spiritually heightened communication which weaves a psycho-spiritual fabric in which inner phenomena give shape to a mystical "commerce" among souls. It is in this "crepuscular" zone that sociological Islam and mystical Islam distance themselves *de facto* from theological and puritan abstractions in order to participate in a spiritual world of subtle interdependencies in the name of Presence. Henceforth, it is plain that the significance of places of pilgrimage and worship in Massignon's vision of Islam results from concepts and practices of sacred space as a collective and dynamic vector of transcendence.

---

[15] "Our secularisation of urban cemeteries, these proper museums of nothingness, has not reached Qarāfa yet. In 50 years, I got to know its two antithetical aspects for the believer; the dead, whose tombs are brushed by given premonitions of election for some, and damnation for others."

[16] *Ibid.*, p. 241.

\*

\*   \*

We propose to examine now the meaning of some geographical stations, or stages, in the spiritual pilgrimage of Massignon's
life: we will focus particularly on three spiritual centres that are
highly evocative of some of his religious emphases, namely Jerusalem, Ephesus and Ise. Other places also appear on this journey,
but in a less detailed way: such is the case of La Salette,[17] and the
tomb of Quṭb Bakhtiyār, the last pilgrimage site of Gandhi. The
latter two seem to have, incidentally, a complementary value for
Massignon, in the sense that they represent perhaps the short-
est path—but no doubt also the most arduous one, due to the
wild slopes of the nearby Alps—and the farthest place—India,
unfamiliar to the world of Abraham—in the pilgrim's journey
towards a single consummation of love in the Divine Presence.

La Salette in Dauphiné, where two children, Mélanie Calvat and Maximin Giraud, witnessed a Marian apparition in
1846,[18] is a spiritual centre whose importance has particularly

---

[17] La Salette manifests the dimension of mercy which Massignon attributes
to the liberating space of the Marian presence, an antithesis to the
"condensed" and vainly communicative space of modern Prometheanism:
"The proliferation of the intercommunication networks that have been
uprooting us for more than a century (the railway network in France
after 1840) increases our hold on a link of a hopeless chain, wherefrom
we come out dead, thrown out and emptied, like heaps of food cans in
front of warehouses. And it is then that a sporadic, supernatural gleam
starts filtering out: precisely through the hideous mechanism of our
collective incarceration, where our hardened sins had amalgamated to the
equipment of scientific progress and the punishment without pardon of the
transgressed natural laws: annunciation of the hereafter, a Marian promise
for mercy," "Notre-Dame de La Salette," (1948), *OM III*, (Dar Al-Maaref:
1963), p. 753.

[18] The message of the Holy Virgin to Mélanie, dated 19th September, 1856,
emphasises the indignity of priests ("cesspools of impurity") , the scourges
about to fall upon society, and the upcoming civil and natural disasters
that awaited both France and Italy. It also refers to the "duplicitous heart"
of Napoléon III, his ambition of becoming "both pope and emperor" and
his subsequent fall under the "sword" that he wanted "to use to oblige
peoples to elevate him". Another Marian message, to Maximin Giraud,

strong bearings upon the question of the salvation of France as a Catholic nation, bearing in mind that, for Massignon, salvation can only take place by "submitting oneself to the universal",[19] hence, away from any parochialism, not to mention nationalism. From this point of view, Massignon is well aware of the fact that the nineteenth century was a crucial moment in the religious destiny of France. The more or less irreversible political changes introduced by the Revolution—despite attempts at a Restoration, and notwithstanding the bourgeois and Caesarean episodes of the waltz of regimes that succeeded each other until the establishment of the *laïque* Third Republic—were doubtless ultimately less important than the profound and progressive modification of social power relationships and mentalities. One must, however, wait until practically the end of the century—or, more precisely, World War I, which in a sense served as an epilogue to it—in order to observe the ultimate consequences of the aforementioned socio-cultural process with respect to both the secularisation of French society and the weakening of its Christian vocation. Attentive to this national perspective, Massignon has been particularly keen to situate La Salette in an historical context which would do justice to the different moments of the religious and political evolution of France, by focusing especially on a spiritual comparison between La Salette and the apparitions at Lourdes which took place twelve years later. It is a fact that the two respective political regimes that were once "shaken" by these manifestations, namely the bourgeois constitutional Monarchy of July and the Caesarean Second Empire, each have in common—despite their marked philosophical differences—a setting of order and authority outside of the context of spiritu-

---

makes the spiritual crisis of France more explicit: "Three fourths of France will lose the faith, and the fourth part, which will retain it, will practice it lukewarmly."

[19] "Deep down, La Salette remains the pilgrimage of predilection for those tormented by the social health of the nation, in accordance with the spirit of Jeanne d'Arc, and the spirit of Mélanie: the last verse of her 'love litanies' for N.D. of Salette is: 'Because you will save France, I love you.'" *Parole donnée*, p. 177.

al legitimacy which traditionally gave religious significance to the French sector of Christianity. As Pierre Rocalve has rightly pointed out, "there was a latent anti-Orleanism in the Message"[20] delivered to Mélanie in La Salette. This "Secret", later revealed by the children—released from their duty of silence by the Holy Virgin in 1858—contains likewise "an explicit indictment of the powers of the time: one of the paragraphs being explicitly directed against Napoléon III".[21] While taking note of the non-fortuitous implications of such apparent coincidences, Massignon docs not envisage them within the limitative framework of the political perspective of "royalist mysticism". As proof, he does not hesitate—not without some signs of disinclined sadness—to stress the corrupting influence of political literalism in matters of heavenly messages, specifically that of "desperate legitimists" who transferred all the frustrated zeal of their faith onto the implicit political dimension of this Marian warning.[22] Surely, the desperate faithfulness of legitimism inspires Massignon with some lines suffused with a sense of congenial empathy, be it in the context of monarchic France or in that of persecuted Shī'ism. For Massignon, "legitimism", broadly understood, is indeed a profound religious reality, a sacred testimony; and yet, he cannot but take into account the weaknesses of concrete forms of

---

[20] "Léon Bloy would make use of it in a passage of *Celle qui pleure* ('She who cries'), in which he evokes the bourgeois and material activities of the royal family at the very moment when the Virgin reveals to the children the suffering of her Son." Pierre Rocalve, "Un haut lieu de la foi: la montagne de La Salette," *Les nouvelles de l'ordre*, July 1997, n. 45, p. 19. Cf. *Celle qui pleure* (1908), devoted to Our Lady of La Salette, and *Vie de Mélanie* (1912) are two major books by Catholic writer Léon Bloy (1846-1917). Let us recall that "*Orléanisme*" refers both to the dynastic preference for the younger branch of the Bourbons (the Orléans) and to its political "liberalism", in contrast with "*Légitimisme*", based on an attachment to the eldest branch of the royal family and a political philosophy informed by a desire for a return to the *Ancien Régime*.

[21] *Ibid.*, p. 20.

[22] We are referring here more particularly to the "survivalist" interpretations (the partisans of Baron de Richemont and those of Naundorff, who saw in these two characters respectively a survival of Louis XVII).

legitimist engagement, especially when it comes to cautioning against the temptations of sectarian eschatological mythologies. These corruptions of legitimism derive from an ignorance, or a neglect, of the margin of human—and *a fortiori* divine—freedom vis-à-vis the prospective and conditional potentialities of the future (*"les futuribles conditionnels"*), but also, no doubt, from a tendency to set the particularity of a miraculous occurrence aside from its most profound and universal spiritual context.

Massignon's first pilgrimage to La Salette took place on Christmas Eve in 1911, when the mountain covered with snow offered to the Marian pilgrim the penitential perspective of a true Way of the Cross.[23] The experience of La Salette was such that it would draw him closer to the popular piety of his countrymen,[24] as well as to the spiritual roots of his precursors and intercessors. Indeed, this is the place where one of his major inspirers and "substitutive" guarantor, the novelist Joris-Karl Huysmans, was converted—a conversion much indebted to the living example of the French peasantry's impetus of faith, as representative of a kind of people today virtually, if not actually, extinct. In this sense, La Salette would appear to Massignon, in many respects, as a spiritual "protestation", flowing from the most profoundly religious elements of national identity, against the fictitious promises and real threats of a mercantile world order, one whose economic foundations rely on an implicit, if not explicit, hatred of any notion of a human "poverty" before God.

---

[23] "I arrived last night by way of Corps and the cliff road of St. Julian, and I thought I was going to perish in the thick and soft snow. Rarely have I been in such a definite danger of death. On a dark night, after a pale, extraordinary, rose-like sunset, above the last rusty valleys, the last dark blue rocks, in complete whiteness and definitive isolation. Thus I had to walk for more than one hour and a half, stumbling, falling and catching my breath every five or six steps! I thought of sitting and letting myself go ... at that moment a pure and fine crescent rose between two clouds." *Massignon*, Christian Destremau and Jean Moncelon, Paris, 1994, p. 94.

[24] Thus, in one instance he notices how the "profound and intense faith of some women's pilgrimages of the Dauphiné mountain" had left their very vivid mark on Huysmans too. Cf. "Notre-Dame de La Salette et la conversion de J.K. Huysmans," (1946), *OM III*, p. 750.

Very far away from the French Alps in terms of geographical distance, but in many ways near them in spirit, one of Massignon's farthest and most "universalist" pilgrimages as regards its reach led him to India, where he would follow the steps of Gandhi's last pilgrimage to the tomb of Qutb Bakhtiyār, near New Delhi. This high spiritual place epitomises the "passion of unity" symbolised by the spiritual master buried therein, who was the guide of Iltrumish, the sultan of Delhi, "who had treated Muslims and Hindus equally", and whose spirit Gandhi wanted to recapture. By making this site the destination of his pilgrimage of witnessing, Gandhi expressed his conviction of the "profound unity of all religions".[25] In fact, on 27th January, 1948, the Mahātma accompanied a group of Muslim women to the shrine of the Sufi saint as a sign of non-violent protest against the violence of the Hindus on Muslims, as a prelude to his speech in favour of peace; three days later, on 30th January 1948, he fell under the bullets of Godse, a Hindu political activist who considered his fraternisation with Muslims a treason. Gandhi's sacrifice retraces the main characteristics of the universal vocation of witnessing that is one of the hallmarks of Massignon's spirituality: these include non-violent "substitution" out of compassion, inner hospitality towards the other, and the gift of self for the sake of truth to the point of martyrdom. Gandhi's last witnessing journey might thereby typify the perfection of pilgrimage as a "journey to the heart" by outlining the pilgrim's most universal horizon, as well as its maximal dramatic intensity as the final term of a "curve of life" entirely informed by a quest for Justice. Falling under the assault of one of his own people for the love of others, Gandhi embodies and epitomises the fundamental de-centring which resides at the heart of all authentic spirituality, and which is retraced in physical space by the journey of the pilgrim "in spirit and in truth". The previous paragraphs suggest that La Salette and the tomb of Qutb Bakhtiyār may be deemed to represent, at each end of Massignon's spiritual itinerary, the two major symbolic dimensions that pilgrimage can assume: the

---

[25] "La signification spirituelle du dernier pèlerinage de Gandhi," (1956), *OM III*, p. 342.

discovery of the divine Stranger in the barren, rustic and abrupt proximity of the familiar sanctuary supernaturally transmuted by divine grace, and the unveiling of the Self in and through one's loving movement towards the maximal otherness of the distant and the foreign.

\*

\*   \*

On our journey through the symbolical places of Massignon's itinerary, the categories and glossary of Sufism provide us in many ways with a language fit for the elucidation of the spiritual meaning of these places which aligns with the universalist vocation that Massignon perceived in Muslim mysticism. This is so because of the profound influence upon Massignon's spiritual sensibility o the mystical conception of pilgrimage rooted in a meditation on the work of al-Hallāj. It is also worth noting, more generally, that the importance of pilgrimage has without any doubt a more marked character in Islam than anywhere else; in fact it constitutes a canonical obligation for every Muslim endowed with the physical and material means to undertake it; this is the *Hajj* that constitutes a kind of periodical collective spiritual regeneration of the *Ummah*. In contrast, one could say that in Christianity the centrality of the Incarnation and the sacramental economy that flows from it tends inevitably to relativise the importance of the Holy Place; the latter is in a sense available anywhere by virtue of the ubiquity of the mystery of the Eucharist. However, Massignon categorically refuses such a relativisation of sacred space in the name of the Incarnation. For him, the historical event of the Incarnation suggests a "precise formal object" for any Christian *élan* of love. In other words, the presence and Passion of Christ in Palestine implies the efficiency of a specific *barakah* which must determine the geographical orientation of Christians.[26] Henceforth, quite paradoxically, one

---

[26] "There is in this (Christian) love a precise formal object, a magnetic pole, which is oriented towards a specified situation and a determined Holy Place," "La pèlerinage," (1949), *OM III*, p. 820.

may take the risk of suggesting that Massignon "Islamises" in some way the Christian perception of space and of pilgrimage by tracing it back to the concrete *locus* of the fundamental Mystery that lies at its foundation.

Moreover, in a kind of reverse analogy, Massignon seems at times to "Christianise" the Muslim vision of pilgrimage. This is so inasmuch as he does not perceive in the *Hajj* primarily a legal obligation or even a pious commemoration; rather he directs attention to a mystical dimension and to an eschatological horizon pertaining to pilgrimage. The latter enables us to perceive the pilgrimage as a "social phenomenon which is a precursor of humanity's consummation into a final unity".[27] The colourful mass of Muslim pilgrims of all origins and ethnicities suggests this universal finality of worship, in which human differences are as it were abolished in the pure witnessing of transcendence. Furthermore, with Hallāj, mystical interiorisation takes this canonical institution as a central theme of a meditation which reveals the deepest significance of the *Hajj* in the spiritual economy of Islam. From a spiritual perspective, it is a matter of aiming for a place—but not simply resting therein, but thenceforth exceeding it: the destination of the pilgrim in its most profound sense is a symbol of an inner place (*maqām*) transcending the tendencies of the ego. It is in this context that we see fit to recall that one of the reasons for Hallāj's indictment was his inner interpretation of the *Hajj*. One of the letters written by Hallāj and condemned by his enemies expresses in a very direct manner the principle of an interiorisation of the rite:

> ....If you want to perform the Hajj, use a room in your own house, stand at its door, just like you would stand on the *wuqūf* at the door of the Ka'ba, and enter in the dress of the *muhrim*; after entering, go in another spot of your house, offer two rak'ats there, and this will be as if you prayed at the *Maqām* (Ibrāhīm); run from this spot to the door of the room where-

---

[27] "El-Hallâj, mystique de l'islam," (1949), *OM II*, p. 224.

from you entered, and this will be as if you ran between Safā and Marwa.[28]

The principle of pilgrimage "in spirit" can hardly be expressed more clearly. In the same line of thought, one should also mention the chief accusation concerning the culminating point of the Hajj, the rite of the *waqfa* of ʿArafāt, at the moment when the pilgrims bear witness before God and supplicate Him to forgive the sins of their loved ones before making the great sacrifice of the holocaust of the sheep in remembrance of Abraham. Yet for Hallāj the only sacrifice which truly matters is that which is realised in the subjective freedom of *ikhlās*, or perfect sincerity, a sacrifice which is nothing but the spiritual death of the martyr: "The others offer animals, whereas I offer the blood of my arteries."[29] In other words, the true pilgrimage is an inner reality by virtue of the mystical principle that leads the Sufis to have a "tendency to envisage even their obligatory duties as pure actions of grace, wherein the plain freedom of the knowing heart is offered to God *willingly*...."[30] That being said, Massignon also underlines that Hallāj appears particularly scrupulous in the performance of his canonical duties, especially when it comes to pilgrimage. The physical execution of this rite implies a blessing which touches all the orders of reality, including the physical order. Between the pole of an utter interiorisation and that of the pious scruple, the solution of the apparent paradox resides in the Hallajian doctrine of canonical rites, which distinguishes religious obligations regarding the intermediaries (*wasāʾit*) from those concerning the realities (*haqāʾiq*). The obligations regarding the "intermediaries" appeal to a call to transcend their transitory or relative reality which ultimately leads to their annihilation. Hallāj expresses this necessity with respect to the Hajj and the Kaʾba in the following way (as translated by Massignon):

---

[28] *La Passion de Husayn Ibn Mansûr Hallâj*, I, p. 586.

[29] "El-Hallāj, mystique de l'Islam," *OM II*, p. 223.

[30] *La Passion de Hallâj*, III, p. 243.

The first sacred site established for man is that of Bakka (= Mecca), the blessed site.... Insofar as you are attached to this site, you will remain separated from God. But when you really detach yourself from it, you will reach the One who erected and established it; then, meditating on the (destroyed) temple in yourself, you will attain the real Presence of its Founder.[31]

There is little doubt that Massignon's Christian perspective tends at this point to orient his choice of texts and his own reading of Hallāj. That is how the Muslim rites are conceived by him as purely "collective" and "temporary" realities in their literality, "having no sacramental character in themselves, nor conferring divine grace, *ipso facto* ... and destined to be interrupted, during the consummation of the mystical union in Paradise".[32] However, the question remains: why cannot the reciting, and pious assimilation, of the Qur'ān, which irrigates the greatest part of these rites, be considered to involve a properly sacramental grace by virtue of the Scripture's own privilege of direct revelation? Be that as it may, the final reality is an inner event, but—with Hallāj—this inner event necessarily falls under the sanction of the Law, a sanction of death which purifies it from the "highest mental representations" of God which the mystic's conscience could taste and enjoy during total *tawhīd*, at the risk of interposing them like so many idols between him and God: "It is a matter of supreme expatriation, a mortifying asceticism, and the apex of divine desire."[33] In other words, it seems that the penalty of the Law must be the necessary fulfilment of perfect asceticism, the "crucifixion" of the intellect. As a result, by virtue of the principle according to which "the letter kills and the spirit vivifies," the sacrifice of the mystic before the Law—like that of the Redemption which "springs forth" from the Passion—is also a kind of spiritual fertilisation of the community by means of the blood spilled from its saintly sacrificial victim.

---

[31] *La Passion de Hallâj*, Vol. I, p. 589.

[32] *La Passion de Hallâj*, Vol. III, p. 244.

[33] "El-Hallâj, mystique de l'islam," *OM II*, p. 225.

\*

\*  \*

In the spirit of the universal desire laid out by the Hallājian pilgrimage, we wish to show how the high places of the Spirit that were dear to Massignon, in parallel to the spiritual depths whose paths they open up, denote an ecumenical geography that may provide us with the keys of a fruitful meditation on a convergence of the various religious traditions of humanity. On this "global" plane, as on that of a soul's history—and beyond the definition of sacred space given by Eliade on the basis of the notion of *axis mundi*,[34] Massignon draws the compelling contours of a spiritual geography characterised by a dynamic tension. This geography is first and foremost, as we have already intimated, orientation and movement; the tension immanent within a desire for God in both the objective and subjective senses of a human longing and a divine, essential Desire. This spiritual motion—grounded in a receptive submission to the *fiat*—is clearly opposed to the modern collective imprisonment, or spiritual alienation, that is determined by the agitated and ultimately sterile dynamics of the quest for a largely illusory individual freedom. Ever inclined to place an emphasis on the spiritual motion towards real, sacred space, Massignon goes even so far as to assert the pilgrim's tension towards the place of his magnetised desire as an imperative which no "sacramental ubiquity"[35] can defer or subrate. There is no doubt that it is from this spiritual tension of *ʿishq*—or ardent love—that flows Massignon's sever-

---

[34] "It must be said at once that the religious experience of the non-homogeneity of space is a primordial experience, homologisable to a founding of the World. It is not a matter of theoretical speculation that precedes all reflection on the world. For it is the break effected in space that allows the world to be constituted, because it reveals the fixed point, the central axis for all future orientation." *The Sacred and the Profane*, Paris: Gallimard, 1965, p. 21.

[35] "It is a matter of going to the Holy Land for a 'service of love', no affirmation of whose ubiquity of the sacramental presence exempts us from participating in the Second Coming of our Judge and Friend." "Le pèlerinage," (1949), *OM III*, pp. 819-820.

ity towards any quietism (such as his little respect for the state of "permanent passivity" of Madame Guyon)[36] and his lively and largely unwarranted reluctance towards the Sufi *wahdat al-wujūd*, "non-dualism of the essence", which he never ceased to refer to as an "existential monism",[37] as if the exclusive Reality of God as the Essence of universal reality abolished the dynamic multiplicity of creatures on their own level. For Ibn 'Arabī, for example, the Unity of Existence does not invalidate distinctions and separations among discrete beings, nor does it bridge the ontological and spiritual gap between the servant and the Lord, the lover and the Beloved. Unity and distinction are both real: "the transcendent Reality is [at the same time] the relative creature, even though the creature be distinct from the Creator."[38] Moreover, in this Akbarian perspective, there cannot be anything fundamentally static about spiritual wayfaring, since the Divine is both undelimited in its Essence and delimitated in its theophanies. The supreme spiritual station cannot but be, therefore, a "station of no station" (*maqām bilā maqām*), since it must be characterised by an experience of limitlessness in limitations and limitations in limitedness. Wary of the spiritual implications of the doctrine of *wahdat al-wujūd*, which he understands as being incompatible with the mystics' burning desire for God, Massignon attempts to disassociate it from the "mysticism of

---

[36] In a letter to Gabriel Marcel, Massignon takes it out on Madame Guyon whom he deems to have "overestimated certain basically mediocre inner experiences, and fabricated with her own means a permanent passive state which proves that the basis of her experience is not divine." *Louis Massignon, mystique en dialogue*, Paris, p. 217. For Massignon, divine life and mystical life are intermittent.

[37] This is the fundamental meaning of the "testimonial monism" which Massignon sees as stemming from Hallāj. Desire, in God, is essential or intrinsic to the Essence (*Dhāt*). "Desire, in the pre-eternity of pre-eternities is the Absolute" (Hallāj). Cf. "Interférence philosophique et percées métaphysiques dans la mystique hallagienne: notion de l'essentiel Désir," (1950), *OM II*, p. 237.

[38] Ibn 'Arabī, in the chapter on "The Wisdom of Holiness in the Word of Enoch," *The Bezels of Wisdom*, translation and introduction by R.W.J. Austin, Paulist Press, 1980, p. 87.

the instant" that he favours by emphasising expressions which, like Jurjani's, appear to extol duration as a mode of "expansion of the divine presence",[39] whereas, in fact, the idea of a renewed creation at every instant is fundamentally congruent with the doctrine of the Unity of Existence.[40] With respect to Christian quietism, which Massignon tends to understand as a betrayal of both the *élan* of love and the spiritual meaning of holy places, it must be conceded that for him the spiritual doctrine of a Jeanne Guyon or a François Malaval tends indeed to relativise, or even minimise, the importance of sacred sites and liturgical times in the name of a perpetual concentration on the divine Presence embracing all things. However, we believe that these divergences result much less from disagreements pertaining to metaphysics than from differences of emphasis that largely depend upon the diversity of spiritual temperaments; it amounts to saying that these doctrines or these spiritual approaches,[41] clad by Massignon in the pejorative connotations of "monism"

---

[39] "Le temps dans la pensée islamique," (1952), *OM II*, p. 609.

[40] "As for those to whom the higher worlds are disclosed, they see that God is manifest in every Breath and that no [particular] Self-manifestation is repeated. They also see that every Self-manifestation at once provides a [new] creation and annihilates another. Its annihilation is extinction at the [new] Self-manifestation, subsistence being what is given by the following [other] Self-manifestation; so understand." Ibn 'Arabī, *Bezels of Wisdom*, in the chapter "The Wisdom of the Heart in the Word of Shu'aib," p. 155.

[41] "By not accepting to divide anything, the doctrine of the *wahdah* refuses to separate the Absolute from the contingent—two terms which are linked into a reciprocal necessity by their logical opposition—as well as to consider as really possible the union of the creator with his creature, since they have never been but one." "Ana al-Haqq," (1912), *OM II*, p. 39. It is therefore clear that, for Massignon, the doctrine of *wahdat al-wujūd* "neutralises" or "annihilates" all essential desire, be it in God or in His creature, this being so because it lays out a unity of essence between the Absolute and the relative. Massignon does not consider that the Infinite Essence envisaged by "non-dualist" Sufism "desires" to manifest itself on the "outside"—which is indeed illusory with respect to It—which is none other than contingence, and that the latter—or rather its human "centre of consciousness"—ultimately tends towards the Source of its own being. The Infinite which "precedes" the Unity of Being is by definition the Essence of Desire.

or "quietism", have, for him, the grave consequence of rendering moot the need for witnessing, the need for pilgrimage, the
tension of the heroic and self-sacrificing soul of the warrior of
divine Love to which he feels vocationally called. This is why he
sees the great flaw of Ibn 'Arabī (in keeping with the Shaykh al-
Akbar's non-dualist perspective) as being, for him, "no longer a
question of preaching and fighting in the Community, but one
of attaining a quietist serenity, wherein there is no longer 'you'
or 'me', or 'we' nor even 'he'."[42] In the logic of Massignon's critique of what he perceives as the philosophical expressions of a
debilitating quietism, we may elliptically hint at the meaning of
his mystical vocation by suggesting that in it the *élan* of Love
takes precedence over the plenitude of Peace. In this perspective, the *Hajj* of the heart,[43] to which he likes to refer in his discussion of Hallāj, can be much more satisfactorily understood as
an ultimate consummation of our orientation towards a specific
collective sanctuary[44] than the inner and essential transposition
of its divine meaning and intent.[45] Hence, Massignon is utterly
distrustful—wrongly, or perhaps rightly so, depending on the

---

[42] "Mystique musulmane et mystique chrétienne," (1954), *OM II*, p. 480.

[43] "Hallāj had understood, in his last *waqfa*, the spirit of the Hajj, this pure
and harrowing call for a 'going beyond' ourselves, which is the basis of all
true pilgrimage." "El-Hallāj, mystique de l'islam," (1949), *OM II*, p. 224.

[44] "On his last pilgrimage to 'Arafāt (around 290/902), during the *waqfa*,
when the pilgrim cries out the names of all those he loves, asking for them
to be forgiven, Hallāj, repeating the call of the crowd, *labbayk* ('at Your
service'), asked God to make him even poorer, to make him unknown and
banished; so that God would be the One to thank Himself through his
lips." "Perspective transhistorique sur la vie de Hallaj," (1955), *OM II*, p.
325.

[45] The sacred form is as it were "sublimated" and "transmuted" at the very
culmination of its "realisation", rather than being *a priori* the object of an
interiorisation by virtue of meditation on its essence as in Frithjof Schuon's
perspective of "quintessential esoterism". It remains nevertheless true that
the two perspectives may be deemed to differ in emphasis rather being
essentially exclusive of each other, since both involve an awareness of the
ontological bond between form and essence, and since both of them give
precedence to the latter.

case—of spiritual and intellectual "abstractions", even to the point of claiming a powerful "corporeal" attachment to his own country, as testified by his constant refusal to be considered—he who was such a relentless traveller of all "the caravans of divine Love"—"a cosmopolitan without a country."[46]

*
*   *

As we have begun to show, the dynamic tension of Massign-on's spiritual geography results from its resolutely affirmed link with meditation and the practice of pilgrimage. It is in fact in and through pilgrimage that the qualitative essences of both space and time converge in a reality which is Reality itself.[47] Pilgrimage is a kind of "apocalypse" of time and space. It is a return to the time of the origin, "which 'does not flow' because it does not participate in profane temporal duration, and is constituted by an endlessly retrievable eternal present."[48] And it is through the monotheistic pilgrimage *par excellence*, that of Jerusalem (which Massignon would perform no less than twenty-eight times), that this convergence of time and space is revealed most directly, a convergence which is also a kind of reduction by fire. There is in fact in the journey towards Jerusalem a double consummation: the pilgrim's space is as it were subsumed within the "absolute" instant of Eternity which is the end of his journey, whereas the consummation of time in sacred History gives "place" to the endless or "absolute" space of the ultimate Jerusalem. It could

---

[46] "One must stress here a point which was dear to his heart and which he would tackle repeatedly with those close to him: he was horrified to be taken, because of his love for the Arabs, for a stateless person, a cosmopolitan without a country. Quite the opposite, he felt, he saw himself as an ardent Frenchman, profoundly rooted in his land and its dead." Vincent Monteil, "Tel qu'il était en son vivant," in *Louis Massignon, mystique en dialogue*, Question de, n. 90, Albin Michel: Paris, 1992, p. 21.

[47] "For religious man, space is not homogenous; he experiences interruptions, breaks in it: some parts of space are qualitatively different from others," Mircea Eliade, *Le sacré et le profane*, Paris: Gallimard, 1965, p. 21.

[48] *Ibid.*, p. 77.

also be said of the pilgrim that he "recharges" his time in the non-temporal space of his sacred destination. There is therefore simultaneity between a reduction into ashes—or a spiritual death—and a perfected fulfilment—one's life and human norm being recovered in God, which makes of the pilgrim a kind of spiritual Phoenix. The pilgrimage is in this sense just as much a journey towards death as a journey towards oneself.

On the eschatological plane, it is as if space were being devoured by time—just as when Abel is slain by Cain (as in René Guénon)[49]—thereby resuming its rights at the end of times, but in a way that is as it were "sublimated". No doubt, one should read in this final "victory" of space over time the "victory" of the infinitude of Mercy over the absoluteness of Wrath. Indeed, space opens one onto the Infinite, whereas time compels us to submit to the Absolute.[50] The ultimate space of Peace incarnated by Jerusalem would therefore appear like the supreme and es-

---

[49] Cf. "Caïn et Abel," ch. XXI, in *Le règne de la quantité et les signes des temps*, Paris: Gallimard, 1945, pp. 195-204. Latest English edition: Guénon, René, *The Reign of Quantity and the Signs of the Times*, 4th ed., Ghent, NY: Sophia Perennis, 2004. "Only, in order that this proximity may be actually realised, the temporal condition must necessarily be suppressed, because it is the unfolding of time in conformity with the laws of manifestation that has brought about the apparent separation from the centre, and also because time, according to the very definition of succession, cannot turn back on its course; release from the temporal condition is always possible for certain beings in particular, but as far as humanity (or more exactly a humanity) taken in its entirety is concerned a release from time obviously implies that the said humanity has passed completely through the *cycle of its corporeal manifestation*: only then can it, together with the whole of the terrestrial environment that depends on it and participates in the same cyclic movement, be really reintegrated into 'the primordial state', or, what is the same thing, into the 'centre of the world'. This centre is where 'time is changed into space', because it is where the direct reflection in our state of existence of the principial eternity is found, and thereby all succession is excluded," p. 163.

[50] According to Frithjof Schuon, space and time, as "containers", come under the Infinite, whereas existence comes under the Absolute (Cf. *Survey of Metaphysics and Esoterism*, Bloomington: World Wisdom Books, 1986, p. 27). From another point of view, time manifests necessity and space freedom, or the Absolute is pure Necessity, and the Infinite pure Freedom.

sential "Here" which is like the complementary aspect of the es-chatological "Now" of Judgement, which is, for man, at once to-tal poverty and illumination by grace. Now, in keeping with this eschatological meaning of the pilgrimage, history converges on Jerusalem as on the ecumenical Promise *par excellence*. Islam's "distant" *qiblah* thus expresses the delay of a "return" wherein, according to the Qur'ān, human beings shall be enlightened re-garding their differences:[51] *Unto every one of you have We appointed a [different] law and way of life. And if God had so willed, He could surely have made you all one single community: but [He willed it oth-erwise] in order to test you by means of what He has vouchsafed unto you. Vie, then, with one another in doing good works! Unto God you all must return; and then He will make you truly understand all that on which you were wont to differ"* (5:48); *And had thy Sustainer so willed, He could surely have made all mankind one single community: but [He willed it otherwise, and so] they continue to hold divergent views* (11:117).

Beyond these providential oppositions (*mutafādila*, or the vying of the divine Names, according to Ibn 'Arabī), Massign-on can thus speak about Jerusalem, and correlatively about the Prophet of Islam, in terms of an "ecumenical Grace".[52] Jerusalem should not be a site of fanatical opposition over land, but a place of vying for grace.

Whether upstream or downstream of the eschatological events associated with Jerusalem, the "consummated" space of

---

[51] The Qur'ān equally emphasises, in the matter of religious diversity, the vying in good deeds which this diversity should inspire among believers (5:48). On this subject, the following article by Father Sydney Griffith will prove useful: "Sharing the Faith of Abraham: the 'Credo' of Louis Massignon," *Islam and Christian-Muslim Relations*, vol. 8, no. 2, 1997: "In the Hijrah of Ishmael he (Massignon) spoke of thirteen centuries during which Islam confronted Christianity, and he said that for these hundreds of years Islam has been 'the angelic lance which has stigmatised Christianity,'" p. 202.

[52] "And al-Aqsā is the Place where Muhammad received the Law of Islam in a dream, making of Jerusalem the place of an ecumenical Grace, beyond the Sakhra of the privileges of Christian Passover and Jewish Passover." "L'oratoire de Marie à l'Aqçâ...", (1956), *OM I*, p. 593.

our pilgrimage to the Centre is already a foretaste, *hic et nunc*, of the very Judgment and the Apocalypse, and herein lies its deepest meaning. This is why and how "the prophetic charisma, in Elias above all, is not limited to the serene unveiling of future landscapes, but also makes the present explode axially in a 'flash'."[53] Thus Massignon reminds us that Islamic time, like the time of Christian mystics, is not a "continuous duration" but a "milky way of instants",[54] in which every star is the "*yawm al-dīn*" (the "day of judgment") of the Exordium (*al-Fātihah*). This conception of time is intimately linked to a concrete consciousness of each and every creature's dependence *vis-à-vis* God at each instant, independent of any secondary causes. With Massignon, this consciousness unveils the ultimate meaning of what may be called an ecumenism of "verticality" and "immediateness". Herein also lies the meaning of the Eliatic archetype of the "telescoping",[55] or collapsing, of historical time which Massignon judiciously identified as the modal hallmark of Qur'anic enunciation. The prophet Elias manifests himself vertically and not horizontally, hence his affinity with the discontinuous and the sudden. Similarly, the divine discourse of the Qur'ān seems situated in an eternal present that subverts the mundane diachrony of an idolatrous mankind.

This axial "ecumenism"—to return to a key term of the Massignonian vocabulary—brings to the fore a cardinal distinction within the modes of traditional dispensation or, more generally, among ways of the Spirit. Massignon insists on this distinction, because it appears to be essential to his vocation and to the spe-

---

[53] "Elie et son rôle transhistorique, Khadiriya, en Islam," (1955), *OM I*, p. 161.

[54] "For a Muslim theologian therefore, time is not a conscious duration, but a constellation, a 'milky way' of instants (likewise, space does not exist, there are only points)." "Le temps dans la pensée islamique," (1952), *OM II*, p. 606.

[55] "By making Elias a physical contemporary of Moses, this trans-historical 'concertinering' is part of those brief and hard 'piercings' of the Qur'ān, which through an anticipated reversal of the Doomsday Book, take us back to our origins." "Elie et son rôle transhistorique, Khadiriya, en Islam," (1955), *OM I*, p. 143.

cific mode of giving his "word". The first mode of transmission, which might be called horizontal, is formal, institutional, at once necessary as the "sufficient" or underlying grace—a grace that satisfies the needs of conversion but can be resisted by the soul, and yet "insufficient" as far as the essential is concerned. From this point of view, Massignon's spiritual inspiration is very removed from the formal rigour, and some would say the quasi-administrative rigidity, of the definition of spiritual and initiatic transmission given by René Guénon, as well as being quite distant from the traditionalist accentuation of certain of Guénon's supporters.[56] It is much closer to the spiritual point of view of Frithjof Schuon and that of Henry Corbin. His roots are less "traditional" than "spiritual", to the extent that these two terms can be put in contrast without jeopardising the integrity of either. What is meant by such a distinction is that the vertical transmission (for which al-Khidr is the "verdant" Prophet), in comparison with the horizontal one, enjoys the freedom of the wind (the light breeze of God's presence enveloping Elias on

---

[56] Cf. René Guénon, *Aperçus sur l'initiation*, Éditions Traditionnelles, Paris, 1976. It would not be out of place to say a word on the relationship of Massignon with the "gnostic" and traditionalist current represented by Guénon, Coomaraswamy and Schuon. If it cannot be said that Massignon ever subscribed to the theses of these authors in their entirety, it should however be recognised that—notwithstanding his strong reservations concerning some of the perennialist positions—he was far from denying the spiritual values conveyed by this current. Regarding the "gnostics", "cabbalists" and "theosophists", Massignon would even write: "....some [authors], Schuon, Guénon, and Vulliaud, have a certain style, the sense of the mystery, and a respect for our vocation." "Soyons des Sémites spirituels," (1949), *OM III*, p. 823. Let us note—and this can hardly be a matter of chance, given the clearly greater notoriety of Guénon over Schuon in France—that Schuon's name is the first to be mentioned in this enumeration. Indeed, the relationship between Massignon and Schuon is characterised by much greater harmonic resonance than that of Massignon with Guénon, the affinities between the former—who actually met—being very distinct in certain respects. One can refer the reader, regarding this point, to the interesting study by Jean Moncelon, "Louis Massignon et Frithjof Schuon, une rencontre posthume," in *Dossier H Frithjof Schuon*, L'Age d'Homme, 2002.

Mount Horeb).[57] Inspiration, or the vertical "flash" testified by the consecrated places of the Spirit, opens up a space of higher "freedom" that may become a virtual pole of "convergence". In such a perspective, a spiritual vocation is not defined exclusively in terms of an "attachment" a traditional lineage, but also—and above all—in terms of a "detachment" and a "surrender" to the divine *fiat*, such inner dispositions being at the foundation of a genuine "liberation" and "expansive openness".[58] From this point of view, Massignon's spirituality is akin to that of the solitaries (*afrād*) who find themselves awkwardly positioned and out of step vis-à-vis the normative economy of their traditional world.

Distrustful of the more or less unconscious idolatries of ecclesiastical institutions, Massignon is in this regard extremely sensitive to the precariousness of "contracts" with Heaven which would lack an ever-kindled consciousness of the demands of the ever-present infusion of grace. Thus, it is clear that for him the horizontal mode of inspiration cannot really be independent from a vertical aspect: "It is only in appearance, and very provisionally, that institutions like the sacraments and the religious orders establish an authentic spiritual continuity and offer us access to the wonders of divine grace in this world."[59] His occasional claim to "gnostic"[60] affinities—as paradoxical and even

---

[57] In the First Book of Kings, Yahweh reveals Himself to Elias neither in the hurricane, nor through the earthquake, nor the fire, but in a "gentle blowing" or "low whisper" (I Kings, 19:12). This is the symbol of the "intimacy" of grace in its "secret" or "esoteric" inspiration, the discreet gentleness of which contrasts with the spectacular and cosmic scale of the manifestations of outward Revelation.

[58] Let us remark incidentally that this liberation through submission to the *fiat* finds a rare expression in Abraham's laughter. Massignon, though being clearly closer to a mysticism of tears than to one of laughter, remarked in this regard that Isaac signifies "laughing" and defined the "perfect laughter" of Abraham, "henceforth ready for everything ... axial in relation to the divine source", an unusual but suggestive expression of Sufi *faqr*. "La syntaxe intérieure des langues sémitiques," (1949), *OM II*, p. 580.

[59] "Elie et son rôle transhistorique....", p. 42.

[60] We are referring here to the surprising but revealing anecdote in an

29

contradictory as it may sound, considering most of his written stances—was probably related to this instinctive distancing from the potential narrowness of formalistic orthodoxy. In fact, from a profoundly gnostic point of view, just as there appears to be a temporal continuum from a point of creation, while creation is actually and metaphysically renewed at each instant,[61] there is also an "appearance" of spiritual transmission while it is in reality the divine *fiat* which informs the operative function of the rite. The vertical presence is always defined "above" the Law which it fulfils and exceeds at the same time. This is one of the meanings of the well-known Qur'anic episode of the Chapter of the Cave, in which Moses, as a prophet of the Law, is guided by a mysterious and amoral guide often identified with *al-Khidr/al-Khadir*.[62] The Qur'ān introduces this significantly anonymous character as a "servant" who had received directly and vertically a "mercy" (*rahmatan*) and a "science" (*'ilman*) from his Lord. This "mercy" is none other than the vertical grace of inner understanding of the "providential contradictions" of the *mutafādila* (11:118-19), and is the proportional inward complement to the "servitude" (*'ubūdiyya*) of al-Khidr/Elias. Only a true servant can be filled with the mercy of the Lord. Al-Khidr leads Moses through the three stages of a type of initiatic test throughout which the scope

---

interview by Jean Moncelon with Robert Amadou. According to Amadou, Massignon retorted to a lady who had warned him to be wary of Robert Amadou referring to him as a "gnostic": "But, Madame, I am a gnostic myself." (Available online at www.saliege.com/occident/amadou.htm.)

[61] On this important question see Toshihiko Izutsu's *Unicité de l'Existence et Création Perpétuelle en Mystique Islamique*, Paris 1980. *Creation and the Timeless Order of Things: Essays in Islamic Mystical Philosophy*, Toshihiko Izutsu, White Cloud Press, 1994.

[62] "In the middle of *Sūrah* XVIII of the Qur'ān, which may well be called 'The Apocalypse of Islam', Islam invokes another dialogue, between these same two characters: Moses, the prophet, and an anonymous Sage (Khadir-Elias, according to tradition). A dialogue on predestination, religious vocation, and the spiritual guide (*murshid*). Elias, the anonymous Sage, becomes the spiritual guide of Moses." "Elie et son rôle transhistorique....", p. 143.

of his vision exceeds the literality of Good according to the Law.[63]
He therefore appears as the secret prophet of the divine ruse of
God as *Khayr al-Mākirin* (the best of plotters or tricksters).[64] The
essence of ruse in general is actually the capacity to consider the
ultimate ends independently from the nature of the means and
intermediaries which enable one to reach the former. From the
divine point of view, ruse is a kind of play with secondary causes
in function of the final End which is also first Cause. Because
they are able to play on this principial register and its manifestation in contingent beings, Elias, or al-Khidr, is seen as the
prophet of freedom in God, which is none other than the other
side of servanthood. Servitude towards God at each and every
instant is actually the pathway to a spontaneous and potentially
infinite freedom. As a concomitance of this most genuine freedom, Massignon explains that "Elias transcends race and trans-
figures the Law," thereby reaching universality beyond culture
and religion in their limitative dimensions.

If the path of the "legalist" perspective (Henry Corbin's *religion légalitaire*) finds its expression in the time of transmission
that links us to the Origin, that is, to the historical Revelation,
the Eliatic inspiration is more like an instantaneous incision into
space. According to Massignon, Islam, due to its emphasis on
"the public fact of an indirect transmission" and "a pact transmitted by an authorised ambassador"[65] cannot accept the latter
way in the normative framework of its traditional orthodoxy:
in fact, exoterically, it can only condemn it as *hulūl*, an incarna-

---

[63] "Elie et son rôle transhistorique, Khadiriya, en Islam," *OM I*, p. 161.

[64] "They plot, but God (also) plotteth; and God is the best of plotters"
(*Qur'ān*, 8:30). Most interpreters and translators of the Qur'ān do not draw
all the meaning available in the root MKR in their rendering of the Holy
Book. This root is definitely associated to the meanings of "cunning" and
"trick", which most translations do not fully acknowledge because of their
lack of metaphysical perspective and their moralistic outlook.

[65] "God guarantees the social value of the *wahā* through the public fact
of an indirect transmission, of a written text, of a pact transmitted by an
authorised ambassador. In Islam, the theory of *hulūl*, which is directly
opposed to that of the Qur'anic revelation, could only be excommunicated."
"Ana al-Haqq," (1912), *OM II*, p. 36.

tionist and Christianising infiltration. The case of al-Hallāj is, in this respect, emblematic and, one may almost say, archetypical. The inner freedom of Mansūr al-Hallāj—which stands at the antipodes of all individualist license—amounts in this sense to a perspective of "spiritual nomadism", following in the steps of al-Khidr, whose vagrant ubiquity no folkloric and popular geography could settle. The mystic escapes the limitations of outer geography, and enters the imaginal configurations of the myth. It is in this context that Massignon likes to emphasise that Elias's appearances are akin to a prophetic "nomad's", a nomad who is perhaps even an Arab.[66] The ambiguity of identifying the characters of Elias, Idris and al-Khidr, much like the latter's eventual anonymity, is in itself the symbol of the "universality" of the spiritual function they embody. This anonymity may be deemed to be connected to the mystery of servitude (*'ubūdiyyah*). Massignon relates to this spiritual reality when noting Ibn 'Arabī's statement according to which in the virtue of *'ubūdiyyah* the only name left to the lover is "that which is given him by the Beloved". When asked for his name, the servant can only respond: "Ask the Beloved. My name is that by which He named me, because no name belongs to me! I am ignored and unknown, and I am the indetermination that is not determinable."[67] In I Kings 17:1, by virtue of such anonymous servitude, Elias directly expresses his function as a messenger of the vertical graces symbolised by water and rain, "By Yahweh, the living God of Israel, whom I serve, there will be neither dew nor rain in the next few years except at my word," following quite significantly the episode of the ordeal by fire (death and life) (I Kings, 18:30-46). He also prefigures the esoteric graces of Christ, especially through the multiplication of flour and oil (I Kings, 17:16) and the res-

---

[66] "Precursor of Justice (and therefore of the Messiah), patriarch of the Essene hermits, rescuer of those in despair unto whom he inspired prophetic dreams, the Jew Elias—and this is very remarkable—has been perceived by the great Israelites who have seen his premonitory apparitions, as a nomadic Arab, a Bedouin: before the founding of Islam" ("Elie et son rôle transhistorique....", p. 143).

[67] *Traité de l'amour*, p. 252.

urrection of a dead boy (I Kings, 17:22). Elias drinks from the torrent of the East and is fed by crows, a bird which often symbolises the solitary vocation of the *afrād*, those who have chosen to live in *l'alta solitude*, the "isolated" ones of Sufism.[68] Unlike Elisha, who would wear his mantle—thereby manifesting the impersonal ubiquity of the Eliatic function, Elias remains a solitary prophet (II Kings, 2:4). He is also the Eternal Adolescent,[69] not rarely mocking mundane illusions (I Kings, 18:27), always situated at the interstice, dying and being born constantly, reappearing here and there. Al-Khidr's "youth" flows from his immediate relationship with the Fountain of Knowledge: "One is ever young in the Intellect."[70] Sensitive to this dimension of immortal youth and mercurial mobility—this is the divine "sudden surge" that Massignon likes to refer to—popular folklore transforms the spiritual and guiding ubiquity of al-Khidr/al-Khadir into a "geographical map of annual displacements of Khadir in the world".[71] It is not without significance that this popular geography, expressive as it is of a spiritual archetype of which the people become the receptacle and the vehicle, *vox populi vox Dei*, finds its origin and its end in Jerusalem, a consecrated site of high concentration of his grace: "He normally resides in the

---

[68] Cf. the article "Corbeau" in *Dictionnaire des Symboles*, Jean Chevalier and Alain Gheerbrant, Paris, 1969. Let us also mention the fact that the Carmelites (Elias is the spiritual guide associated with Mount Carmel) introduced a colourful, black and white or brown and white, garment in the West, close to the *muraqqa'a* of the *malāmatiyah* Sufis, who were considered "wandering monks and eccentrics" and also called "magpies" (*pica*), "colourful crows".

[69] "Max von Oppenheim (*Von Mittelmeer zum Persischen Golf*, 1900, vol. II, p. 240) observes: 'Khidr-Elias (the two names here are conjoint) is called the Eternal Adolescent....'", ("Elie et son rôle transhistorique....", p. 146). The "Youth" of al-Khidr is due to his immediate relationship with the Fountain of Knowledge: "In the Intellect one is absolutely young" (Meister Eckhart, "Adolescens, tibi dico, surge," in *Sermons II*, ed. Ancelet-Hustache, Paris: Le Seuil, 1978, p. 84).

[70] Meister Eckhart, "Adolescens, tibi dico, surge," in *Sermons II*, ed. Ancelet-Hustache, Paris: Le Seuil, 1978, p. 84.

[71] "Elie et son rôle transhistorique....", p. 151.

Temple (*Haram*) of Jerusalem."[72] Thus, a central sacred location and spiritual ubiquity correspond, in the sense that the former is nothing but the crystallisation or the supernatural condensation of the latter.

The eschatological role of al-Khidr is also related to a periodical filling of the cracks of the traditional edifice, in accordance with the vertical relation that aligns tradition with its foundation: "Each year, Khadir visits the Wall (*Sadd*) of Gog and Magog, and repairs it."[73] The traditional reading of the *Sūrah al-Kahf* (the Chapter of the Cave) every Friday functions, moreover, in parallel to this repairing function on the eschatological plane in the liturgical economy of Islam.[74] Al-Khidr appears as

---

[72] "Normally he resides in the Temple (Haram) of Jerusalem, in the northern part of the ancient wall (which dominates the Cedron and Gethsemani): between Bāb al-Rahma—now the 'Gilded (blocked) door' and Bāb al-Asbāt." "Elie et son rôle transhistorique....", p. 151.

[73] 'Elie et son rôle transhistorique....", p. 151.

[74] This is also the function devolved upon the prophet Dhū'l-Qarnayn in the same *sūrah*: "They said: O Dhu'l-Qarneyn! Lo! Gog and Magog are spoiling the land. So may we pay thee tribute on condition that thou set a barrier between us and them? He said: That wherein my Lord hath established me is better (than your tribute). Do but help me with strength (of men), I will set between you and them a bank. Give me pieces of iron—till, when he had levelled up (the gap) between the cliffs, he said: Blow!—till, when he had made it a fire, he said: Bring me molten copper to pour thereon. And (Gog and Magog) were not able to surmount, nor could they pierce (it). He said: This is a mercy from my Lord; but when the promise of my Lord cometh to pass, He will lay it low, for the promise of my Lord is true. And on that day we shall let some of them surge against others, and the Trumpet will be blown. Then We shall gather them together in one gathering" (18:94-99). "This apocalyptic text is recited, for prophylactic motives which render it more and more 'unappealing' to 'enlightened' Muslims, but which is exposed in the following way by an immemorial tradition: this weekly recitation repairs the cracks made in the Wall of Gog and Magog ... by the barbarous hordes bearing this name, and its irruption should provoke the End of the world. An 'eschatological' event whose prodromes are exposed in the rest of the *sūrah*, and whose deadline should be delayed by the prayers of the believers." "Les 'Sept Dormants', apocalypse de l'Islam," *OM III*, p. 104. On the "hordes" of Gog and Magog and the cracks in the wall of tradition, see also René Guénon's *The Reign of Quantity*, chapter 25, "The Fissures in the Great Wall."

God's most central instrument, albeit the most hidden, in the economy of the divine Reminder. At the end of times, this function of reminder is revealed in all its plenitude. According to some traditional Muslim sources, Al-Khidr will return together with the seven privileged witnesses—the seven Sleepers of Ephesus—who are associated with him in the spiritual context of the eighteenth *sūrah*. Freed like them by grace from the limitations of time and space, the prophet of verticality will join the witnesses of inwardness. Massignon reminds us that, according to such sources, "Al-Khadir will be leading the avant-garde of the Mahdi's army, in order to guide it all the way to Jerusalem and to join Jesus son of Mary there,"[75] and the Islamic tradition associates him, therefore, with the *'īsawiyya* spiritual family of Zachariah, John and Jesus.[76]

\*

\* \*

It is in the same spirit, and within the same framework, that Massignon contemplates the relationship of Islam and its Prophet to Jerusalem. The fact that Massignon denotes the holy city and, more precisely, the relation of the Prophet to al-Aqsā—the place of his *mi'rāj* and his receiving the Law of Islam—as a "love from far away"[77] must be understood in a context that has

---

[75] 'Elie et son rôle transhistorique....", p. 152.

[76] "And Zachariah and John and Jesus and Elias. Each one (of them) was of the righteous (*sālihīn*)" (*Qur'ān*, 6:85). According to Massignon, this filiation can be read in Mihrāb Zachariah ("the Niche of Zachariah, the place of the only substantial miracle mentioned in the Qur'ān, the provision of supernatural fruits to Mary by the angels, in support of her fast," in "L'oratoire de Marie à l'Aqçâ, vu sous le voile de deuil de Fatima", [1959], *OM I*, p. 593) and in the retreat of Mary and of Saint John in Ephesus (*ibid.*, p. 595).

[77] "Jerusalem is the Qibla of the heart of Muhammad as a Prophet, the 'remote' goal of his desires, '*amor de lonh*', since, being no longer the Place of Expiatory Sacrifice at the Sakhra, Jerusalem remains the Place wherefrom the dew of Divine Grace and Mercy drops over the victims of the Abrahamic sacrifice, all the way to 'Arafāh, before the immolation

35

much more to do with time than with space, for at the end of time Islam envisages a transfer of the *qiblah* to Jerusalem. The distant Jerusalem is in a sense the symbol of the exile of Islam. But in mentioning *"l'amor de lonh"* of the troudabour Jaufré Rudel[78] (who would become a crusader in order to pay his loving respects to the Countess of Tripoli, whom he had loved without ever meeting her, having merely heard of her outstanding virtues), one of the most striking examples of the Troubadours' spiritual ethics of courtly love as expressed in a lover's pilgrimage to the East, Massignon already places the experience of "ecumenical grace" under the sign of the Eternal Feminine. The tradition that sees the conception of Fātimah taking place upon the "return" of the Prophet from al-Aqsā,[79] under the sign of a mercy associated with Jerusalem, places this rapport in the same light. The presence of the Niche of the Holy Virgin at the site of al-Aqsā, at the Mihrāb Zakariyā, as well as its "inner" signifi-

---

itself." "L'oratoire de Marie à l'Aqçâ....", p. 593.

[78] The historical uncertainty concerning the object of the love of a troubadour like Jaufré Rudel indicates, moreover, an opening onto the divine dimension of the Eternal Feminine. "Thus with respect to Geoffroi Rudel and to the *amor de lonh* he sang with such a sound art and such a captivating nostalgia: is it really a woman, and if so, which one? The countess of Tripoli of the legend having seemingly been excluded, one rightly thinks of Queen Eleanor. But isn't she a pure symbol instead? According to K. Vossler, it is Helen of Troy. (Unfortunately, we are not in the second Faust!) For Grace Frank, it is the Holy Land (after all Rudel was crucified, and very serious exegetes have admitted that, in the Song of Songs, the Beloved could be an allegory for Palestine); for Carl Appel it is the Holy Virgin (but, isn't this anachronistic in the first half of the twelfth century?); and finally, for others, perhaps God Himself?" Henri Irénée Marrou, *Les Troubadours*, Paris: Seuil, 1971, pp. 162-63.

[79] "It was during one of the nights of the 'desire for Jerusalem' that Muhammad's monogamous wife, Khadīja, conceived a daughter from him. The tradition of Muslim women relates how in that night there was provision from the Angel Gabriel to the Prophet, bringing with him in a state of dream (*Isrā*) from Jerusalem an apple (*tuffāha*) plucked in Paradise; and how Muhammad ate it before approaching Khadīja." "L'oratoire de Marie à l'Aqçâ....", p. 593. This "apple" is like the inverse analogue of the "forbidden fruit", and hence it participates in the mystery of Mary as a "reversion" of the tendency embodied by Eve.

cance, manifests this self-same inspiration as a fundamental spiritual and eschatological reality. In the same context, Massignon reminds us that the Turkish sultans who took Constantinople wrote on the *mihrāb* of all the churches which were converted into mosques the extract of verse thirty-seven of the third *sūrah*, "*Kullama dakhala alayha Zakariyā....*", as an omen of "the transfer of the Qibla to Jerusalem."[80] From a strictly essential spiritual perspective, Massignon reads in the Mystery of al-Aqsā the sign of a "voluntary sterility" intended for a begetting of the Word. At al-Aqsā, Mary appears as pure receptivity to the Word, or pure virginity perfectly "submitted" to the divine *fiat*. Hence she testifies to the "passively active" nature of woman—that is, a vocation that manifests itself actively by virtue of its inward and "passive" source of inspiration, a "passive activity" in which Massignon saw—together with Gandhi—the Mystery of Femininity: "....Woman was not made to claim a right, but to bear witness to a privilege, the privilege of the humiliated and the oppressed; the privilege of knowing the secret of history because she is the one making it."[81] Fātima shares with Mary the privilege of being

---

[80] "....the Turkish sultans who took Constantinople, the City of the Marian Triumph, ordered that in the niches of all the churches, which they turned into mosques, the verse *whenever Zachariah entered the sanctuary....* (3:37) be inscribed, restoring to the Jewish Virgin of Transcendence the sanctuary where the Incarnation of her Son had often been renewed in a sacramental way, because the capture of Constantinople is among the apocalyptic signs, precursor of the transfer of the Qibla to Jerusalem." "L'oratoire de Marie à l'Aqçâ....", p. 596.

[81] Extract from a radio interview on France-Culture in 1958, quoted by François L'Yvonner in his article "Une histoire épiphanique" in *Louis Massignon, mystique en dialogue*, Question de, n. 90, Paris: Albin Michel, 1992, p. 121. This vision of the spiritual mission of woman, exempt of all cynicism—this goes without saying with Massignon—is more "interiorist" than "dolorist", inasmuch as it implies the primacy of the "freedom of the heart" over the "necessity of the letter". The apparent inferiority which strikes woman in Islam—the incapacity to perform the ritual prayer during her cycle, the veil and claustration, the "almost optional" character of fasting—draws us back, according to Massignon, to the spiritual eminence of the "supererogatory" and the "secret". "Man bears witness whereas woman conceives. The *Shahādah* (bearing witness that God is One) becomes in woman a *dhikr khafī* (remembrance of the heart)." "La

a *"compatiente"*: *"fiat mihi secundum verbum tuum"* (Let it be done to me according to your Word) (Luke, 1:38). Massignon loved to translate this *fiat* by the Arabic feminine imperative *kunī*, rather than *kun*, although the latter is more frequent in the Qur'ān, in order to indicate the feminine nature of the soul in relation to God. Fātima represents in this sense the mystery of "private in-ward prayers", "able to conceive the Grace that must sublimate the literal Law".[82] Along with Mary, she is "co-spouse" of the Muhammadan Light. She is also Fātir,[83] "the point of genealogic junction of the Prophets and the Saints". Furthermore, she is, in a very profound and enigmatic way, *Umm Abīhā*, "mother of her father". Massignon considers her a substitute for Amina bint Wahb, the mother of the Prophet who lost her husband while pregnant, as well as *thaklā* (a mother deprived of her infant) at the Prophet's death, just like the Virgin, *mater orbata* (bereaving mother) after the Crucifixion. It is possible to think, in the light of some Shī'ite traditional data, that as "mother of her father"— Hallāj's "my mother has given birth to her father"[84]—she is iden-tified with the feminine "informal" pole of prophecy, hence with the "Mother of the Prophets". From this supereminent place she embraces the origin and the end of the human vocation. She represents and embodies the *Fitra*, "the mark of the predestined ones"[85] or the original, primordial, norm; and she is also by the

---

signification spirituelle....", *OM III*, p. 344.

[82] "'Umar committed the political mistake of entering into a duel with a woman, an inferior being, exempted from obligatory Muslim activities, and veiled with social despicableness; but apt to take refuge in private prayer and secret vows (an essentially feminine thing, especially in the Qur'ān), and able to conceive Grace, which must sublimate the literal Law." "L'oratoire de Marie à l'Aqçâ....", p. 598.

[83] "Fatima will be resurrected among men, even more, among prophets and the Saints (Imams), for she is the point of their genealogic junction, as indicated by Marandī." "L'oratoire de Marie à l'Aqçâ....", p. 606.

[84] Cf. Henry Corbin's commentary on Hallāj's enigmatic line as an allusion to the "Creative Feminine". *Creative Imagination in the Sufism of Ibn Arabī*, Routledge & Kegan Paul, 1969, pp.169-70.

[85] "The Perfect Woman, *Mathal A'lā*, 'Supreme Sign' of the Predestination of the Elect, representing the *Fitra*, the mark of the predestined ones,

same token the mother of the Mahdi: "The soul of Fātima, at the end of her solitary agony while being abandoned in contempt was visited and consoled by the messianic hope which is ridiculed by those who find happiness in this world. This hope is political and mystical at the same time, and it shattered the rigidly legalistic framework of the Sunni state, *opening Islam to a universalist perspective* and the ecumenical horizon foreseen by the Fatimid missionaries."[86] A central inspiration in the works of Massignon, the "femininity" of the soul, is therefore operative at all levels of the drama of existence. It nonetheless pertains first of all to our will, *fiat voluntas tua* (Let Thy Will Be Done), while reaching thereby the most profound meaning of Islam as surrender; a surrender that cannot be fully understood save in terms of the will, since the latter must let itself be informed by the divine Law. The "Marian sign"[87] pointed out by Massignon should constitute precisely, for this reason more than any other, the rallying point of the three lines of the Abrahamic family, hence the essential character of the Immaculate Conception in the ecumenical meditation of Massignon. Such a convergence on the Immaculate Conception is not only related to the spiritual imperative of inner "poverty" that is the fundamental calling of all children of Abraham, but also to a kind of "pre-decarnali-

---

who conceals the corresponding Divine Name, *Fātir*, under the parental relations of humanity." "L'oratoire de Marie à l'Aqçâ....", p. 612.

[86] "L'oratoire de Marie à l'Aqçâ....", p. 600.

[87] "Hence, it is not so much a matter of having them (Muslims) discern the eternal generation of the Word, as it is to suggest to them that, by allowing the virginal birth of the Messiah, the Immaculate Conception is the sole protection of pure monotheism (it "pre-decarnalises" the Incarnation): Christ (and the elect who are his adoptive members) will be born neither from blood, nor from the will of the flesh, nor from the will of a male. It is so because the entire Muslim protestation against the Incarnation bears against a carnal paternity while the entire Muslim witnessing for the Immaculate Conception bears for a virginal maternity, this "supreme parable" of God in Woman (*Qur'ān*, 16:62), who conceives the *fiat* (*kun*), mentioned eight times in the Qur'ān, referring in each case to Jesus son of Mary and to the Judgment." "Du 'signe marial'", 1948, *Louis Massignon, mystique en dialogue*, Question de, n. 90, Paris: Albin Michel, 1992, pp. 49-50.

sation" of the Incarnation that opens a theological space for an ecumenic communion in the "pure monotheism" which Islam intends to preserve until the end of times. In this regard, Massignon understands the Islamic rejection of God's begetting, exclusively focused on the masculine lineage of the flesh, as being compatible with a sense of spiritual engendering according to pure feminine virginity, as expressed by the example of Maryam in the Qur'ān.

\*

\* \*

It could be argued that the whole mystical thought of Louis Massignon revolves around the symbolic notion of "displacement". This notion, and its corollary, that of "displaced person",[88] determines all the planes of Massignon's thought and action, from mystical psychology to sociology. When considering the spiritual peaks of the human experience, the encounter of man and God, Massignon is so substantially Christian—despite what has been discreetly called his "temptation of Islam"—that he cannot conceive of the Divine, and the relation of the Divine with the human, except as a motion, a displacement, an incarnation. Hence, with regards to the meaning of the word "God" and its human representation, Massignon speaks in terms of a "fragile Host", a "Stranger", a "visitation", a "*fiat*",[89] and a "commotion", all of which are terms expressing movement, exchange, dynamic manifestation and interaction:

---

[88] However, there is a distinction between a voluntary "displacement"—that of the mystic who "makes room" for God through acceptance and sacrifice, and the forced "displacement" of the expatriate groups, or "refugees", who find themselves uprooted and abandoned without a shelter in spite of "progress" and "development", disseminated as they are to the four winds of modern socio-political and moral confusion.

[89] For Massignon, too, the divine *fiat* and the human "commotion" are essential notions in the spiritual anthropology of Islam, and they actually go back to the existentiating divine order (*kun* or *kunī*) and to the *khashiyya* (reverential fear) taught by the Qur'ān.

This fragile Host (the Lord) whom she (the soul) carries in her bosom determines (by her acceptance of the fiat) all her ways of being. This is not an invented idea which she develops as she pleases according to her nature; rather it is a mysterious Stranger whom she worships and who guides her: she devotes herself to Him.[90]

For Massignon as a Christian mystic, God is a stranger in this world: He is the "Light which shines in the darkness and which the darkness comprehends not." He became flesh so that man could be restored in His Divine image and likeness as *to zôon to theoûmenon*.[91] He neither integrates, orders nor governs the world extrinsically according to his Word; He does not structure and orient human reality according to the simple, but multifaceted, economy of His Law as in the case of Islam. He bears witness to the Truth, and His defeat or "folly" in the eyes of the world is overriding evidence of His Victory and Wisdom in the Spirit.[92] Since God has been "displaced" by the Incarnation and through the Divine Sacrifice, the soul must respond to His *fiat* by a "displacement" which is averred by her hospitality towards the Stranger, a welcoming of the divine Visitor. That is why the essence of hospitality is to give oneself in acquiescence to Grace, in a spirit of "poverty" vis-à-vis the divine Stranger and the thousand faces He chooses to assume in order to meet us, that is to say, our "neighbours". In the economy of grace, the Muslim Other has certainly constituted for Massignon[93] the

---

[90] "Réponses de Louis Massignon à deux enquêtes sur Dieu," in *Bulletin de l'association des Amis de Louis Massignon*, n. 6, September 1997, pp. 28-30.

[91] "Divinisable animal", as Jacques Berque proposes to translate this expression of St. Gregory of Nazianzus. *L'islam au défi*, Paris, 1980, p. 141.

[92] Pascal saw in the temporal triumph of Islam the sign of its "falsehood", and in the humiliation of Christ and his crucifixion the most profound proof of his truth. One cannot be more Christian than this, in a sense which, of course, does not embrace the whole of Christianity.

[93] As Amira El-Zein has shown in her study "L'Autre dans la spiritualité massignonienne (The Concept of the Other in Massignon's Spirituality)," in *Louis Keryell, Luis Massignon au Coeur de notre temps*, Paris, Karthala, 1999,

divine Host inviting to a "de-centring", the spiritual sting forcing him to a change of existential plane through conversion. The
hospitality of the Alusi family during his stay in Baghdad from
1907 to 1908 was the catalyst of a spiritual assimilation of this
de-centring that informs any genuine conversion.[94] This is the essence of Massignon's spirituality, and the secret of his existential
debt towards Islam.

*
* *

One cannot understand in depth Massignon's positions concerning the identity of Israel and its relationship with the question of Jerusalem without being fully aware of the spiritual connection binding together displacement and election. Everything
begins with the observation that spiritual election calls for and
requires acquiescence, and follows from a recognition that there
is no acquiescence other than in and through the "de-centring"
of the soul and its new "concentration" on God. Now, for Massignon, Israel's divine election is, by definition, a source of "displacement". Being chosen by God, Israel is summoned to let go
of itself as a natural, "carnal" reality, and is thereby "displaced".
This is why and how Massignon sees in Israel's destiny a holy
manifestation of the spiritual archetype of consent. At its highest level, this reality is denoted by the scriptural expression "the
virgin of Israel" (*Amos*, 5:2),[95] that is, the mystical essence of Is-

---

pp. 29-43.

[94] "The Alusi family, who pleaded as a warrant for the Frenchman before
the police, has considerably facilitated his research...." *Massignon*, Christian
Destremau and Jean Moncelon, Paris, 1994, p. 49.

[95] "Hear ye this word which I take up against you, even a lamentation, O
house of Israel: The virgin of Israel is fallen; she shall no more rise: she is
forsaken upon her land; there is none to raise her up. For thus saith the
Lord GOD; The city that went out by a thousand shall leave an hundred,
and that which went forth by an hundred shall leave ten, to the house of
Israel (*Amos*, 5:1-3, King James Version).

42

rael which is also the divine Presence, *Shekhina*.[96] On the level of historical reality, Israel's consent, which is nothing but faithfulness to the Torah, must be constantly renewed in the "return" (*teshuvah*) towards God. As a Catholic, Massignon cannot but underline the fundamentally Marian character of the archetype of Israel, as already indicated by the aforementioned traditional reference to the "virgin of Israel". The Holy Virgin being "displaced" too, she renounces her own will in order to be a "servant of the Lord". She is "chosen among all women", just like Israel is chosen among all the nations. Mary is the model of pure submission to God, and as such a symbol of the perfect soul exemplifying passive, virginal and feminine perfection.[97] If Massignon saw in the Immaculate Conception the rallying "Marian sign" of the three religions of the Abrahamic family, it is because, in the first instance, the virginity of the soul obedient to the divine *fiat* is the essence of Abrahamism as a consent to sacrifice. As we have suggested above, Massignon also envisages the "pre-decarnalisation" inherent in the "Marian sign", the supernatural and predestined purity of the Holy Virgin, as the spiritual and dogmatic locus of a spiritual ecumenism, inasmuch as it "attenuates" Christian incarnationism by a supernaturalisation of the "flesh", thus leaving untouched and inaccessible the divine transcendence that Jews and Muslims have jealously preserved as a privilege of their divine endowment. Hence Massignon's sometimes zealous, if not excessive, passion which he shows by his harshness to the attitude of some Jews and Jewish traditions on the Virgin Mary.

---

[96] The Zohar interprets the verse of Amos ("The virgin of Israel is fallen; she shall no more rise") to mean the total incapacity of Israel to "rise" by itself. The salvation of the "fallen virgin" is utterly in God's hands: "Whenever previously she was in exile, at the appointed time, she was wont of herself to return to the King; now, in this exile, the Holy One, be blessed, will go and take her by the hand and raise her, and give her comfort, and bring her back to his palace." *Zohar—The Book of Splendor*, ed. Gershom Scholem, New York, Schocken Books, 1977, p. 85.

[97] Massignon likes to remind his readers that before God "the soul feels feminine."

It is worth noting in this context that, if Mary is a woman, she is so in a "supernatural" and exemplary sense, while her "femininity" cannot be separated from her consent to the *fiat*, so that it is difficult to speak with Massignon of a "Marian feminism" without abuse; for the French Islamicist, femininity always refers, in the continuity of all monotheist traditions, to a masculine ontological centre, both directly as divine *fiat*, and indirectly as a "representative" human reflection of a sexual and social character; unless femininity be understood in a purely metaphysical and spiritual sense, perceived as the essence of man, *Ewig Weibliches,* the Eternal Feminine, which is expressed mystically by "the final Promotion of woman, the first, stainless 'Conception', of this frail sex that elevates us, setting us ablaze, in the end, like the hidden Mirror of Amaterasu-Omikami, into the Fire of the Burning Bush."[98]

In a sense that is not without analogy to Marian election, Israel is a nation chosen among all nations, but precisely to the extent that she has been attentively "listening" (*Shema Israel*) to her Lord. The "naturalism" of the nation is thus transcended on the level of a collective supernatural predestination. In contrast, all Jewish "nationalism" is but ethnic and "natural", and it can therefore only reveal its being a radical perversion of the divine election. One could even say that the "virginity" of Israel consists in its refusal to consider itself, or to be considered by others, as a "nation" in the purely natural, nativist, and therefore "carnal", sense of the term.

Herein lies, precisely, the crux of Massignon's critique of Zionism. Let us first of all pre-empt a possible error of interpretation regarding his way of thinking: if Israel is "displaced" by a kind of holy predestination, it does not mean at all, in and of itself, that this spiritual de-centring need be an obstacle, and an objection, to a Jewish return to the Holy Land. However, the whole matter lies in an assessment of the "spirit" in which this

---

[98] "Méditation d'un passant aux bois sacrés d'Isé," *Parole donnée*, p. 420. Cf. Massignon, Louis, *Testimonies and Reflections: Essays of Louis Massignon,* Notre Dame: University of Notre Dame Press, 1989, for Herbert Mason's translation of this text.

return may be achieved. Is it a return "in truth" and "in spirit", a return in all humility and in the hope and expectation of the Promise, or is it rather a collective rush—courageous, surely, and often efficacious in its horizontal realism and its technical ability—but bearing the sign of a civilisationist, not to say colonising, bias, and thereby wholly reducible to building a bridgehead for the modern world in what still remained of the Biblical world over half a century ago?

Massignon remained very ambivalent in his assessment of such a return to the Holy Land.[99] Initially, he did not exclude the possibility that this return could correspond, for pious Jews, to the fulfilling of a divine promise. However, the events of April and May 1948, especially the massacre perpetrated in Deir Yassine by the Zionists of Irgun, Lehi, and the Haganah paramilitary troops, not to mention the subsequent building of a Jewish neighbourhood on the site of the village a year later, increased his awareness of the incompatibility between inhumanely violent means and sacred ends. The holy purpose of a return to the Holy Land cannot be combined with means which bring about terror, contempt, and hatred of the Other. In fact, the peak of this realisation took place in July 1948, with the symbolic capture of Nazareth by Zionists on the 16th of that month. On this occasion, Massignon and his Egyptian Melkite friend Mary Kahil did not hesitate to interpret the passivity of the Occident as a true apostasy.[100] As for the military actions of Irgun, they were interpreted by Massignon as a profanation which, at the height

---

[99] "Are they still those 'Hovevei Zion,' those poor 'Lovers of Sion,' chased by the pogroms, who joined through the centuries the sublime wailers of the Wall of Lamentations? Or rather those racists with cruelly atheist skills who, in order to have the monopoly of an impious colonisation of the Holy Land, make themselves voluntarily slaves to large colonising American firms and dream that they can create the New Adam there like a supreme robot, and the Kingdom of God like an atomic laboratory?" "Le pèlerinage," *OM III*, p. 820.

[100] "How could Europe allow the bombardment of Nazareth? On the apostate Europe I shake off the dust of my shoes...." Quotation of Mary Kahil in Destremau and Moncelon, p. 290.

of transgression, recreates the pagan violation of the Sacrosanct Mystery:

> Zionism, which neglects the Hebraic holy liturgy, does not understand that by taking Nazareth with its bloody hands, it essentially imitates Antiochus or Pompey looking for the God in whom they did not believe behind the curtain of the temple.[101]

It is therefore the absence of "recourse" to God that spells the fundamental tare of the Zionist enterprise, a radical flaw which, as Massignon reminds us, lies at the foundation of the condemnation of Herzl's Zionism as a Jewish heresy by Orthodox rabbis on the occasion of the first Zionist Congress convened in Basel in 1897. One may also surmise that Massignon, as a Christian disciple of the humiliated *Rex Judaeorum*—the much-derided "King of the Jews," could not consider the earthly triumphalism of dejudaised Zionists without quivering. In the "logic" of his spiritual sensibility, there are worldly victories which cannot but reveal their collusion with the *princeps hujus mundi*. In such a context, the lack of a "recourse to God" cannot but result in degrading the idea and practice of pilgrimage into a kind of colonial enterprise, the latter being none other than the inversion of the former, according to Massignon; for if pilgrimage is indeed a displacement of the self towards the centre, an inner retreat towards that which all of a sudden invests us and displaces our self, opening us thereby to the Stranger, then colonialism—a profanation of sacred hospitality—amounts in contrast to a displacement in the form of a conquest, and a violation with no inner horizon but a Promethean illusion of power, inspired and reinforced by a fragmentary and planimetric knowledge akin to an apprentice sorcerer's. Far from providing one with spiritual sustenance, as does the pilgrim's land, the "colonised" land is debased to the status of an object of systematic exploitation, a debasement which is also a desacralisation, as the Native Indians of America have tragically experienced, and repeatedly emphasised in their testimonies. Even graver, in

---

[101] "Nazareth et nous, Nazaréens," (1948), OM III, 492.

the perspective of Massignon, is the colonialistic turning of the "host" into a "slave" condemned to industrial hard labour. "He is being substituted to work hard on production," whereas hospitality is, on the contrary, a substitution of oneself for the sake of the other; and likewise, "he (the other) is expelled on occasion as a displaced person,"[102] whereas the movement of hospitality is a displacement of oneself. According to this logic of appropriation, the "positive", practical and "realisational" knowledge trickling from phenomenalist idolatry, and the type of shallow relationship with the world that it founds and reinforces, not to forget the collective bedazzlement before its technical achievements—in the temporary oblivion of its less glorious impending fall-out—all of these elements legitimise, in the eyes of the "big colonial animal", the crushing of the Other, or his reining in and forcing him in step with civilisationist and technological idolatry. In contrast with this "Western" figure of the Jewish exodus, Massignon refers readily to Judah Magnes, the first president of the Hebrew University of Jerusalem and instigator of Ihud, the Jewish movement advocating parity between Jews and Arabs in the framework of a bi-national state.[103] Magnes' thought was based on a sort of "spiritual patriotism" that postulates access to the universal beyond the temptations of nationalism through a comprehensive meditation of traditional roots. The very earthly metaphor of Jewish identity—"the roots firmly planted in the soil"[104]—which reformed Jews have, according to Magnes, sacrificed under the superficial pretext of a lukewarm "universalism", suggested the path of a genuine spiritual Zionism that received but a very limited echo in Israel.

It is appropriate to recall, in this context of spiritual rootedness, the cultural and symbolic importance of the question

---

[102] "Le pèlerinage," (1949), *OM III*, p. 819.

[103] "Parity, we contend, is the one just relationship between the different nationalities of a multi-national state," in "Palestine, divided or united?" J.L. Magnes, *Oral evidence before the UN special committee on Palestine, 14 July 1947*, 1983, p. 33.

[104] "After you have rooted yourself in your nation you can overcome nationalism," *Dissenter in Zion*, Harvard, 1982, p. 226.

of language. Massignon advocates a return to the spirit of the Semitic languages in and through spiritual practices. This is neither a superficially pious conservatism on his part, nor a historical or archaeological concern; it is rather one of the most direct expressions of his longing for a radical primordiality, to a spiritualisation of language informed by a fundamental relationship with being. In such an ontological framework, language is not a mere tool of communication, nor a "manufacturer" of culture, nor a symbolic system of exploitation; it is, rather, an articulation of being, a prolongation and a multiplication of the Invocation of Divine Presence. This ontological reality of language takes us very far from the scattered contingencies and endless shifts of contemporary semiotics and its "whirling dervishes" of nothingness. Now, for Massignon, Arabic is the language that has remained the most faithful to the Semitic genius, a language marked by the fire of the Divine Presence. It is also the language of his conversion, the language of a principial relationship with God, and of the witnessing of the truth;[105] hence its importance for the Jewish community, which must revive its own Semitic genius. *A contrario*, the victory of modernist and colonial Jewish identity was sealed by a very symbolic victory on the linguistic level:

> (Arabic) still remains the language of Sephardic and Yemenite Jews today, but they were unfortunately not able to make their technical Arabic vocabulary prevail over the technical European vocabulary at the time of the formation of a scientific modern Hebrew in Palestine.[106]

With regard to the need for a spiritual rootedness in language, Islam "urges" Jews to reaffirm their faithfulness to their own linguistic, and ultimately mystical, substance.[107] This role

---

[105] "I remember my first prayer in prison when I was tied and I had nothing of mine on me, I spoke to God in Arabic...." "L'involution sémantique du symbole," (1960), *OM II*, p. 629.

[106] "La sauvegarde des cultures dans leur originalité," (1948), *OM I*, p. 206.

[107] It is therefore not surprising that the Kabbalists are often the most

of Islam as a spiritual "inciter" also reveals its pertinence with regard to a Christianity that Massignon deems to be spiritually "dozing" and even idolatrous. Thus, aiming at Christians who, having been converted by Western "civilisation" and its technological faith, and have forgotten their essential spiritual identity through their political "alliance" with Israel, Massignon does not hesitate to set the record straight:

> I have the duty to send a strong reminder that between, on the one hand, a state of Israel that rejects the Messiah, holds Jesus in suspicion and casts doubts on his Mother's honour, and on the other, a Muslim "fanaticism" that canonically chastises whomever doubts the sanctity of Jesus and the virginity of His Mother, my choice as a Christian is made.

The unexpected importance of the Holy Virgin in the question of Israel may surprise. Transported by a confessional zeal that is perhaps more "mystical" than "objective", Massignon attaches an utmost "symbolic" importance to some negative positions of the Jewish community of Nazareth towards Mary.[108] The truth is that Massignon always remained somewhat reluctant to recognise the largely obsolete character of these extreme positions, shocked as he was by the passionate reactions of some members of the Jewish community of Jerusalem and of Nazareth. Similarly, almost trembling with indignation, he recalls

---

Islamophile of all the Jews. Cf. Martin Buber or Gershom Scholem, whose thought and action were parallel to those of Judah Magnes.

[108] "Neither in Palestine, nor elsewhere, will the world ever find peace and justice as long as Israel does not revisit the case of the Mother of Jesus. So must it be, not so much regarding the gross calumnies of Sefer Toldoth Jeschu (and of their Talmudic reverberation), as with respect to a canonical judgment by the Jewish Community of Nazareth (*"mischmar cohenim"*, let us not forget this) which disbarred—before Barcochebas—the name of the legal father of Jesus ("a so and so") in the genealogical rolls (*megilloth juschasin*), with the marginal gloss "son of an adulterous woman"; a gloss pointed out by R. Schim'on bar 'Azzai; this is a canonical judgment which the conscience of Israel must erase if it wants to live again." "La Palestine et la paix dans la justice," (1948), *OM III*, p. 470.

the day when he heard a Jew from Jerusalem refer to Jesus as a *"mammser"* (bastard) and call for the destruction of the Holy Sepulchre. Later, in an interesting dialogue with a Jewish interlocutor, Massignon explains in a most direct manner the premises of his bold and intransigent stance on the question of the integrity of Jesus and Mary in the eyes of the Jews. In response, his Jewish interlocutor emphasised that the lack of respect towards Mary is a virtually unknown phenomenon in the world of Judaism. Notwithstanding, a consistent and orthodox Jew cannot accept the virginity of Mary without contradicting his own faith. This does not mean, however, that he has to translate this theological rejection into a defamation; the question simply does not arise for him, since it does not touch at all upon the spiritual integrity of the tradition in which and from which he lives.[109]

For Massignon, on the contrary, the question of the virginity of Mary is crucial, especially with respect to Jews, because the Immaculate Conception is the condition *sine qua non* for linking the Christians to the Abrahamic family: "Our position on Abraham is terrible according to you; you cannot accept Christians because they are not children of Abraham; we are not children of Abraham except if Mary is a virgin." The *fiat* of Mary is indeed for Massignon the stumbling block of the whole Christian edifice: questioning her virginity amounts to severing the bond connecting Christians to Abraham since it implies denying the only filiation which matters for them, namely the spiritual filiation. Massignon cannot imagine that Jews might be perfectly indifferent to this argument, precisely because he cannot envisage it in a perspective where Christianity would just be a "prepa-

---

[109] Here we quote the clarifying response from Massignon's Jewish interlocutor: "I know all the Jewish milieus of the East and Europe, and I have never heard a single insulting word against Mary by a Jew. This is a testimony that I can make before God. If, as a Jew, I am asked whether Mary is a virgin, I say no. But my "no" stops there, and this is a silence of the same kind as the silence of Eastern Christians that you mentioned earlier. It is not up to us to raise the problem; it does not concern us, it is all about the mystery of God vis-à-vis the Christians." Unpublished lecture, "Le front chrétien."

ration for the future accomplishment" among others. On this point the position of Massignon is totally uncompromising and without qualification.

In a similar fashion, Massignon interprets the extremist Jewish opinions concerning Mary—which are in no way representative, we repeat, of Jewish communities in general—as the very symptom of a lack of spiritual conformity on the part of Israel. He held that the recognition of Mary's purity was the necessary condition for a Jewish revival in the spirit of Abraham, nay, a prerequisite for all peace. This was a matter of spiritual integrity: "Honour your father and your mother if you want to live (have a long life on earth)"; for Massignon, Israel is at fault with regard to this injunction of the Decalogue. This is why he did not eschew denouncing the capture of Nazareth by the Zionist forces in 1948 as both a patricide and matricide:

> Before the Crypt of the Annunciation, Zionism comes up against the Fourth commandment of the Decalogue: "Honour you father and your mother" if you want to live. Honour the true parents of the Messiah, the Spirit of God, and the Virgin of Israel.[110]

This messianic kinship constitutes an allusion to the three Christian, Muslim and Jewish notions through which Massignon seeks to define a Marian ecumenism: the expression "Spirit of God" is a direct reference to the Qur'anic expression *Rūh Allāh*, Spirit of God), which pertains to Jesus; as for the "Virgin of Israel," it goes back, as we have seen, to the most profound spiritual reality of the Elect People by connoting its link to the Marian mystery. Massignon's reading is therefore completely representative of his spiritual approach, which consists in interpreting the religious positions which he denounces as betrayals of the very principles that found the spiritual and moral integrity of the traditions under discussion. However, it must be said that, in the particular case at hand, the argument presented by Massignon, apart from the fact that it cannot apply to the whole

---

[110] "Nazareth et nous, Nazaréens, Nassara," (1948), *OM III*, p. 493.

of Israel, is principally determined by a Christian orientation which, from its own point of view, the Judaic tradition has every right to ignore. In a way, Massignon is forced to acknowledge this impossibility, in an effort of supra-confessional objectivity which bears witness to his intellectual integrity. Indeed, the crux of the problem is that Judaism cannot accept the virginal conception of Mary without accepting *ipso facto* the Christian Incarnation, *quod absit*:

> Israel cannot come to recognise that Mary is a virgin because that would mean for Israel to become Christian.[111]

These difficulties and tensions demonstrate the extent to which the spiritual economy of Christianity informs Massignon's approach to spiritual realities, including non-Christian religions. This is why inter-religious dialogue is based, for him, on a clear awareness of the chief principles of one's own religion, without which an approach to the other can only be vitiated through a kind of indifference or a culpable recklessness. Notwithstanding these incontrovertible difficulties that are the ransom of the religious phenomenon as such, one's main concern should be to keep from all sterile inter-confessional polemics, so as to preserve—or promote—a perfume of serenity and sacred respect in the garden of the other as in one's own.[112]

Be that as it may, the mystical equation between the reality of Mary and the essence of Israel worked out by Massignon stands at the heart of the question. For Israel, just as for Islam and Christianity, the main problem is to keep from bearing witness against one's own spiritual reality, against the "mother of one's own being", in the Arabic sense of essence and perfection. It is doubtless in this sense that one should understand that which Massignon denotes as the "outclassing" of the state of Israel by

---

[111] Unpublished text of the conference "Le front chrétien."

[112] Let us specify that this failure to be in conformity with one's own foundations is by no means an exclusive flaw of the Jewish community, as Massignon makes it clear in his occasional "treatment" of other believers, first and foremost Christians.

Mary. The Queen "outclasses" the country because she is, "by divine right", the "original seed" of the homeland. She represents the spiritual principle which presides sacrificially and quasi-sacramentally over the social and "natural" body. This principle being acknowledged, one will find it less surprising, or perhaps less unsettling, to read into the ways Massignon connects the two seemingly irreconcilable figures of Miriam of Nazareth and Queen Mary-Antoinette[113] of France; for in point of fact, the persecuted Queen is the figure *par excellence* of sacrificial destiny, a figure of the spirit being persecuted and sacrificed in the flesh. Massignon notes that Marie-Antoinette embodies the mystery of the foreigner and the misunderstood, the humiliated person that cannot be "assimilated" by the nation and its purely natural standards, values and preferences. As such, the reviled Queen assumes an eschatological function as a "proxy" in view of the ultimate advent of God's "Justice". We are here at the heart of a profoundly Christian vision of the world's spiritual economy, one in which the suffering of *compatientes* (those women who suffer the passion for others) is fuel for the revelation of Truth in history.

Then what does Jerusalem represent in the economy of Justice? It is clear that for Massignon the Holy City epitomises the apparent paradox of a "centre for de-centring", if one may say so. Like all pilgrimage sites, it "places" the soul by displacing it, therefore dragging it out of its individualistic idolatry in order to reveal to her the *qiblah* of the heart.[114] Jerusalem is also a pilgrimage site in a more particular sense. It is the Holy City (the root *q-d-sh* or *q-d-s* of the Saint of the Saints of the purest inaccessibility) where the three lines of the Abrahamic family converge. It is the place of "de-centring" wherein each community must realise its own desire for justice by sublimating it, because "one can

---

[113] "The Israeli state has not understood yet that Miriam of Nazareth outclasses it.... Mary-Antoinette brings out the indignity of Woman, who will testify on the last day against all the persecutors—just like in ancient times, when She used to have the last word before the judge in China."

[114] It is by virtue of this principle that, based on a *hadīth*, Islam defines the *Hajj* as the "monasticism" of Islam.

possess spiritually only that which one has renounced materially here-below."[115] It is at this point, and at this point only, that the true meaning of the Abrahamic descendance of the three religions is realised:

> There (in Jerusalem), I understood that Abraham was the father of all beliefs, that he was the pilgrim, the "stranger" [Hebrew: ger], he who left his close ones, he who made a pact of friendship with the foreign countries where he went for pilgrimage, (I understood) that the Holy Land was not the monopoly of one race, but the promised land for all pilgrims like him.[116]

Conversely, or as a shadow cast by the Divine Light, Jerusalem is also one of those places of clashing contact where the desire for Justice emerges fully in its most violent intensity:

> These zones of grief are naturally located on the surface of friction and osmosis between the two cultures; these apocalyptical, eschatological cries, of those hungry for Justice, however strange they may be, can be interpreted and given their true value after discovering that they hold in common, on both sides, a memory of past promises that becomes, in trial, a desire for the advent of Justice, or more simply, the need for an intelligible coincidence between the remembered promise and its fulfilment: "you will not look for me, if you had not already found me."[117]

This is the sense of the Absolute, the essence of the desire for Justice, that springs forth with all the more intensity in the relative domain where the impossibility of its realisation is confirmed. Henceforth, far from being a mere immediate conver-

---

[115] "Ce qu'est la Terre Sainte pour les communautés humaines qui demandent justice," (1948), *OM III*, p. 474.

116 Excerpt from *Trois prières d'Abraham*, quoted by Pierre Rocalve, "Louis Massignon et Abraham", Luqmân, vol. 13, n. 2, 1997, 26, p. 30.

[117] "Le Mirage byzantine dans le miroir bagdadien d'il y a mille ans," (1950), *OM I*, p. 126.

gence, the ecumenism of Massignon appears, in its collective substance, like an "ecumenism of opposition", an ordeal in view of Justice. The only truly transcendent solution would consist in recognising the Absolute, and therefore one's own thirst for Justice in so far as it relates to it, in the affirmation by the other of that which contradicts one's own. Here the supreme spiritual paradox is that this opposition reveals a desire for Justice which the level of opposition cannot provide: it calls for a vertical displacement which is the condition *sine qua non* of all peace. We can understand in what sense—a profound and infinitely more "pertinent" sense than all geopolitical considerations—Massignon considered that the world's destiny would be decided in Jerusalem. Conceived as a mere place of bodily, geographical "displacement", the Holy City cannot but serve as a means, or even a pretext, for "denying" the other in the name of the sense of the Absolute that animates our faith, a sense of the Absolute which today is, in fact, adulterated and marred by all kinds of idolatry and a host of religious parodies and perversions. The exclusive claims of "religious nationalism" (whichever it may be) cannot but exacerbate the violent cycle of action and reaction resulting from an incapacity or unwillingness to "displace" oneself, a failure to realise what Frithjof Schuon refers to as "objectivity", the capacity to look at oneself from the outside, to renounce one's illusory self-centredness, and to die to oneself.

The whole question amounts to knowing whether a religious community, in all its social and psychological relativity, is capable of such a "displacement". On this point, we should comment upon two passages by Massignon that may allow us to gain an insight into what could be referred to as his "mystical-political eschatology". It seems that one may identify in his work, in the purest Catholic tradition based on the cardinal distinction between the earthly Church and the mystical Body, on the one hand a collective mass, a sociological raw matter more or less determined by a principle of inertia, and on the other hand, a supernatural dimension of the collective, a "supernatural entity" crystallised at the point of convergence of all the spiritual "pilgrims" whose interiorisation has "displaced" them towards God, or whom God has displaced by inviting them to a spiritual interiorisation. If there is a "collective salvation", it cannot but proceed from the latter pole:

> I profoundly believe that, despite and through all errors, scandals and crimes, the final reality of human history is built with the sum of our ultimate personalities, which our thirst for suprahuman justice unites, and thereby immortalizes.[118]

History is therefore finalised by God's will, which prevails in the end over all the turbulence and rowdy unrest of collective idolatry. Massignon goes so far as to speak of a "construction"—starting from the "premonitory signs" crystallised by the fulgurating and discontinuous encounters between Heaven and earth—of a trans-historical entity that is for him like the mystical secretion of our earthly identities vowed to the Eternal:

> This is how the ultimate, supra-historical physiognomy of each person, each city, each group, is constructed; through a series of unheralded observations, "surprises" and converging "recognitions", which Jung, from Zurich and the most judicious of Freudians, minimises by reducing them to cyclical reappearances of natural archetypes. It is not in nature, in the cadre of wild landscapes, that these constructions are sketched here below, but in the artificial and moving décor of the cities' social life, those Babylons that the supernatural Jerusalem will cause to crumble, ending with their ruin and the "voices of the city" overwhelmed by the solemn sound of the wailings of the parturient pain of apocalyptic water fairies.[119]

Let us note that the principle of this apocalypse is less collective than personal; it builds up starting from the individual as its soul's consent to the Divine *fiat* before radiating into the collective dimension: "Man was not created for works of outer charity; but to worship *first* in his heart the divine Host, in the present

---

[118] "Ce qu'est la Terre sainte....", *OM III*, p. 472.

[119] "Le Mirage byzantine," (1950), *OM I*, p. 128.

56

moment." It is by virtue of this inner welcoming of God in the instant, without which every external activity is like "sounding brass", that some religious "poles" with a particular social vocation can somehow magnetise a beam of efficient spiritual forces. Thus, concerning India and the function of Gandhi, Massignon would write:

> I believe very deeply in the authentic social radiation, throughout the centuries, of some saintly religious personalities who are at the origin or at the knots of these lines of spiritual force.[120]

The pole to whom Massignon refers is therefore an "intermediary" personality, bridging in a way the gap between the inward and the outward. This situation is therefore somewhat different from the case of "invisible" saintly persons on the model of the Eliatic initiation—whose "action of presence" remains for the most part occult—since it involves remarkable souls who are in one way or another involved in socio-political contingencies, and therefore no doubt more spiritually "mixed", in the image of Gandhi. It remains to be determined at which level, and up to which point, the "reminder" of these "saintly religious personalities" can make Justice emerge. Whatever the answer, it is certain that Massignon's eschatology tends to see Justice "descend" into human history through and in its final ends. Some may be of the opinion that the concrete engagements of Massignon led him to give to the reign of Justice some determinations and bases that are perhaps too terrestrial. If that is so, one must conclude that his vision of an incarnation of Justice was certainly connected to, and informed by, his own vocation, his inner "vow" and, even more so, his outer oath and "destiny". The commentary of the Zohar to which we made an earlier reference seems to suggest to us an answer to the difficult question of the collective salvation of Jerusalem that is at the same time more elliptical and more ingrained with "spiritual realism":

> Whenever previously she was in exile, at the appointed time,

---

[120] "Ce qu'est la Terre sainte....", *OM III*, pp. 472-73.

she was wont of herself to return to the King; now, in this exile, the Holy One, be blessed, will go and take her by the hand
and raise her, and give her comfort, and bring her back to his
palace.[121]

Israel's spiritual recovery—and by extension, the recovery
of all "fallen" and perverted religion in its terrestrial manifestation[122]—cannot be its own working. It is plain to see, following
Amos, the extent to which the "army" of Israel is "decimated";[123]
and the Kabbalah echoes this observation by emphasising the
increasing rarity, in times of confusion, of true *Mequballim*—
those who receive, conserve and transmit the genuine message
of God.[124] Far from drawing pretexts for some gloominess or any
kind of despair, the Zohar teaches us how to find in this most
marked disequilibrium between human weakness and divine
Mercy the most beautiful and profound reasons for hoping for
the day when "Yahweh shall be One and his Name shall be One."

\*

\* \*

As an inner prelude to this eschatological affirmation of the
One, the soul's pure receptivity to the Divine *fiat* and to the "axial

---

[121] *Zohar—The Book of Splendor*, ed. Gershom Scholem, New York Schocken
Books, 1977, p. 85.

[122] Massignon would certainly have become indignant at the liturgical
improvisations and the profane demagogy of many manifestations of the
post-conciliar Church, and no less at the abominations of hateful violence
emanating from some sectors of the contemporary world claiming to
represent Islam.

[123] We may not be far from the moment when, according to a *hadîth*, "of
Islam only the name shall remain."

[124] "The 'pillars' of the exiled people....appear to have become a negligible
minority in the era of the triumph of 'Edomite' civilisation, this modern
world of ours which has even been transplanted to the Holy Land itself."
Leo Schaya, *The Universal Meaning of Kabbalah*, Sophia Perennis, 2005, p.
146.

explosion" is also described by Massignon in terms of "fission"[125] and a "miracle within", expressing the prodigy of what Meister Eckhart denoted as the birth of the Word in the essence of the soul.[126] Therefore the axial experience is first of all an experience lived in the intimacy of the spiritual heart. The perfect praying servant at al-Aqsā, Zachariah, joins the Seven Sleepers of Ephesus in this "miracle from within". The presence of Mary in Ephesus—attested by popular tradition and by the Council of Ephesus[127]—associated with Saint John and Mary Magdalene, and the integration of this chosen site into the "interiorist" and sapiential legacy that also includes Heraclites at the temple of Artemis, marks the place with an "ecumenical" imprint that takes us well beyond anecdotal evidence and supposedly fortuitous coincidences. Massignon perceives in this symbolic place the spiritual "parturition" of the Holy Virgin and the contemplative path of Saint John.[128] The "mystery of Mary, John and Mary Magdalene of Ephesus"[129] to which he refers must be understood as an allusion to the inner and silent testimony, imbued with suffering, of the witnesses of the Resurrection; for the miraculous sleep of the Seven Sleepers in the Cave and the perfect orison of the Virgin described by the verse of Zachariah are clearly parallel manifestations of the inwardness of the Religion of the Heart. Inwardness is here intimately connected with an "*esseulement*" (a

---

[125] "Méditation d'une passant sur la visite aux bois sacrés d'Isé," (1959), OM III, p. 715.

[126] "For God operates the work of his birth within the soul; his birth is his work and his birth is the Son." Meister Eckhart, "Ecce ego mitto angelum meum," *Sermons II*, ed. Ancelet-Hustache, Le Seuil, Paris, 1972, p. 9.

[127] The Council actually took place at the Church of Mary in Ephesus.

[128] "I have been very interested in Ephesus lately. I have understood the importance of this "august" site looking out to the sea (towards Patmos), wherein the aging John secluded himself, praying for the whole Church, because it is there he had hidden his adoptive mother, who was entrusted to him on the cross by a sentenced person." "L'involution semantique", *OM II*, p. 636.

[129] "Le culte liturgique et populaire des Sept Dormants Martyrs d'Ephèse," (1961), *OM III*, p. 123.

spiritual solitude or *solitudo*) of the soul in the divine Presence, a principle that some Islamic brotherhoods or *turuq* have integrated into their initiatic method in the form of the *khalwah*, or spiritual retreat. Massignon also sees in it the "seeds of Christian eremitism". Ephesus is identified in this sense with a place of exile, a site of awaiting death and resurrection, very much akin to the "otherworldliness" of Our Lady of Soledad, our Lady of Solitude awaiting the Resurrection. Following a parallel spiritual orientation, Massignon was able to find in the desert spirituality of Père de Foucauld a very direct symbolic expression of this mystery of holy solitude under the gaze of the One. This is so inasmuch as the desert presents us indeed with both a saving and a destructive, or at least implacable, dimension; it is the maternal welcome of the oasis, but also the inalterable purity of the sun and death. Massignon's inner experience is fundamentally marked by this blazing gaze of the Transcendent on the naked and sinful soul of the pilgrim:

> Then nothing; save the vow of His sacred inward solitude; a recognition of my original indignity, a transparent shroud between us two, an intangibly feminine veil of silence which disarms Him, and which becomes iridescent through His coming, under his creating Word.[130]

Solitude is thus a sign of virginity, or inner poverty of the soul in obedience and surrender to one's only Lord. In a French translation of remarkable beauty, Massignon finds in Hallāj symbolic expressions of this mystery: "In their secret, our hearts are a single Virgin wherein no dreamer's dream can penetrate (*Nos coeurs en leur secret, sont une seule Vierge où ne pénètre le rêve d'aucun rêveur*)."[131] In addition, the "deep sleep" of the seven young men of the cave transcends the texture of every dream.

---

[130] *Parole donnée*, pp. 282-83.

[131] This is the "virgin heart", centre of grace at the heart of every human being. For this "virgin heart" ("point vierge"), one may refer to the beautiful study of Dorothy C. Buck, "Mary and the Virgin Heart," *Sufi*, 24, 1994-95, pp. 5-10.

The transcending of the "worldly" dream thus amounts to a holy "deafness" that shields the soul in the "cave of the heart" from the "sirens' song" of the existential veil: *Then We sealed up their hearing in the Cave for a number of years* (*Qur'ān*, 17:11). In this case, time and space are reduced to a moment and a point, beyond all determination of "where" and "when", a point also echoed by Hallāj's meditation: "My essence is made explicit to the extent that 'whereness' is no more."[132]

However, if the ecumenical inwardness of the Seven Sleepers could so profoundly influence Massignon's life and work, it is also by reason of its exteriorisation by a return to the world as a witnessing: having come out of the cave, the martyrs returned to life to become living witnesses of the miracle of faith. Herein perhaps lies the essence of the spirituality of Massignon: utter surrender and perfect witnessing. In a letter to Mary Kahil written during the last months of his life, Massignon counts among the achievements of his work for his substitutive sodality of prayer and friendship with Muslims, the Badaliya, "the defence of the act of Abrahamic abandonment of the Seven Sleepers of Ephesus, the seven Lazarus, related to Mary Magdalene's act, she who was the apostle of the Resurrection, and the guardian at the threshold of their cave."[133] The Byzantine tradition in fact situates the cell where Mary Magdalene—the beloved disciple of Christ and the companion in exile of the Holy Virgin and Saint John, the *Ahl al-Bayt* of Christianity, so to speak—spent the end of her life at the entrance to the Cave of the Seven Sleepers. Hence, the convergence of Mary Magdalene and the Seven Sleepers confirms that the mystery of inwardness has two faces: the strictly inward one of complete reliance upon God (*tawakkul*), as well as an outward one pertaining to faithful witnessing in the world. In this context, Mary of Magdala embodies that "excess of love" that seeks none but Christ. Bérulle has described this totality of Mary Magdalene's love by addressing Jesus in the following terms:

---

[132] Cf. "Interférences philosophiques et percées métaphysiques dans la mystique hallagienne: notion de l'essentiel désir," *OM II*, p. 228.

[133] Quoted from Jacques Keryell, *L'hospitalité sacrée*, Paris, 1987, p. 323.

During your journeying and public life in Judaea, she was the first who sought you for love. You have sought the first, and the others have sought you for their particular needs and their extreme necessities, looking for your miracles more than for yourself.[134]

It is this love that leads St. Mary to become the guardian of the threshold of the "cave" and that of the Holy Sepulchre, in mere expectation of her Lord. And it is precisely this love that constitutes the foretelling of the Resurrection. It is she who, in her extreme poverty as sinner, is in a position to communicate in all humility the Good News: she expects nothing good from herself, and cannot claim any "talent" save that of Love.

In the Qur'anic account of the Chapter of the Cave, it is the dog who—analogically—plays the role of guardian at the entrance of the cave; as a creature often endowed with a bad reputation in Arab Islam—but subject to a positive symbolism as a paradisal animal (*al-kalb*), the dog actually embodies in this passage the highest spiritual function of the inspiring guide. Some Shīʿite interpretations go so far as to see in this dog the figure of ʿAlī, whereas the Druze identify the dog with Salmān and al-Khidr. In any case, what emerges from these diverse symbolisms is the image of the dog as an initiatory and teaching figure, "invested in relation to them (the Sleepers) with the spiritual role of al-Khadir."[135] The bad reputation of the dog in exoteric Islam—analogically to the figure of Mary Magdalene as sinner—can therefore allow us to read into this surprising identification a kind of esoteric occultation. Indeed, the witnessing in the world that we have been discussing is not necessarily exteriorised in a way that would be recognisably perceptible or outwardly comformable.

On the plane of inner realities, the Seven Sleepers epitomise the pillars of the world and those of the community of believers: Massignon stresses their identification with the *Abdāl*, the

---

[134] Bérulle, *Élévation sur sainte Madeleine*, Grenoble, 1998, p. 89.

[135] "Les Sept Dormants apocalypse de l'Islam," (1950), *OM III*, p. 107.

"substitutes", the just or righteous ones whose occult presence in the world is also intercessional and spiritually foundational; they are, furthermore, the "Posts of the Holy Land,"[136] without whom the religious community would collapse, as if deprived of grace, since it belongs to them to be the "axial" guarantors of a harmonious relationship between the world above and the here below. Their eschatological function is therefore central and parallel to al-Khidr's, he who actually presides over their assembly and "contains" the tides of Gog and Magog.[137]

The Qur'ān also makes mention of the Sleepers being "turned" by God during their sleep, giving thereby the impression that they are actually awake. This principle of alternation has sometimes been interpreted by Muslim apologists as referring to the historical changes that have characterised the Christian world, especially the various tribulations and catastrophes marking the history of Byzantium, historical "turns" expressing the providential mystery of divine purpose. One can also read herein, on a more directly spiritual plane, and even following the Qur'anic text literally, an allusion to the Divine All-Powerfulness which turns and returns those men who are perfectly surrendered, having them follow the cosmic rhythm of the motions of the sun, as the correspondence of terms in verses 17 and 18, *dhāta'l-yamīn dhāta'l-shimāl*, seems to indicate. God "turns" the hearts of men just like He turns the sun and the stars. In other words, the perfect abandonment of sleep—which resembles *prima facie* a "death"—is in fact accompanied by a "life" that is completely dependent upon divine activity. After waking and coming out of the cave, the young men wonder how long their sleep

---

[136] "They are the *Awtâd*, the Pillars of the Holy Land, who cast sparks against crimes....according to Ghazāli...; the *Abdāl*, supporting Pillars of the world here below...." "Les 'Sept Dormants' apocalypse de l'Islam," *OM III*, p. 107.

[137] Massignon has pointed out various devotional practices in Baghdad that evidence this protective function attributed to al-Khidr, conjoined to that of the *Abdāl*: "In Baghdad, workers suffering under their tasks, say, instead of the usual Muhammadan Tasliya: *Yal-Khidr, ya' Bû Mhimmèd*; and mothers pacify their frightened babies with the words *Yammak Khidir Eliyās, yābah*."

has been, but the uncertainty of the duration (a day, a part of a day?) and its disproportion to the historical time that has actually and "outwardly" elapsed evidently points to a relativisation of temporality. Abandonment to the Divine *fiat* does not pertain to perpetuity, but to eternity: "It is the instinct of desire for the essential which constitutes the only bearable manner of envisaging eternity, and not this indefinite prolongation of time."[138] Eternity is understood in accordance with the non-temporal axis of abandonment to the Divine Will, oftentimes coinciding with this immediate present which is its door. Curiously enough, the Sleepers' uncertainty about time—which is resolved in verse 25 (309 years)—is replicated by another uncertainty, namely that of the number of the Sleepers themselves. One may also fathom in this a sign of God's transcendence, and the incognoscible depth of His ways: *qul rabbī a'lamu bi'iddatihim ma ya'lamuhum illa qalīl* ("Say: My Lord is best aware of their number. None knoweth them save a few" 18: 22). The number of the predestined cannot be known by people who judge by the forms they have been given to know conventionally: *Spiritus ubi vult spirat.* Thus, the pillars of light remain at least partially invisible to the fleshly eyes of the world.

The Breton pilgrimage of Vieux-Marché, extending a practice common to the Muslim and Christian worlds, has become since 1954 a witnessing echo of Massignon's devotion to the Seven Sleepers of Ephesus. Massignon has listed the many manifestations, both Christian and Muslim, of popular devotion towards the Seven Sleepers in an appendix to his article on the subject published in 1961.[139] The ubiquity of the Spirit is herein suggested—namely, that of al-Khidr and Elias—informing the popular and folkloric imagination that serves readily as its vehicle and support. The active universality of the Spirit is projected onto the passive universality of the collective human psyche, and is thereby reflected in it; and this is needless to say "a hyphen between East and West." In parallel to such popular testimony, the

---

[138] *L'hospitalité sacré*, p. 323.

[139] "Le culte liturgique et populaire des VII dormants martyrs d'Ephèse," (1961) *OM III*, pp. 134-41 & 151-59.

pilgrimage likewise expresses, over the cycle of time, the perennial return of witnessing, the periodic rebirth in the "Water of
Youth" of divine Presence, the spring of al-Khidr, the "verdant",
whose grace of ubiquity is also a privilege of perpetuity; this
is an "horizontal" perpetuity, linking in an invisible thread the
manifestations of its "knowledge", but also, and above all, giving access to Eternity, by making the soul born again into that
which she is in truth *sub specie aeternitatis.*

*
*  *

The green (in Japanese, *midori*), verdant nature of the truth
of the initiator *par excellence* constitutes precisely the symbolic
hallmark of our last stage, that of Japan and the sacred woods
of Ise. We are referring to the trip Massignon made to Japan
on the occasion of the 9th World Congress of the International
Association for the History of Religions, held four years prior
to his death, in 1958, and about which he has left us a spiritual
testament with his text, published in English, "Meditation of a
traveller on his visit to the sacred forest of Ise."[140] Notwithstanding his extraordinarily intuitive incursions within the domain of
what he calls the "human beauty" of "the Aryan Path," Massignon did not cease to affirm the transcendent "pre-eminence" of
Abrahamic monotheism,[141] doubtless because he did not find in
the sapiential disciplines of the East (including Platonic Greece)
the devouring fire of the love of the divine Person. When Massignon mentions the God of India, it is the name of Ishvara, the
personal Deity, which comes to his pen, and not that of Atman,

---

[140] "Méditation d'un passant sur la visite aux bois sacrés d'Isé," (1959), *OM
III*, pp. 714-22.

[141] "Whatever may be the human beauty of the Greek or Indian "Aryan
Path ", upwardly trodden by heroes towards the Unknown God's
heaven, or the common touch of pure melody met with among the most
humble Polynesian or African tribes, the "pre-eminent" value of Semitic
monotheism transcends." "Tu vertex et apex," (1937), *OM III*, p. 788.)

the transpersonal Subject.[142] Advaitin or Mahayanic non-dualism could not "speak" to this compassionate interlocutor of the God of Abraham. It is, however, significant that Massignon needed to go all the way to Shinto Japan to find the nearest parallel to the most intimate dimensions of his personal reality: those of his country, his roots, but also, and more profoundly, the mythological archetype of the soul's rectification in the mirror of God. Thus, we surprisingly and wonderfully discover a genuine alchemy in this spiritual exploration of the distant depths of a Shamanic mythology, for folkloric "mythology" is understood by Massignon as a reservoir of archetypes bearing upon the most personal "salvation". Massignon approaches the mythological reality of Shinto with "the illiterate mind of a foreigner"; which is to say with the "virginity" of a host to the Rising Sun, while remembering that for the Japanese the sun is "feminine". Therefrom, the vernal ambience evokes the kake-monos "of spring blossoming trees" contemplated by the traveller before his departure for Japan, a legacy from the bedroom of his childhood, where his father, Pierre Roche, a "Japanising" artist, had placed them. That the Far East of the Ancestors may have left an impact on Massignon in the way of a catalyst for a recollection of the origin and memories of his childhood is certainly not a coincidence. The inspiration of the text, at least partial if not wholly, is founded on an immemorial reminder of our Paradisal Origin, the primordial innocence of a simple and—in the true, undeprecative sense—naïve conscience. The rehabilitation of the pre-mystical intuitions of Massignon's father constitutes the most personal mark of this return to the sources of the Promise.

With regard to Ise, Massignon is particulary sensitive, as Bernard Frank reminds us,[143] to the "lively contrast" between the "light green" of the rice fields and the "velvety green" of the

---

[142] "India has always cast a spell on me. God hides himself in a way. We have to find him. Ishwara hides in us. We are his shrine." "'Gandhian' outlook and techniques," (1953), *OM III*, p. 375.

[143] Bernard Frank, "Louis Massignon et le Japon," in *Louis Massignon et le dialogue des cultures*, Paris, Cerf, 1996, pp. 357-64.

pines and thujas. The two are experienced as a reassurance; it is the green of the eternal spring of a certain Shamanic primordiality, but also that of a nostalgia for one's country of birth. Hence, the colour green places meditation under the sign of the mirror, it becomes the "silvering" of the mirror wherein the real self of he who is no longer a traveller but a pilgrim is reflected. More precisely, it seems that the contrast of the two shades of green—light and dark—calls for this "remembering", as if through a sort of reflective exchange between the two shades, evoking the interplay of the present and the past, the current "self" and the earlier, long-established "self", the witnessing of the pilgrim and the ancestral vow (P. Roche). The light green of rice fields evokes the virginal benediction of the agricultural labour of men, "a wonderfully artistic paradox ... dear to (Pierre Roche's) thought",[144] whereas the more dense green of the forest already evokes the retreat of the sanctuary, the cave of Amaterasu-Omikami, the Shinto goddess of the sun who had withdrawn into her grotto as a response to the wild pranks of her brother Susano-o-no-Mikoto, before being lured out of her retreat for the sake of "enlightening" the world; herein lie the two dimensions, one collective and the other mystical, of the Virgin of Transcendency: the pull of inwardness and the gift of light to the world.[145] Hence, Massignon recognises in Susano-o-no-Mikoto's solar sibling "the Virgin of Transcendence—foreseen, intimated as a common archetype, from the Greek cave of Persephone (of the Eleusinian Mysteries) to the Japanese cave of Amaterasu-Omikami. She is the Virgin with a Mirror (not one of 'feminine sexuality', but rather of ecstatic abandonment), and a sword (not one of 'virile sexuality', but

---

[144] "The wonderfully artistic paradox of non-violated Virginity blessing the tools, the crops, the harvest, and cattle, was dear to his (Pierre Roche's) thought," "Méditation d'un passant....", p. 716.

[145] "Not precisely the Jewish Virgin-Mother of conscious Christendom, but her prototype, the immemorial Witnessing Virgin of Transcendence—foreseen, as a common archetype, from the Greek cave of Persephone (Eleusinian Mysteries), to the Japanese cave of Amaterasu-Omikami." "Méditation d'un passant....", p. 716.

rather of angelic nudity and purity), both blazing with fire like as within Joan of Arc." The two aforementioned negations "desexualise" the attributes of the solar and immaculate Virgin by taking them back, as it were, to the archetypes that they reflect in an inverted manner. The narcissistic mirror of the introverted eroticism of post-lapsarian woman is supplanted by the mirror of exteriorisation of the heart in its faith in God—which makes us let go of ourselves in order to find our true self; while the sword of terrestrial judgment through action is outclassed by that of the incorruptibility and inviolability of pure being. The myth specifies that when Amaterasu, goddess of the Sun, hid herself in the cave in order to escape the furies of Susano-o-no-Mikoto, the mirror was one of the instruments used by the gods to lure her out in order to enlighten the world, hence the idea of an "ecstatic abandonment". Frithjof Schuon identifies the Mirror to "the Intelligence governing the physical world" which "focuses" the principial Light in the material universe.[146] In the Shinto rite, the sacred mirror is thus the theophanic site of the goddess, the epiphany of a virginal and solar archetype. Through a rapprochement with a few Muslim customs such as the *Ayīné-i-Bibi Maryam* (the mirror of our Lady Mary),[147] in which two newly-weds see their reciprocal images reflected, and thereby "rectified", in a mirror, Massignon emphasises the

---

[146] "In order to avoid the violence of her brother, the solar goddess hides herself in the celestial Cavern, causing a total obscuration of all regions of the Universe; then the 'eight hundred myriads of gods'—refractions of the intelligible Light now cut off from their divine Source, and so to speak deprived of life—cause Amaterasu to come forth by playing with a mirror symbolising the solar disc. This mirror, which is none other than the Intelligence governing the physical world (the Virâj of Hindu cosmology) 'draws out' the Light towards the cosmic labyrinth, whose arteries—receptacles of light like the mirror—are precisely identified with the 'myriads of gods'." Cf. Frithjof Schuon, *Images de l'Esprit: Shinto, Bouddhisme, Yoga*, Paris: Le Courrier du Livre, 1982, pp. 42-3.

[147] "The mirror is hung on the back wall of the meeting hall; the newly-weds have to enter through two opposite doors, and, instead of looking straight at each other, they must look askance at the Mirror. Doing so they meet as in Paradise, seeing their faces 'redressed' (the right eye on the right), not 'inverted', as in this world." "Méditation d'un passant...", p. 719.

function of the mirror as a symbolic means to the personal archetype as willed by God. Man cannot know himself except in the "mirror" of God, since—according to Ibn al-ʿArabī in his *Fusūs al-Hikam*—he cannot see God but in his own form, since "contemplation of the Reality without formal support is not possible, since God, in His Essence, is far beyond all need of the Cosmos."[148] In a sense, the mirror draws the divine projection "outwardly" ("I was a Hidden Treasure and I wanted to be known, therefore I created the world"), the world and man thus being mirrors of God; and while delimiting the Divine to be mirrored in its cosmic reflection, it simultaneously interiorises the one who contemplates God in the latter, hence unveiling his most profound reality in the creative intention: his archetype or "restored" image, to use Massignon's beautiful expression. In Massignon's words, "it is the restored vision (Mary) enjoyed, as Primeval Virgin, before the creation of bodies, seeing all those of the Elect, from inside the heart of her shadow body, in God's own Word."[149] The outermost—and therefore the mirror of the innermost—is by this token the key to this "vision of oneself", which is like the "reverse" of contemplation of God in His Creation, in the unfolding of His dimension of Infinitude, in His feminine Reality. In this sense, the feminine means both the most inward and the most outward, the Essence and Manifestation, the one being nothing but the "inversed" dimension of the other.[150]

Massignon reads in these archetypal symbols—particularly the mirror and the sword—that guided his visit to Ise "the original and permanent truth of these folkloric Archetypes.... that open the door of escape for Humanity out of the servitude of the Laws, out of Space, Time, and all our axiomatically

---

[148] *The Bezels of Wisdom*, translated by R.W.J. Austin, p. 275.

[149] "Méditation d'un passant...", p. 719.

[150] Manifestation is like the display of the Infinitude of the Essence towards the "exterior". The two realities, the innermost and the outermost, are therefore "feminine" and this commonality takes us back to the paradox of the Eternal Feminine, or to the duality of Eve and Mary.

crystallised universe, in its expansive prism."[151] Hence, these archetypes spell, as it were, the language of the universal initiator, previously recognised in al-Khidr, a metaphysical language always and everywhere available for human souls capable of attending attentively to its significance, and disposed to reading it "in spirit and in truth". If those archetypes free us from Laws, they do so in direct accordance with the innermost truth, and therefore also with their attunement to the miracle and the vow, gushing forth from the divine Inwardness through the crust of the world and the shell of the self; and this makes plain why, for Massignon, the inner vow must be considered as feminine and "open", whereas the virile oath must be seen as "stopping" at a legal sanction.[152]

*<br>*　*

In following the order we have chosen for the exposition of the contents of this chapter, we have in a certain way reversed the chronological time sequence, for if Jerusalem is the crest line of the Future, and Ephesus the reminder of the most immediate and profound Present—the instant of eternity—Ise unveils the message of the Origin, the message of archetypal Memory, which is like the infallible intellection of human collectivities. However, this reversed chronological order may be appropriate to suggest the dynamics of Massignon's life and work, insofar as the latter testify to a desire constantly magnetised by its Divine Object, and a kind of impatience for its Advent. If one were to offer a synthesis of these dynamics by means of the major moments of his lifetime, one could write that Massignon's work amounts to a message of the imminence of the Advent in the Present of the Divine *fiat* wherein is concealed our predestination

---

[151] "Méditation d'un passant....", pp. 714-15.

[152] "In contrast with the vow, the oath is more masculine, the oath is a kind of virile ordination, whereas the vow is a feminine sacralisation.... While the vow remains open to the unexpected, the oath stops at a legal sanction." "Le vœu et le destin," (1957), *OM III*, p. 691.

in the Origin. Massignon's Sufism is that of the Witness of the Moment (*ibn al-waqt*). It provides us with the keys to a genuine ecumenism which is neither a flattening down nor a quick fix. We have encountered the principles of this ecumenism through our analysis of Massignon's three major stations of pilgrimage. It engages, first of all, a respect and love for the living tradition in its most present and concrete manifestations, those whose bearing is most collective as well, hence the rejection of all forms of vague sentimental syncretism and comparative abstraction. Herein dwells the foundation and the condition of the "graveness" of inter-religious convergence. Secondly, an emphasis is placed upon the spirit of prayer and retreat, a spiritual interiorisation of the message, which is a condition for any real and substantial encounter: "this opening of the soul through prayer to the foundations, through devotion and liturgy, this opening through to the essential realities that sustain faith."[153] Next comes a devotion to the Virgin of Transcendence and Mercy, of which the Virgin Mary is a manifestation and a vehicle, a meditation on *Ewig Weibliche*, the Eternal Feminine, as the only real Promotion of Woman; hence also a receptivity to divine intentions as read through the supraformal, and thereby feminine, dimension of reality as a principle of unification and continuity. Finally we must mention, without any prejudice to concrete and highly effective engagements stemming from vocations or functions that pertain to the secret of particular souls, the rigorously charitable dispelling of any illusion as to a "carnal" or "political" salvation, an illusion that can only be a crude substitute or a downgraded religious hope.

---

[153] "Réponse à un ami musulman," in *Louis Massignon, mystique en dialogue*, Question de, n. 90, Paris: Albin Michel, 1992, p. 197.

2

# INWARD FEMININITY

The meditation on the nature and function of woman in the work of Louis Massignon is a complex question touching upon theological, aesthetic and psychological matters that can hardly be dissociated from the spiritual personality of the Islamicist. Although, as far as we know, this question has never been dealt with directly by critics and commentators, it occupies a central position in Massignon's work, especially insofar as it allows us to better grasp the articulation between the inner vow (vis-à-vis God), existential engagements (vis-à-vis our fellow men), and the eschatological ends that draw the crest of history in the spiritual vision of the author of *The Passion of al-Hallāj*. In a wholly general manner, one can suggest that, according to Massignon, woman is associated with spiritual inwardness, the "Kingdom of Heaven which is within you," hence with all that participate in the domain of the essence, and so with the extra-legal religious reality. Here, the essence refers to spiritual life in what is most profound, but also most secret within it. Its reality is therefore not reducible to a relationship with religious law, nor with a social sanction, nor even with an external visibility of any kind. This is to say that for Massignon the spiritual truth of woman bears no direct relationship with the world of action, a world which it transcends. Hence, it would not be an exaggeration to say that, from a spiritual point of view, the inner world of Massignon is essentially a feminine world, in the sense that it is always characterised by an inner primacy and freedom of grace with respect to the forms that are its provisional vehicles in the world. Massignon therefore distinguishes most often between the "spiritual technique" and the "inner disposition" of the soul towards grace. The former, exalted above all by India, seemed to him to derive from a perspective that is all too "natural", and bears no relationship with the supernatural except in a tangential and, so to speak, accidental way. In fact, the spiritual guarantees of traditional and sacramental forms are clearly apprehended by him as both conditional and outward: "It is only in appearance, and very provisionally, that institutions like sacraments and religious orders establish an authentic continuity which gives us access to the marvels of divine grace."[1]

The spiritual heroines of the inner universe of Massignon, silent witnesses of these "marvels of divine grace", are most often denoted by the term "*compatientes*".[2] The term implies an idea of substitutive participation in the collective destiny, or even an historical sacrificial function, and a mode of surrendered receptivity, or even passivity, in relation to the Divine. It is through this double vocation of substitutive participation—consisting in offering their suffering for the sake of others, particularly the outcast—and of abandonment to the divine *fiat* that the *compatientes* envisaged by Massignon constitute in a real sense the most solid links—albeit often the most secret ones, to the extent of being invisible to many—in the chain of history as a painful advent of Justice. In this sense, Mary, Fātima, Sītā, Sainte Christine the Admirable, Anne Catherine Emmerick, Marie-Antoinette, Mélanie of La Salette and others participate in the same mystery, inaccessible to the "rich" in spirit and the powerful of this world, but whose impact is both spiritually powerful and eschatologically determining.

Without any doubt, Massignon has pondered upon the Qur'anic expression that defines woman as enjoying the privilege of *hafizat al-ghayb*, "keeper of mystery", a holy guard of the mystery of the divine Presence that is also an indelible remembrance of the Spirit. Woman therefore enjoys the privilege of be-

---

[1] "Elie et son rôle transhistorique, Khadiriya, en Islam," (1955), *OM I*, Paris: PUF, 1969.

[2] Sacrificially compassionate souls. The author has proposed to use the English neologism "compatient women" to render this term adequately. [Translator's note.]

ing a powerfully silent witness; for her silence is not just a contingent fact, the social and psychological consequence of a legal or exoteric status that subordinates her to man, and—according to Massignon—humiliates her; it is also, and more profoundly, the expression of a "*compatient*" vision of the occulted side of history. A woman's silence is nothing but a close and often suffering attention to the hidden meaning covered by the turmoil of external events. Massignon insists: the silence of woman is consent, whereas in man it is the word that constitutes consent, silence being instead, for him, a refusal. Man promises by his word, whereas woman gives herself and transmits through silence; under the universe of the word which is like the visible shell of intentions and desires, the silence of women is the site of the truth of the hearts. Silence is also an allusion to the feminine privilege of inwardness at the service of peace: woman can take us back "before the break-up between brothers", for she is the matrix and the locus of the perennality uniting them.[3] Massignon has particularly pondered the role of the silence of women in the transmission of spiritual truths. It is in India, in the principles that Gandhi struggled to propagate, that Massignon found the most profound meaning of this reality. By emphasising the crucial function women have in the spiritual health of India, Gandhi sensed that woman played a determining role, as a silent witness, in the permanence of tradition. Woman is the mysterious element that nurtures deep within the invisible spiritual link that establishes and preserves the foundation of all family kinships.[4] She is the hidden reverse of the family as an external entity; she is also the secret and occult side of the nation and of history. She is above all the hidden centre, a personification of the Divine Essence often referred to by Sufi metaphysicians; she is the immanent Substance which unites all realities in her bosom. Thus Jacobus Wardenburg has managed to express a

---

[3] "La Rawda de Médine, cadre de meditation musulmane sur la destine du Prophète," (1960), *OM III*, pp. 287-88.

[4] "Woman is the silent permanence of wisdom, between her parents, her husband and her brothers, and her children." Preface to C. Drevet, *Gandhi et les femmes de l'Inde*, (1959), *OM III*, p. 385.

77

very profound understanding of Massignon's outlook and work when writing: "Although the form of history was being revealed to him as a process of justice, its substance was that of a Love drama."[5] Indeed, behind eschatological Justice, which is a basically extrinsic manifestation of *al-Haqq*, the exclusive truth of God that requires and justifies the appearance of "compassionate" witnesses at the "judicial" court of history, it is Love and Mercy, as fundamental and ultimate dimensions of the Divine, which manifest in the last analysis as the moving force and the final secret under the labyrinth of events and motions that shape history. In this unfathomable yet fundamental sense, history is a profoundly feminine reality.

We can therefore rightly wonder whether it is in the question of woman, symbolically speaking, that one should look for the foundations of Massignon's Christian vocation. It is a fact that Massignon refers on many occasions, in too categorical a formula to be understood literally without betraying his overall thought, to—in his own words—"the humiliating status of woman in Islam." The very special attention he pays to the sacrificial figure of Fātima follows a parallel concern; this is also witnessed *a contrario* by his more or less explicit distrust regarding the polygamous marriages of the Prophet and the outward profile of a Prophet's wife like 'Aishah. The latter, "the favoured wife" of the Prophet, and one of the most important figures of early Islam, both on the spiritual and social planes, appears to be identified by Massignon with the all too external contingencies of the "flesh" and the "tribe". At the opposite end of the spectrum, and in a contrast that most acutely reveals at the highest level the typically Christian vision of Massignon, Fātima is placed indubitably in the same feminine spiritual group as her mother Khadīja: she represents the purely spiritual orientation of femininity in Islam. Associated, like her mother, with the privilege of monogamy, Fātima is thereby singled out by the Prophet with a distinctness that frees her from the purely social and psychological connotations of her sex:

---

[5] *Mémorial*, Cairo: Imprimerie de l'Institut Français d'Archéologie Orientale, 1963, p. 116.

Her father set up for her the conjugal ideal which he had lived
with her mother; Fātima is exempted from divorce, and remar-
riage, whereas it is licit for the best women in her entourage,
her sister married to the caliph 'Uthmān, 'Asmā, and many others, to be *murdafāt* [divorced].

If Massignon is so profoundly sensitive to the sacrificial figure of Fātima, this is partly because his sensibility is foreign to
the Muslim excellence of the *kafāf*, that is, the domestic ideal
of the economic support of women, and—more profoundly—
because he is averse to the idea of a traditional matrimonial
relationship which would not be unique and chaste according
to the Catholic model. Concerning the first point, he suggests
that the economic difficulties affecting the marriage of 'Alī and
Fātima, with a series of negative consequences on the domestic life of the Prophet's daughter, can justify, in the context of
an average Muslim mentality, a critique of an alleged idealism
and "lack of commercial spirit" on 'Alī's part.[6] This possibility
would be excluded from the Christian point of view, given the
purely spiritual character of Christian sexual morality, which
is unrealistic and prone to hypocrisy from a Muslim point of
view. As for the second point, polygamy, divorce, *mut'a*,[7] that
is to say, all the legal adjustments of Muslim sexuality in the
sense of an integration, sometimes maximally realistic, of the
most diverse dimensions of *eros*, these are always singularly and
exclusively conceived by him as the aberrant consequences of
natural interferences testifying to a moral deficiency. Here too,
Islamic realism clashes with the Christian's spiritual sensibility
and expectations.

---

[6] "L'oratoire de Marie à l'Aqça," (1956), *OM I*, p. 600.

[7] He is therefore delighted to find in Fātimid Islam "a little of that cryptical
tendency of Islam, religion of Tawhīd, vis-à-vis monogamy", in the same
religion where, according to him, "masculine egoism imagined, as an
antidote, the very shocking 'temporary union' called *mut'a*." In "Préface
aux lettres javanaises de Raden Adjeng Kartini," Parole donnée, Paris,
1962, p. 396.

Be that as it may, one should certainly caution against any exclusively sociological, or even simply moral, reading of this component of Massignon's work. One cannot be satisfied with the remark that Massignon reproduced the vision of woman in Islam presented by Orientalists. In fact, whatever may be the status of this supposed or real "humiliation" of Muslim woman, its spiritual significance cannot be fully understood independently of the adoption of an inward point of view—a perspective doubtless nearer to any authentic Christian sensibility—that reverses the "carnal logic" akin to the social ordering of this world. Indeed, to suppose that woman is socially "humiliated" in Islam—making a gross abstraction of the fact that the latter still constitutes a decisive improvement of women's lot in comparison with pre-Islamic Bedouin customs, and regardless of the extreme diversity of regional sociological contexts in the Muslim world—amounts for Massignon, in a certain way, to the affirmation of a feminine privilege—exalted by Christianity, and basically ignored by legalistic Islam, at least in practice, if not in principle. This privilege is that of inwardness. Massignon returns on many occasions to this notion of privilege which, in itself, points to the obligations of a higher status or function. He saw in these obligations the fundamental marks of feminine identity. Thus did he express the ultimate, unfathomable truth of the "*point vierge*" that refers for him to the pure essence of the soul, even when the latter has been touched with impurity.[8] This

---

[8] "I remember one day, there was an unfortunate woman—God knows that she was not interesting at all—who came to see me during my course at the Hautes Etudes, because she had allegedly given birth to a child of one of my students who had been recommissioned to Iraq. Without saying a word, all stiffened, she brought a medical certificate that attested that she had been caught, with lightning-like speed, by a case of severe tuberculosis.... And then, at that very moment, simply, two tears slipped from her eyes ... I know that women cry at will ... I know, I know, I know all the dramatic forms that women are able to give to their claims. But what about this kind of last call for grace by this unfortunate woman who told me: 'I know that you will vaguely help me, in memory of this child who—incidentally—may not have been fathered by your friend; still again, I believe that this foreigner had been tricked. But there it is: I have nothing anymore. I am assailed and cornered.... So? Is there no pity?'" "Le vœu et le destin," *OM*

"*point vierge*", through which the soul is in contact with God, is the feminine part of being, the seat of consent to the Truth.

The importance of virginity in the work of Massignon, especially in its relation to femininity, definitely stems from this essential reality. This is why prostitution, and above all the sexual commerce that feeds on it, constitute for him ignominious symbols of the deepest disrespect for the sacredness of woman. Massignon did not forgive the British and French military institutions their tolerance, and even encouragement, of prostitution, especially in the colonial context. The institution of "*bousbir*", in the garrison towns of North Africa and the Middle East highlighted, for Massignon, a particularly nefarious moral compromise on the part of Western powers.[9] Faithful to his spiritual intransigence in favour of justice, Massignon accepted neither the argument that sees prostitution as a guardrail—for example, as a means of curbing homosexuality in a military milieu, an argument put forth by Saint Thomas Aquinas among others—nor that of sexual realism—according to which all the human tendencies and practices existing *de facto* should be in any way integrated, and therefore in a sense neutralised, by social institutions. It is perhaps more astonishing, bearing in mind his meditation on the figure of Mary Magdalene, that he did not take a glimpse into the mystical paradox of the conjunction between virginity and prostitution, as expressed in the institution of the *devadasi* of India, for example. The spiritual archetype of prostitution has here been, in fact, related to the "virginity" of the pure Substance "giving itself impersonally" and univer-

---

*III*, pp. 701-02.

[9] "Here it is not a question of justifying Islam ... but of noting that it is the European colonisation which is responsible for the methodical creation of public houses in Islamic lands.... The paternalism of the barracks by the military leaders considers procurement an 'auxiliary force' that is indispensable to the administrative services, and this I have observed in the French Colonial Army, where I ended up becoming a battalion commander. In addition, they confide to the 'profane' that this is done in order to avoid worse, namely homosexuality, this undisclosed cancer of the French Army in Africa, spotted by Foucauld in Mascara, and by Psichari in Atar." "L'islam et le témoignage du croyant," (1953), *OM III*, p. 590.

sally as *materia prima*.[10] If institutional prostitution, understood symbolically, cannot sometimes—and not without historical and cultural ambiguities—refer to a kind of universal compassion marked by a profound poverty and humility (a perspective that Christianity itself, in the logic of its penitential perspective, does not hesitate to glorify in the sanctity of Mary Magdalene), it is first and foremost its connection to monetary profit that affects it with scandal, according to Massignon. Simony—the merchandising or exploitation of the sacred—is the sin *par excellence* in the vocational universe of Massignon, and everything coming under the category of a trade of souls and bodies is nothing but an attack against the "secret" of the creature and its inalienable purity "fresh from God's hands". In a certain way, the disrespect and humiliation of woman constitutes an external sign of a betrayal of the "virgin heart", the soul's essence. Massignon concurs with Gandhi in recognising in history an abusive treatment of woman by man, which is parallel to a neglect of the "heart" as a consequence of the Fall. Woman can therefore be envisaged, in a certain perspective, as the "noblest being" of the two, insofar as she embodies an inner fidelity to the truth (*satyagraha*) that man readily violates under the intoxicating influence of his will for power.

\*

\* \*

When attentive to this purity which is none other than her deepest nature, woman realises most profoundly the spiritual meaning of religion and sacred history in its secret and "supererogatory" dimension. And it is in Islam that this vocation appears in its full light from the very fact of the distinction be-

---

[10] On a purely profane level, this sort of chaste impersonality was reflected, in a way, in the fact that in most lands the prostitute would not normally "sell" her mouth, which symbolises the sacredness of her person: she would only sell her sex, that is, in a sense, the most "universal" and impersonal part of her body. From another point of view, it is this "impersonal" dimension of sex that refers to the highest mystical symbolism of union.

tween the obligatory (*fard*) and the supererogatory (*sunnah* or *nāfilah*). The very concept of a "supererogatory" practice seems, in contrast, totally out of place in the spiritual context of Christianity, which is centred upon Love, therefore essentiality and totality. What could a supererogatory act of Love be when Love embraces and penetrates all there is? This is why this principle can only reveal its deepest meaning in the framework of an *a priori* legalistic religion like Islam. Basing himself analogically on the principles and practices known in some sectors of Sufism, Massignon interprets the legal exemptions from religious duties enjoyed by women (with respect to *jihād,* for example, or the omission of the *salāt* during the menstrual cycle) as paradoxical signs of a spiritual privilege: "It is through the *nawāfil*[11] that one draws near God spiritually."[12] This is a perspective which one may rightly consider as a mystical reading of Islam, since the *sharī'ah* emphasises above all the common religious practices and the dutiful performance of the obligatory rites. Hence, the supererogatory practices that Massignon highlights must not be understood primarily, as they are most often, as a quantitative supplement or an emotive intensification, but rather as a synonym of inwardness, *ihsān,* and spiritual sincerity. This can be seen, among other revealing examples, in the fact that Massignon associates the *shahādah* with man and inner *dhikr* with woman; and this is a fundamental illustration of the polarity between the oath and the vow that we have been encountering in several domains of Massignon's thought.[13]

The *shahādah* is the first pillar of Islam, its most evident as well as most outward reality, since it is a testimony by the tongue

---

[11] "In the love inherent to supererogatory works (*nawāfil*) God is the sight, the hearing, etc., of His servant, whereas in the love which is proper to the obligatory works, the servant is the sight, the hearing, etc. of God." Ibn 'Arabī, *Traité de l'amour,* p. 223. In the *dhikr,* God "prays" in man, in the *salāt* man prays to God.

[12] "La signification du dernier pèlerinage de Gandhi," *OM III,* p. 344.

[13] "Man testifies whereas woman conceives. The *shahādah* (bearing witness that God is One) becomes in woman a *dhikr khafī* (remembrance of the heart)." *Ibid.,* p. 344.

before others. To say the *shahādah* means to enter Islam or to attest one's adherence to Islam. It means bearing witness in front of the *ummah* or its representatives for the occasion. Hence, the *shahādah* is like the keystone of the edifice of the *sharīʿah*, an edifice that encompasses and frames, at least in principle, the totality of the existential space of the believer. In contrast, *dhikr*, the invocation of the Name of God which stands at the centre of the methodical practices of Sufism, is ultimately an act of the heart that remains mostly secret, even though it is most often first relatively exterior as a mention by the tongue or a remembrance of the mind. Be that as it may, even when the practice is mental or vocal, it is at any rate almost inaudible, and sometimes combined with breathing or the beating of the heart. The Sufis often refer to the Qur'anic expression *wa-la dhikruʿLlāhi akbar* ("the remembrance of God is greater") in order to illustrate the spiritual excellence of inner jaculatory prayer. Yet this practice is not listed with the numerous legal obligations of Islam; it is supererogatory with respect to the Law. This is why, in fact, it can even be considered with distrust, or even outright hostility, especially in the modern context of puritanical reformism and revivalism, by the "doctors of the Law" or the outer authorities who have a definite tendency, whatever might be their intentions, to reduce the spiritual reality of Islam to its outward, active and legal dimension. Often associated by the mystics with *ihsān*, or "the beautiful way of being" of the virtue of sincerity of which it is, as it were, the divinely operative complement, the *dhikr* represents a mode of supra-legal inwardness akin to the spiritual climate of Christianity, to such an extent that Islamicists like Asin Palacios have quite abusively postulated that Christian influences might have been seminal and determining in the development of Sufism. Although Massignon rejects such interpretations by emphasising the Qur'anic roots of the inner life in Islam, he is well aware of the major affinity relating Christianity and Sufism. This affinity arises from a typically esoteric reversal of the ordinary perspective by equating the supererogatory to the spiritual dimension, while the obligatory might be limited to the formal surface of the tradition; and woman is spiritually identified with the former inasmuch as she is envisaged as "conceiving" in her heart. Let us add that *dhikr*, a practice of invocation which is well-known to the Eastern churches,[14] is directly assimilated by Massignon to the spiritual reality that "makes the *fiat* in Mary engender Jesus in us".[15] Far from being a mere mechanical or "magical" practice arising from a technical precept of spirituality lacking in "soul"—as many contemporary believers given to all sorts of activisms and prisoners of paralysing psychological complexes think—*dhikr* is in fact an "enclosure" of the soul in view of the reception of the divine Presence. It practice implies quite clearly a work of inner assimilation, a mystical "impregnation" that opens onto the depths of union (*ittihād*).

The aforementioned contrast between "masculine tradition" and "feminine inwardness" must not however be hardened in a simplistic way to the point of neglecting or ignoring the reality of reversed correspondences. It is one of the highest merits of Sachiko Murata's beautiful book, *The Tao of Islam*,[16] to have emphasised the perils of an obsessively unilateral vision of the relationships between the two sexes in Islam—perils from which Massignon's work itself is unfortunately not exempt. By virtue of the Far Eastern symbolism of the *yin-yang*, a principle of cosmological alternation which implies a fluid interpenetration of the two masculine and feminine principles, one can actually understand how each sex somehow integrates the reality of the other without renouncing the prerogatives of its own identity. Hence, for example, the concept of the chain of transmission (*isnād*), which founds the "institutional" edifice of Islam in its "masculine", formal definition, can also be connected to a

---

[14] "I have often seen people who, quite simply, without any education whatsoever, and not even familiar with the exercise of attentiveness, utter the prayer of Jesus with their mouths, without stopping. I have seen them reach the point where their lips and their tongue could not stop saying the prayer. It brought joy and light to them, and it turned negligent and weak people into accomplished ascetics and models of virtue." *Le pelerine russe*, Bellefontaine, 1976, p. 95.

[15] Quoted in Jacques Keryell, *L'hospitalité sacrée*, Paris, 1987, p. 323.

[16] *The Tao of Islam: A Sourcebook in Gender Relationships in Islam*, Albany: SUNY, 1992.

modality of *dhikr* that is not without spiritual affinity with the "feminine path". We are referring here to the privilege of oral tradition, transmission through audition, which, when contrasted with the world of writing, reveals major resonances with the modes of feminine conception. As Massignon highlighted, there is in Islam, in everything that pertains to the traditional life of women, a primacy, or even an exclusiveness, of oral transmission, whether the latter be expressed in folkloric lullabies or in the custom of reciting the Qur'ān in cemeteries. In such contexts the word is primarily understood as a means of preserving; it receives and transmits the traditional legacy, and this is one of the functions in Islam arising from the woman's world. The contemporary psychologist Daniel Sibony has referred to what he calls "the incantation of the *ummah*"[17] as constituting a sort of fundamental feminine "substance", a maternal linguistic matrix that is literally foundational within Islam as a spiritual, psychological and societal experience. By daily contact with expressions found in the Qur'ān, such as *al-hamdu-li-Llāh* (praise to God), *in sha'a Allāh* (God willing), and many others, there occurs an emotional, affective sharing of language and communal denotations and connotations that binds the "brothers" and "sisters" into a family of religious siblings within a warm, inclusive, almost sensual relationship with Islam as a metaphorical "Mother". Within this oral, communal reality, one must certainly distinguish the "maternally conservative and fusional" function that we have just mentioned, one of quasi-instinctive religious participation, and the more formal, codified oral tradition of argumentation, or legal and theological edicts. For Massignon, though the former corresponds to some extent at least to a more fundamental layer of tradition, that which arises from "the path of hearing, *sam'*, or remembrance, *dhikr*"[18] is understood here as connoting a direct,

---

[17] *Les trois monothéismes*, Paris, 1980.

[18] "(The Qur'ān) ... mentions the unanimity of the revealed facts that have been transmitted, down the generations, through oral tradition, *khabar*. This is the path of audition, *sam'*, of remembrance, *dhikr*." *La Passion de Hallâj*, p. 63. It is worth mentioning that these two Arabic terms are used technically in a more specifically "mystical" context in Sufism.

immediate participation in the *barakah* of religious transmission. These so to speak "feminine" realities are thus connected to the very nature of tradition, even in its "masculine" and exterior dimensions of legal and social practices. Inversely, the mystical instantaneity of the *kun*, or the Eliatic "flash" of direct inspiration, notwithstanding its affinity with "feminine" inwardness, arises indubitably—in its mode of operation—from a "violent" and "absolute" discontinuity loaded with masculine symbolic values, as it tends to break conventional or conventionally-lived forms and fertilise, like rain, the traditional "fields" that have been far too long dried up by formalism and forgetfulness of the essential, as in the Biblical prelude to Elias' mission.

\*

\* \*

Not without analogy to our preceding considerations, the relationship between the world of woman and the world of the confessional community and its tradition is revealed in that the hidden weft of history illustrates the privilege of woman as inner "keeper" of the secrets of destiny, whereas the chain that makes visible the appearance of historical fates and facts is, albeit in a quite illusory way, man's making. This is not unconnected to the fact that Massignon does not shun from associating the outward "male" realities to a sort of material thickness and a measure of closure to grace. In the educational domain, for example, Massignon stresses the imbecilic brutality that characterises masculine institutions and practices, such as "hazing": "men are brutes."[19] Men are identified with instinctual aggressiveness that must be transcended by self control and sacrifice. This is the path that is often shown by women, as historically evidenced, among other examples, by their support for the *ahiṃsā* advocat-

---

[19] "When men get together, it is like a school hazing in preparatory classes to Polytechnic School or Central School or even at the School of Fine Arts, where I have known people who died from disgusting tortures inflicted upon them in the name of the corporate friendship of the student association." *Conférence de Toumliline*, 1957.

ed by Gandhi. It is on this most concrete level that Massignon deems women to have a crucial role to play in the "salvation of the world".[20] Indeed, behind the brutal and largely illusory history spelled out by men, there is a "real", albeit occulted, history, a spiritual history that is like the invisible background of literal and factual history. Such history does not make the newspaper headlines, since it is connected to the collective "energy" stemming from the sacrifice of the heart—*historia feminarum*, the history of "compatient women", but also of the "righteous ones", or the "Forty just men" of the Jewish tale who are the true spiritual poles of collective fate. They are the *abdāl* of Sufism, the *apotropaic* souls who make up the invisible but necessary pillars of Creation. The Greek word *apotrépein*, from which derives the "apotropaic pole" that is so central in Massignon's "spiritual sociology", refers to the spiritual or magical function of diverting evil. The apotropaic soul takes evil upon herself, as it were, in order to divert it from others, thereby protecting them from its harmful influence. As explained by Naquib Baladi: "Technically used in grammar for one named in apposition, the *badal* denotes one of the pillars of religion in Muslim mysticism, one without whom the earth would crumble, to the extent that if one of them dies, God will put another in his place."[21] Now women, inasmuch as they remain aware of their function—and men insofar as they make themselves "feminine" before God—are in resonance with this hidden side of history in which they collaborate eminently but secretly as "substitutes". Substitution, a very central spiritual element in the path laid out by Massignon, amounts to offering oneself to God for the redemption and salvation of those who have strayed. On this point Massignon is most probably

---

[20] In his preface to C. Drevet's *Gandhi et les femmes de l'Inde*, Massignon quotes a remark made by a taxi driver in Paris, worried as he was by the development of nuclear weapons: "One must make sure that women raise their voice, as they were made to give life and not to take it away." *OM III*, p. 384.

[21] "Louis Massignon et la pratique chrétienne de la substitution," in *Mémorial Louis Massignon*, Institut français d'archéologie orientale, Cairo, 1963, p. 18.

indebted to the work of Huysmans,[22] whose Catholic themes led him to sense this spiritual mystery. Commenting upon St. Christine the Admirable, "substituted" mystic of the thirteenth century, Massignon quotes a passage devoted by Huysmans to St. Lydwine of Schiedam—a fifteenth century Dutch saint—that sheds light on the mystery of substitution:

> Each one of us is, up to a certain point, responsible for the mistakes of others and should also, up to a certain point, expiate them; and each one can also, God willing, attribute, to a certain extent, the merits ... he acquires to those who ... do not want to collect any.[23]

The question, therefore, demands nothing less than one's participation in the Redemption through Jesus Christ, or to use Massignon's terms, "a universal and triumphant proof of the sacrifice of Jesus". Unacceptable from the general legalist Muslim point of view, since one soul cannot in principle be responsible for others in the exoteric literality of Islam, substitution is no less "absurd" and "scandalous" than the Incarnation and the Passion. If one accepts that God can be incarnated and sacrificed in order to redeem man, one can also accept that man has the capacity to collaborate in this redemption by substituting himself for some of his fellow human beings. Moreover, a major segment of Massignon's meditation on Islam pertains to this function of substitution, to such an extent that Muslims are

---

[22] Mary Louise Gude has emphasised this filiation in her work *Louis Massignon: The Crucible of Compassion*, Notre Dame, 1996, p. 9: "Massignon arrived from Béarn on the afternoon train October 7 (1900) and spent six hours with Huysmans 'listening to the strange confession of the new convert and struck by it to the extent of being astonished.' Among the topics touched upon was Huysmans' forthcoming biography of Saint Lydwine of Schiedam, whose life exemplified the writer's belief that one could atone for the sins of others by offering up one's sufferings on their behalf. If this notion of mystical substitution made little impression at the time on the seventeen-year-old boy, it later became one of the cornerstones of his Catholic faith."

[23] "S^te Christine l'Admirable," (1950), *OM III*, pp. 637-38.

often apprehended by him as the "forsaken", or those who have been "excluded" from the Abrahamic Promise which is theirs also. For Massignon's substitutive sensibility, a Christian soul aware of this exclusion can only offer itself for them and for their salvation.

In its universal dimension, substitutive redemption is none other than the most profound meaning of history: some souls suffer for others; and herein is the privilege of women *par excellence*, namely that of "knowing the secret of history because they are the ones making it",[24] a secret of history which is Redemption through the Saviour and his Church. Massignon develops from this point a vision of woman that is indebted to the works of Léon Bloy.[25] As Jean Sarocchi has demonstrated, "If there is a point where Massignon is without any doubt indebted to Bloy, it is precisely this crucial matter of history centred upon the Passion, and continued, until the end of time, by the collaborators of the Passion, the *compatients*."[26] Now, these compatients are first of all, as Sarocchi himself makes it plain by his use of the subheadings of Massignon's biography by Christian Destremau and Jean Moncelon, compatient women.[27] The novel *La femme*

---

[24] Extract from a radio interview on France-Culture, 1958, quoted by François L'Yvonner in his article "Une histoire épiphanique" in *Louis Massignon, mystique en dialogue*, Question de, n. 90, Paris: Albin Michel, 1992, p. 121.

[25] Léon Bloy (1846-1917) was a French novelist and pamphleteer. Hailing from a Voltairian and rationalist background he converted to Catholicism and became one of the foremost representatives of the Catholic intellectual renewal of the turn of the century. A passionate, polemical and non-conformist writer, he was alienated from the world of bourgeois and progressive intellectuals, and lived as a quasi-destitute. He is the author of *Le désespéré* ("Despairing") (1887), *La femme pauvre* ("The woman who was poor") (1897), and *Exégèse des lieux communs* ("Exegesis of the Commonplaces") (1902—1912).

[26] "Le secret de l'histoire ou 'l'invention' de Bloy par Louis Massignon," in Jacques Keryell, *Louis Massignon au cœur de notre temps*, Paris, 1999, p. 50.

[27] "Their profoundest connivance, perhaps, suggested by Moncelon in his subheadings (Abraham, Marie-Antoinette, Sainte Jeanne d'Arc, Mélanie de la Salette, Anne-Catherine Emmerick) is intuition, without any shadow of feminist prejudice, which, contrary to the most common belief of the most

*pauvre* is in this sense a source of inspiration for Massignon's concept of the feminine secret of history. Indeed, in Bloy's work woman has access to a kind of "perception from the heart" of history without her necessarily understanding it in the sense of forming a concept of it. In her heart of hearts she discovers intimations of this hidden meaning; so it is with the novel's main character, Clotilde, who responds to her benefactor: "Sir, I believe, indeed, that you have been placed in my path by God's will. I deeply believe so. I am also very certain that no one ever knows what they do or why they do it, and I am not even sure if someone could tell, without fear of being mistaken, *what they are* exactly."[28] There is a mystery of inwardness, the enigma of the *sirr*, the secret of the soul, that is the very domain wherein woman realises a type of knowledge coming from the heart, a knowledge that also entails a profound insight into her destiny. In this context, "I believe" is substituted for "I know", and transcends the latter. Furthermore, as the radiating splendour of the innermost heart, even the female body is for Bloy the "inner garden" of a divine beatitude intimated as a promise, and to which "everything is due". The humiliated is also, by this very fact, the Queen. For, the reversal of the suffering of history is also the doorstep of Joy, the doorstep of women, all of whom, according to Bloy—whether they recognise it or not—"are convinced that their body is Paradise".[29]

Should all the previous considerations lead us to speak of a "Massignonian feminism"? That is very doubtful. In fact, based on his inward understanding of feminine destiny, Massignon deplores that today's women, hypnotised as many are by the norms of outward activism men have imposed on them, dream but to realise their nature backwards, in a sort of frenzied exteriorisation that would insure their recognition as equals of men. Mas-

---

objective historians according to whom history is above all the making of man, the histories of women being the anecdotic, futile reversal (how did Napoleon make love? etc.), means women, in their painful patience." *Ibid.*, p. 58.

[28] *La femme pauvre*, Paris, 1972, p. 94.

[29] *Ibid.*, p. 157.

signon doubts the spiritual value of these "works of zeal, this activity turned towards the outside which women so childishly envy them (men) for today".[30] How could one be astonished, however, at this feminine betrayal of the inward in favour of the manifold lures of outwardness, given that redemptive inwardness has no place in a cultural and social vision that would not know what to do with it, unless it be reduced to a superficially psychological layer of the person? Indeed, the externalisation resulting from the desacralisation of modes of thought and being can only lead to an absurd and foolish headlong rush. Deprived of all inner recources, and bereft of any way of realisation that would compensate for, let alone transcend, their status of external and "provisional" subordination, women are often condemned—or they condemn themselves—to run the risks posed by the illusions of outwardness. A fascination with power and the understandable, but often delusory, desire to be in perfect command of one's social status and one's sentimental and matrimonial destiny do the rest. Yet, for Massignon—and this makes his views largely unacceptable to virtually any contemporary feminist—civic duty is primarily not a feminine duty. Education itself must take this principle into account, and it cannot purely and simply suppress or ignore the differences between the two sexes. Conscious as he is of being an "old-timer" or a latecomer in this domain, Massignon even considers that Islam has a positive role to play as a "brake" on the civic and public exteriorisation of woman in the West. One should pay heed, however, not to simplify his thought on this matter by reducing it to a kind of one-sided reactionary position on women's issues. Actually, his position may be deemed to lie somewhere between the two poles that he seems to equally reject. On the one hand, he strongly criticises the side taken by too many Muslims of the past in their resisting or opposing the education of women, and he sees in it a most reprehensible abuse.[31] Eventually, the exclusion of woman

---

[30] "L'apostolat de la souffrance et de la compassion réparatrice au XIIIᵉ siècle: L'exemple de Sᵗᵉ Christine l'Admirable," (1950), *OM III*, p. 639.

[31] "I am therefore in such a difficult position to explain to you as a professor what I have seen among educators, and in the system of education, and

from the domain of education implies her exclusion from the religious domain and the confines of the Law, since participation in the latter requires a minimum of instruction, be it simply oral. In this sense, the very tenets and worldview of Islam require the defence and development of women's education as the condition for the well-being and equilibrium of Muslim society. However, keeping his distance vis-à-vis some naively modern views of Euroopean-style education as an absolute value, Massignon goes so far as to assert, at this point drawing upon his views the strong disapproval of many modern Muslim women, that the relative and partial ignorance in which educational segregation tends to lock, to a certain extent, the Muslim woman, may be counted as a "blessing" in some real ways.[32] Centred upon the spiritual and mystical priority of a consciousness of God, despite or beyond his educative vocation, Massignon remains aware of the limits, and also the dangers, of a superficially or

---

more generally the principles I have drawn from it. The first principle I drew is that Islam has been very fundamentally and very violently, and in an excessive manner, I admit it, a partisan of education being reserved for men in the process of civic training. So, women did not have a right to be taught, so I remember the *wartassib* of Fez, the old *wartassib*, or if you wish the old custodian of ways and customs in Fez, to whom I said timidly: there should be a Muslim school for girls built—this was in 1923—to which he responded: 'God forbid, Sir!'.... And unfortunately I must say that during 1300 years in Islam, especially Malikī Islam, which is the strictest in this respect. there was no instruction for women. There were isolated cases of women who learned *ahādīth* and transmitted prophetic traditions orally. There is one of the four Sunni legal schools, the Hanbalite school, wherein there exists an education of women; but this was very exceptional, as it was meant to allow them to read prayer manuals by themselves, their eucologue." Text of a speech given by Massignon in 1957 in Toumlinine.

[32] "Therefore this primordial problem of segregation keeps woman in ignorance. And this ignorance—and Muslim women still reproach me for it—I consider a blessing. Here again though, Monsieur Mehdi Ben Barka, whom I like very much, would tell me: Dear friend, you were with me in the Teaching Commission in 1946; you were not a partisan of keeping women in ignorance. So far, fine. But still there is a certain ignorance that the systematisation of school destroys, and that is what I call the surrender of the soul to God.... I believe that in the past there was a reserve of a certain purity, and even of prayer." *Ibid.*

poorly assimilated Westernised education and its potential, if not actual, antagonism toward any sense of inner poverty, and every authentically spiritual vocation. For him, it is clear that the "true science" of woman transcends in more than one way the domain of secular instruction in the strictly modern sense of the term; it arises in reality from a "sense" of truth, love and justice that no technical training can contribute to shape and foster, and that contemporary absolutisations of "education"— so diffuse and unexamined as this term may often be— may even contribute to dull, if not semi-consciously devalue or deride.

Whatever the case may be regarding most contemporary women's ignorance of their highest vocation in the name of an ultimately illusory competition with the modern type of the Promethean male—who is himself cut off from any relationship with his own inner femininity—a woman who is intent on remaining aware of her spiritual archetype remains in a position to realise her "supernatural nature" through and in her function as a freely determined and voluntary compatient being. Obviously, Massignon is conscious of the fact that femininity transcends sexual identity, be it even psychic. The imperative of sacrificial and compatient inwardness is incumbent upon both man and woman, even though woman enjoys a particular ontological resonance with it. Every soul is feminine in relation to God, in the sense that it must be fully receptive to the *fiat* or the *kun* of the divine act: "May it be to me as Thou sayeth."

*<br>*   *

Feminine inwardness, as seat of a spiritual consecration, is connected by Massignon with the nodal theme of the vow. The dialectic of the vow and the oath proves indeed central as one seeks to deepen one's understanding of the Massignonian vision of the rapport between prayer and action. As was suggested earlier with respect to the *shahādah* and *dhikr*, the vow— like the latter—pertains to a secret realm, to the purely intimate sphere of the relationship between the soul and God, whereas the oath represents a type of public testimony. The vow is open,

inasmuch as the modes of its realisation are never totally determined by the literality of a contract. "The vow remains open to
the unexpected";[33] it expresses a type of ductility of the soul, a
receptivity towards the orientations of grace. It therefore presupposes an inner poverty and a surrender allowing for an attentive reception of the divine Other. Moreover, this opening is
not unrelated to the freedom of the Spirit which "bloweth where
it listeth" and the non-delimitation of the Infinite that frees from
the provisional constraints of forms by opening the path of inwardness. In contrast, the oath is masculine, in the sense that
it is formally defined in a more or less public sanction that determines its content and modes. Its structure is determined and
exclusive. The oath tends to absolutise the form that it states
and takes as its chief directing principle the spiritual and moral
planes. In a spiritual complementarity that runs parallel to that
of the two sexes, the vow lies entirely on the secret side of spiritual intention, whereas the oath is related to the law, and therefore to political and social outwardness, to power and public
work. For Massignon, destiny is nothing but the "encounter"
of an inner vow, and the circumstances that make possible, and
indeed necessary, its external manifestation in the form of an
oath, are not without obstacles and sacrifices. Man is first of all
what he is in the freedom of his vow, the spiritual dimension
of his nature, and he "builds himself" on the basis of this vow
and the external determinations guiding the latter. Every human being is therefore first of all a "woman" before becoming a
"man" in the layout of his outward life. The "premonitory signs"
(*intersignes*), significant and allusive coincidences of the natural
and the supernatural, are none other than the external manifestations most pregnant with the meaning of one's inner secret,
as it gradually emerges in the outward and public dimension.
Put in other terms, and deploying one of Frithjof Schuon's most
striking formulae, "man becomes what he is." He becomes what
he is to the extent that he exteriorises the inner reality that he
has reached through spiritual interiorisation. Man is principally
and imperatively a "spiritual animal"; he cannot "do" anything

---

[33] "Un vœu et un destin: Marie-Antoinette," (1955), *OM III*, p. 654.

real before truly being "as he is in himself", or in other words, "as he is in God". Let us specify, in order to remove any ambiguity, that while the secret vow, which is like the unsaid essence of destiny, is the glorious privilege of woman, this cannot mean that women are not meant to realise themselves as sacrificial witnesses in the public arena. In the latter case, woman will even be understood in a certain way independently from all relationship to man, as a primordial and predestined substance, preceding all creation and all salvation. Such is the case for example of Marie-Antoinette as far as the history of France is concerned, a historical model to which we shall return in more detail in the following pages. The self-effacing King Louis XVI and his somewhat subordinate position vis-à-vis the Queen of France expresses an historical manifestation of this mystery, as is, in other ways, the "Virgin" Queen, Elizabeth of England. At this at once sacrificial and regal culmination, Massignon sees woman's freedom from her outer dependence on man as signifying no less than a return to her archetype antecedent to the creation of Eve.[34] Indeed, the biblical account of creation implies a relative ontological dependence of woman starting from the moment when Eve is literally made from Adam's rib (*Gen.*, 2:22). Before this separation, mankind is created "male and female" (*Gen.*, 1:27). Furthermore, in her archetype preceding creation, woman is identified with the maternal and virginal Substance. On the plane of the monarchic hierophany, this Substance is identified *mutatis mutandis* with the "original seed" (*goutte-mère*), a reality which is the very principle of hereditary divine right, since the male primogeniture is first "conceived" in the bosom of the Queen. Metaphysically and mystically, this "original seed", the feminine principle and matrix (for Buber, woman's matrix is her *barakah*) of all reality, is situated "before" all her children, or "above" them. She is

---

[34] "This primitive desire in every woman to return to her ideal prototype before the creation of Eve (and outside of her dependence from Adam), to her predestination of being Privileged (the Christian idea of immaculate conception, and the Fatimid Muslim idea of *Fitrah*): to re-enter her feminine pre-nature, wholly made like opal with a lactescent tenderness." "Un vœu et un destin: Marie-Antoinette," (1955), *OM III*, p. 657.

the Queen *par excellence*, *qua* archetypal and glorious perfection. Massignon also mentions, in the same vein, the Nusayri[35] sacralisation of Fātima as "permanent sacralising element of the race" and "prenuptial ablution of all the Nusayrite brides":[36] Fātima is identified with the purifying water as the primordial Substance that sanctifies the male line issuing from her. This sacralisation by the "Virgin Mother" (*al-Bātul*) is all the more expressive in the case of this radical Shī'a sect in that it is connected—in an apparent paradox which reveals in full light its mystical value— with a sort of negation of the immortal soul in women as such. Fātima is thus introduced as a sacralising feminine "exception", being in a sense the unique and only Woman. However, from another point of view, insofar as—still according to the Nusayri—every resurrected woman becomes "male", Fātima too must become Fātir, the Originator, a Name of God (*Fātir as-samāwāti wa'l-ard*) that is also the title of Sūrah 35 in the Qur'ān and used as an epithet of Fātima in Isma'ilism.[37] These contradictions and difficulties seem to result from the interlacing, and sometimes confusion, of diverse metaphysical and spiritual perspectives which envisage the archetypal reality of woman for some and the relative aspects of her terrestrial contingency for others. In fact, it appears that the various aspects of this very special matter converge on the idea that every soul which has entered Paradise assumes a definitive celestial hermaphroditism, which can be understood as a sort of transcendent restoration of the original androgynic state.[38] The symbolism of the Houris, the supernatu-

---

[35] The Nusayri or 'Alawite form a somewhat "radical" Shī'ite group dating back to the ninth century of the Christian era and the eleventh Imam al-Hassan al-Askari. Some of their beliefs, like the divinity of 'Ali, the exclusively spiritual interretation of scriptures, and a form of transmigration take them outside of the normative framework of the Islamic *ijmā'*, or consensus of believers.

[36] "Les Nusayris," (1960), *OM I*, p. 621.

[37] *La Passion de Hallâj*, Paris, 1975, p. 177.

[38] "(The Nusayris ... ) according to whom the resurrected shall be males ... this invests the believing men and women of this sect with an active hermaphroditism, but also capable of deflorating two kinds of virginities,

ral companions of paradise, partakes in the same gender ambiguity, while at the same time affirming the restoration of a paradisal and normative reality of sexuality. As a Christian mystic,
and conforming with certain Sufis like Bistami, Massignon goes
past the immediate meaning of this sexual symbolism, while integrating its essential content, by suggesting a reading of the
Qur'ān that clearly differentiates between the "two Gardens"
of the Muslim Paradise, while emphasising that in the second
"the reward for goodness is aught save goodness itself" (*Qur'ān*,
55:60), a reward that stands beyond the potentially reductionist
imaginary connotations of sexual symbolism.[39]

\*

\* \*

If the mystical exultation of woman is in fact intimately connected to the integration of a masculine element—or even to a
kind of masculinisation—this is precisely because the principial
reality "consumes" the polarisation that unfolds from it. On a
certain level, Eve is "consumed" in Adam and Mary in Jesus, but
on another plane, the supreme Femininity of the Essence transcends the determination of the masculine polarisation of Being.
A terrestrial illustration of this ambivalent hierarchical structure
is found in the episode of the *mubāhala*, the ordeal proposed by
the Prophet to the Christians of Najrān in 631, a cardinal event
often commented upon by Massignon, wherein Fātima is situated at the centre of the group of the five family members, accompanied by her father, her husband and her two sons. Hers is a
spiritually central situation—although outwardly concealed—in
a sacrificial and inner context that may be deemed as constituting a symbolic reversal of the social reality of the Muslim family,
wherein the male is to be found at the centre of the family structure with four female pillars—the Muslim polygamous marriage

---

'unbroken pearls', male and female beings, created at once, the hūris and
the ghilmān." *La Passion de Hallâj III*, p. 177.

[39] Cf. "Mystique et continence en Islam," (1951), *OM II*, p. 436.

extending to the number four, a perfect square representing external stability.

It is in the historical character of Marie-Antoinette that, better than in anyone else, Massignon crystallised this paradox of the woman who is queen and humiliated at the same time, but also somehow "masculinised" by the exceptional eminence of her function. Massignon's readers have not uncommonly been surprised at his profound interest in this ambiguous historical figure, who has often been disparaged or considered with suspicion. For many, Marie-Antoinette appeared to be characterised by frivolity, extravagance, and an aristocratic arrogance, not to say a measure of hatred towards the French. For Massignon, these biased images are all but caricatural fixations of some aspects of the Queen's youth, all of which have been transcended or sublimated in the latter part of her reign, and in her martyr's death. In some respects, this "life trajectory" reminds us of Esther's, leading the sacred heroine as it does from a youth, without apparent spiritual depth, to a mystical sacrifice at adult age. Moreover, it may be that the acerbic criticism addressed to Marie-Antoinette participate in a general tendency to understand the function of queen within the ideological and psychological perspective of a contemporary vision imbued with democratic values and highly suspicious of monarchic institutions; now Massignon's thought largely escapes these types of determination, transcending them as it does by referring to spiritual principles that no political cause can limit or cancel out. For him the matter does not lie in an identification with the outward, dynastic manifestation of a political institution that the passage of time and human indignities may have more or less fossilised as a quasi-archaeological reality. Notwithstanding, it is just as true to say that, for him, an inner and legitimist faithfulness to the Mother of the kingdom remains binding. In the eyes of an external observer whose points of reference would not exceed the socio-political issues of our times, Massignon's generous activism in the service of justice and in favour of the oppressed would seem *prima facia* hardly compatible with any attachment to the principles of divine right and legitimacy as emerges from a number of pages written by the French Islamicist. Here, as elsewhere, Massignon is in quest of a spiritual truth that he is willing to discover under the ambiguous veils of human events and actions. The character of Marie-Antoinette seemed to him to reveal its truth to anyone who would seek to understand it in the meaningful context of the queen's "life trajectory", which is to say that it requires that one manages to grasp the spiritual logic presiding over the crystallisation of her vow into destiny. Massignon identifies in her life the "premonitory signs" of a very high and profoundly feminine vocation. Marie-Antoinette is first a "stranger" in the Kingdom of France where she would reign, a situation that is already symbolically apotropaic in the sense that it contains as a seed her sacrificial predestination as one excluded and made a scapegoat. Then, during the first years of her reign, the observer comes across insinuations and calumnies regarding the life at court of the young queen and the uneven character of some of her friends (like the duchess de Chaulnes-Picquigny and the Princess de Lamballe) rising against her reputation as Louis XVI's wife. There is talk of lesbianism, tribadism, and Massignon does not reject such qualifiers categorically—he has personally meditated on the meaning and flaws of homosexuality, or "uranism", to use the rare term that he favours. However, he deciphers these orientations in a way that frees them from the pettiness of malicious gossip and the strictures of physical nature by suggesting a pondering on their archetype. Taking up implicitly the discourse of Aristophanes in Plato's *Symposium*, Massignon reads in the homosexual temptation attributed to Marie-Antoinette the nostalgia for a "before" the partition of the two sexes; but if for man this primordial state is antecedent to "the wound of Eve on his side,"[40] for woman this is—as we earlier suggested—a "before" the creation of Eve, a prototypical reality of the "feminine pre-nature". Yet it is interesting to note that the latter spiritual mystery surpasses the former, that of the "pure" man whose uranian temptation, the anti-natural illusion of angelism, is the sexual figure. Woman, unlike man, does not seek anything more in this domain than a state of original nature,

---

[40] *Ibid.*, p. 657.

does not attain her most profound reality as woman except in this "beyond" that lies upstream of nature and creation.

*
* *

The preceding reflections inevitably lead us to delve into the difficult question of homosexuality, and sexuality in general, in their relation to the "perfect life", that is, the life of sanctification through prayer and sacrifice. In so doing, we do not wish in any way to reduce the spiritual vocation of Massignon, the nobility of his vow and his engagements, to any psycho-sexual determinism. Here it is not a question of giving in to the speculations and unhealthy curiosity of the "untold history", but rather of understanding the predispositions and the experiences of Massignon as many "premonitory signs" of the path that was his own. Setting ourselves in the spiritual logic of Massignon, we must recognise that nothing must be deemed an insignificant accident in the inner and outward events of the life of the exceptional human being he was. Now in this domain, of his own admission as it appears from part of his correspondence, some sexual weaknesses, particularly those of uranism, were temptations from which Massignon seems not to have always been able to guard himself. A personal letter dated 20th October, 1934, mentions a "feminine liaison carried out in the music-halls in Paris" at the beginning of the century, and above all "aberrations of taste inherent in the lust against nature" to which the young Massignon was initiated by his Spanish friend converted to Islam, Luis de Cuadra. It seems to us that these sexual experiences, that all preceded the conversion of 1908, have marked in a decisive manner the spiritual sensibility of Massignon. According to his own testimony, Massignon had kept "a kind of horror and instinctive repulsion for the act of the flesh, and everything that borders on it—especially for the feminine face". We find a manifestation of this strongly marked reluctance in a text written in 1953 and dedicated to Rūzbehān Baqlī, a tenth/sixteenth century Persian Sufi, whom a brilliant student of Massignon, destined for a most eminent intellectual vocation, namely Henry

Corbin, would have the merit of translating and commenting upon with great insight, situating him in the context of a genuine spiritual *eros* informed by theophanic vision. We shall return to this remarkable figure later. While taking a keen interest in the spiritual biography of this important figure of Islamic mysticism, Massignon found it difficult to reconcile "the spirit of childlike innocence that marks all his writings" and the anecdote relating Rūzbehān's love for a young woman, for whom "he discarded the frock for years",[41] which, in Massignon's Christian parlance, refers to Rūzbehān's unconventional—but not anti-spiritual—apprehension of human love. While Corbin would interpret the episode in terms of an intrepid sincerity of heart that evokes childlikeness by its ingenuous freedom with regard to all adult suspicions and all conventions experienced independently from the love of God,[42] Massignon prefers to attribute this love—which he deems incompatible with his own conception of Baqlī—to the homonym of Baqlī, Rūzbehān Misrī, an attribution which Corbin would totally reject in his *En Islam iranien*. Contemplative sexuality and a spirit of childlkeness therefore reveal a symptomatic incompatibility in Massignon's spiritual universe; doubtless because they are envisaged through the subjective and mystical prism of repulsion towards the flesh. On the biographical plane of his inner development, this repulsion was not overcome until January 1913 when, according to the same document cited above, "a feminine face glimpsed for an instant made the feminine form acceptable to me." It is in the social continuity of this return to the archetype of femininity that Massignon's marriage could take place, not indeed as a theophanic experience *à la Corbin*, but as the consummation of a family obedience, at the same time as the sacrificial assumption of a sacred duty of state.[43] Nevertheless, the meaning of Catholic marriage

---

[41] "La vie et les œuvres de Rûzbehân Baqli," (1953), *OM II*, p. 455.

[42] Corbin does not hesitate to link the vocation of Rūzbehān with that of the Malāmatiyya, "the intrepid ones who, precisely in order to remain faithful to this total sincerity towards themselves, did not fear facing public blame." *En Islam iranien*, III, Paris, 1972, p. 69.

[43] In a letter from 10 April 1934, Massignon alludes to this sacrificial

transcends for him the mere limits of this duty of conformity. In point of fact, it is through a meditation on the Hindu example, and particularly on Gandhi's teachings in this domain, that Massignon revisits the meaning of Christian marriage. For the latter is not only, for him, the psycho-social guardrail and means of channelling of sexual desire. In fact, marriage aims, rather, at an ideal of perfect chastity. Carnal union is not rejected, but it seems to be more like a starting point linked to the imperative of procreation than a norm in itself. In a letter to Gabriel Marcel from 1918, Massignon presents in a rather explicit manner his Catholic conception of marriage: basically it consists in proceeding from the number two of polarity to the number three of synthesis through love, a love that has to go through the "incarnation". The couple is a potential opposition: procreation, as the consent to a third human being proceeding from the two, "gives us a glimpse of the incarnation, as the antithesis of the dilemma, resolved through syllogism, makes us sense that the holy parable addresses us."[44] The syllogism resolves the dilemma through the element that is common to the two terms. The couple receives the "stranger" in the person of the child, thus realising this "rainbow" of life that joins the Spirit and the flesh by having the soul taste the mobile and varied spectrum of the human vocation.

---

character of family demands: "....when the night comes; according to the beautiful thought of the Persian Abū Sa'id, one must get up for prayer at night-time, because it is during the night that the door of love is open: 'Get up during the night-time; it is during the night that lovers converse; they fly swiftly around the door of the Beloved. In every place, at night-time, the door is closed, except for the door of love.' But I should not prevent my family from sleeping, and all the doors of my apartment creak." In *L'hospitalité sacré*, p. 187.

[44] "I wish you a lot of happiness, and above all a lot of fervour: married life is possible only for those who fully understand its force of sacramental symbol: this mutual and great consent to the divine work by us and in us;—this mystery of the division of the sexes, which, through generation, allows us to glimpse into the incarnation as the antithesis of the dilemma, resolved by syllogism, makes us sense that the holy parable is addressed to us;—just like the opposition of darkness and light, resolved by the rainbow, makes us taste the harmony and the contrast of colours." Quoted in *Louis Massignon, mystique en dialogue*, p. 214.

Despite this familial assumption of the "incarnation", what ultimately matters for Massignon, in the line of Gandhi, is the ideal of *brahmacharya*[45]—in marriage or in celibacy, an ideal of chastity ordered to the Spirit that is realised in parallel with a gradual perception of women as diverse manifestations of the celestial Virgin-Mother. "Woman is the Mother of man," in the sense that she precedes him in her spiritual archetype, beyond the sexual polarity that is only secondary in relation to this filial relationship. Sexual love is therefore truly excluded, or rather, exceeded, in the devotion to the Mother. This model of chastity is the condition of the spiritual union that is the deepest potentiality of marriage.[46] Notwithstanding his devotion to this ideal consummated in the sacrament of marriage, there would always remain in Massignon, due to his personal equation, a vivid awareness, painful and fruitful at the same time, of the distance between what he "knew" himself to be and what he very often was thought to be in the eyes of others. This subjective deficiency, fed by a very vivid sentiment of transgression, probably would have been one of the main ferments of an extremely intense sacrificial path of Love.

\*

\* \*

The spiritual critique of homosexuality proposed by Massignon must be explained here. Among the three prayers of Abraham that lie at the foundations of Massignon's meditation, namely, the prayers on Sodom, Isaac and Ishmael, the first prayer of Abraham pertains to uranism, that is "the idealism that delivers one from the yoke of nature and makes one lapse into

---

[45] In Hinduism the term may refer, during teenage years, to the period of celibate and exclusive concentration on the study of scriptures, but also to the ideal of sexual abstinence of the renunciates.

[46] "The ideal of marriage, which is in fact a sacrament, is to reach together a spiritual union, passing through the physical union destined for procreation." Preface to the work of C. Drevet, *OM III*, p. 386.

physical inversion."[47] The choice of the term "uranism" is therefore not a matter of preciosity: it suggests through its oblique reference to heaven, in Greek *ouranos*, a tendency that is less sexual in the physical sense of the term than spiritual in its impulse toward a negation, or a sort of psychic transcendence, of nature. For a Christian, this amounts to an illusory deliverance from the material strictures of sexuality that Massignon contrasts with Abraham's fatherhood. Independently, even from its procreative dimension, sexual differentiation is defined as a "fissure" which prevents the couple from remaining enclosed within itself, and therefore closed to God. On the contrary, Massignon's view of uranism implies a sort of "shared narcissism" that opens itself neither to God, nor to procreation as going beyond the limits of the couple.

Aware as he is of the anthropological and historical realities that testify to a recognition of uranism as a marginal but integrated social possibility, Massignon reads in these manifestations a dangerous spiritual ferment of social dissolution which he relates, in an interesting if not convincing manner, to the phenomenon of "*sociétés de pensée*"; initiatory, private, ideological clubs or fraternities. In such contexts, as among Bantus or Native Americans, altered sex phenomena are indeed of a psychic and not merely physical nature; they correspond to a true vocation, which is most of the time induced by a supernatural communication. This type of vocation gathers its elect in "fraternities" that are the antipodes of the family as a natural structure. These initiatic groups therefore present themselves in potential contradiction with the totality of the organic body of society. However, the fact remains that these "exceptions", unlike some

---

[47] Les trois prières d'Abraham, Paris, 1999, p. 36. On this question see chapter two of Jeffrey John Kripal's *Roads of Excess, Palaces of Wisdom: Eroticism and Reflexivity in the Study of Mysticism*, "The Passion of Louis Massignon," University of Chicago Press, 2001, pp. 98-145. The conclusions of the author that see Massignon's "holiness" and "felt energies" as "sublimated forms of a morally tortured homosexuality" (p.145) are symptomatically and gravely reductionist, but his analyses have the merit of revealing some of the very real tensions of the "Catholic soul".

contemporary vindications, only confirm the rule which they do not question in any way as such and on its own level.

Faithful to both his historical and anthropological method and to his spiritual criteria, Massignon retraces three phases in the development of the social reality of homosexuality, which are as many "degrees of virulence" of the uranist phenomenon: first there are the secret sacerdotal societies seeking to transcend the "wheel of servitudes" and therefore the natural cycle of generation; then follows the classical Greek type of uranism that is "a desire for Heaven, without a desire for God";[48] and finally the "odhrite"—an Arab "Platonic" eros—type, "that is content with just a sign, a glance", a type that is more ambiguous, and also paradoxically more dangerous according to Massignon, because it is more resigned to its non-realisation. As for the Western context, it reveals that "in Christian lands, uranism, which elsewhere seems to succeed in short-lived symbioses with profane culture, is affected, without being able—for obvious reasons—to flourish, by a deadly dehiscence."[49]

The more or less necessary separation of the sexes—especially in the sacerdotal and warrior frameworks—is generally the fostering milieu, if not the cause, of inversion. It must not close in upon itself as segregation. There is certainly, for Massignon, an interference of the archetype of the "warrior" in the uranian protestation against mothers,[50] but the sublimation of profane homosexual love is for him nothing more than a dangerous literary myth. More generally, and beyond the strict question of homosexuality, there is with Massignon an outright rejection of spiritual Platonism.[51] Unlike his student Corbin, a phenomenologist of the amorous "amphiboly" that enables one to grasp the theophany in a beautiful face, Massignon does not perceive a spiritual continuity from the physical to the spiritual, but rather a chasm of metaphysical proportions: "God is not an ordi-

[48] *Ibid.*, p. 40.

[49] *Ibid.*, p. 41.

[50] *Ibid.*, p. 47.

[51] *Ibid.*, p. 45.

nary 'object of love,' and the collections of amorous casuistry accredited among the uranists attest to a refined paroxysm of elated idolatry rather than the direct divinely oriented élan of the only love."[52] The contemplative love of woman itself tends to an analogously perilous destiny in its "vain enterprise" to "climb to the absolute", since truly mystical union is "transnatural" and lies "beyond all created things". In the perspective of pure transcendence that is his own, Massignon is inclined to close his eyes before any beautiful human form for fear of betraying the pure essence of the Beloved.

*<br>*   *

On the other hand, Platonic spiritual friendship consummated in an apotropaic substitution is, next to marriage in its sacrificial dimension, the second response to the sexual *problématique* of his Christian path. The letters to Mary Kahil published by Jacques Keryell in his valuable work *L'hospitalité sacré* (Paris, 1987) enable us to gain a better grasp of the meaning of this path. Let us recall first of all that Mary Kahil was a "distinguished lady" of Egyptian society who was very closely associated with numerous aspects of social mores and education during the period between the two world wars.[53] Thus, she was very directly involved in social action in favour of the improvement of public hygiene and women's rights, as well as Christian-Muslim dialogue and understanding. Her encounter with Massignon was crucial. Their meeting seems to have revealed an extremely creative polarity between the ascetic professor representing French culture on the one hand, and the Melkite supporter of a cultural and political independence of the Arab world, whose personality was, as it seems in contrast with Massignon's, inclined to enjoy a significant measure of social and psychological comfort. Biographers have been struck by the lively and almost

---

[52] *Ibid.*, p. 56.

[53] One can find precious biographical elements concerning Mary Kahil in Jacques Keryell's *L'hospitalité sacrée*, Paris, 1987, pp. 77-132.

aggressive character of their first meeting, as if illustrating the Chinese traditional characterisation of the great love of one's life as "the predestined enemy". Mary Kahil's description of her first meeting with Massignon is very revealing in this respect:

> I found a fine and sinuous young man in front of me, very fine, very serious, a little odd, with a monocle in his eye and a black band on the monocle. He was wearing a black hat, his outfit was black. He spoke to me in Arabic: "*Hal tatahaddathi bil lugha al-arabiya?* (Do you speak Arabic?)" I told him: "*E* (yes)." Then he said that he was professor of philosophy at the Egyptian university. His name was Louis Massignon and he came from Syria, where he had done a lot in favour of French influence. At which I told him: "You are my born enemy."[54]

The portrait of Massignon emerging from this text presents him in a somewhat "disturbing" and unsettling form. The dark and sinuous characteristics of the sketch strike us as close to conjuring up the ambiguous figure of the snake. The sudden introduction of the French intellectual suggests a spiritual intrusion that would threaten *a priori* the well-ordered universe of the young Arab lady. And actually, as it perfectly suits its spiritual symbolism, this beneficent "serpent" would serve as nothing less than a principle of transformation for Mary Kahil. What Massignon actually offered and shared with his female friend throughout the years that would bind their destinies within the same spiritual vocation is a surpassing of the natural sphere into a substitutive self-oblation to Christ. In this common spiritual adventure, love becomes a silent and subtle communication, a shared participation in grace. The souls are united in the coincidence of their vocations; Massignon thus writes to his correspondent:

> When I speak, in the inflexions of my voice, when I fall silent in the detours of my thought, in the desires of my heart, from time to time, I find something that surprises me, expands me,

---

[54] *L'hospitalité sacrée*, p. 93.

loosens me, and I think this is our Angels communicating; this is, in silence, the good fragrance of incense, the wordless prayer of my Arab sister, of Maryam, which ascend to God, reaching me here by a supernatural delicateness of grace....[55]

This communication remains conditioned, or rather predisposed, by an inner vigilance and a call to transcend the self that alone can enable sanctified and efficacious action, and a real influence on the surrounding ambience. Massignon often insists, in his letters to his "Arab sister", on the need not to confine oneself within a more or less unconscious idolatry of a Christian familial or social order. He knows very well that this is a potential trap, particularly for a woman as present in the world and as generous as Mary. Although being himself a man of engagement and action, Massignon complains at times of having squandered his inner life, his relationship with God, on the insignificant surface of the world; thus in a letter to Gabriel Boulad-Schemeil discovered and communicated by Jacques Keryell, he writes:

Since God wants you for Himself, by keeping you away from men, seize this "better part" that Magdalene received. I desired it so much and I am still condemned, as a husband, as a father, as a professional man, to this odious thing that profane conversation with others can be, interviews, letters, and administrative processes in view of goals that are just as perishable as they are ridiculous.[56]

At this juncture, the inner vow is therefore in potential or effective conflict with "the summons of the milieu, the caste, the race, and the class that says: 'You are bound to this milieu, you must not look for anything else....'"[57] Here, Massignon proves to be highly sensitive to the trans-culturally universal and su-

---

[55] *Ibid.*, p. 183.

[56] Unpublished letter from Tuesday, 25th June, 1924, in Jacques Keryell, *Louis Massignon au cœur de notre temps*, Paris, 1999, p. 148.

[57] "Le vœu et le destin," (1957), *OM III*, p. 695.

pernaturally interior dimension of Christianity. Christianity is neither a "family", nor a "nation", much less even a "party". In it, all the carnal and natural, not to say cultural, determinations are as it were burned in the sacred fire of pure charity. Massignon's whole thought and sensibility appears in this sense penetrated by an acute sense of the weighty gravity of the familial, national, social "Great Beast" (*le gros animal*), to use Simone Weil's expression.[58] On the one hand, the truth according to God is not the truth according to men; on the other hand—and this is what a certain humanitarian re-orientation of Christianity tends to veil to many—one cannot do real good to others save by freeing oneself from their unconscious psychic tyranny in and through prayer and sacrifice.[59] At any rate, it is quite clear that for him compassion is neither weakness nor gregarious complacency. In a word, Massignon's absolute demand is like an imperative appeal for inner awakening: "Everything that is not sanctity is vanity."[60] For Massignon, virtue is never a middle ground, and no more is it an equilibrium; in this sense, no thinker is less Aristotelian than Massignon, for whom mystical virtue is dynamic and heroic at the same time.[61] Thus, it is the "perfect life" of the contemplative and sacrificial vocation, and not any sort of psychological and social equilibrium for its own sake, that con-

---

[58] "The "Great Beast" is defined by Weil as follows: "It is the social that throws the colour of the absolute over the relative." Excerpt from *Gravity and Grace*, in *Simone Weil: An Anthology*, edited by Sian Miles, Grove Press, New York, 1986, p. 122.

[59] "Do you think that humans, up there, keep any of these pieces of furniture of the herebelow, made of complacent and lukewarm concessions, that constitute the 'good households', or the 'well-kept convents'...." (*Ibid.*, p. 209); "Trust in my experience: you will not be able to do good to your dear ones except if your sight, perceiving God's superior vision of things in the universal horizon of the Church, remains in peace and serenity" (*Ibid.*, p. 200).

[60] *Ibid.*, p. 173.

[61] "Because virtue ... is essentially heroic, oriented, and dynamic, and not a static equilibrium between two opposite tendencies." "Mystique et continence en Islam," Paris: 1962, *Parole donnée*, p. 273.

stitutes for him the real finality of the spiritual union between man and woman.

Massignonian inspiration relates on this point, implicitly or explicitly, to the practice of *syneisaktism*,[62] as lived during the first centuries of Christianity. This ideal and chaste relationship between a man and a woman is in fact akin to the *vita angelica*, the angelic life through which a purely spiritual communication takes place, outside of any sexual consummation. This type of relationship seems to have been connected, during the first centuries of Christianity, to a total trust in the workings of a grace which constitutes the only guarantee against the deviations and pitfalls to which such relationships could easily lead when considered from a purely natural point of view.[63] This is why Massignon could remain both fascinated by syneisaktism and reserved with respect to this very particular spiritual possibility the mystical promises of which he seems to have intimated while also keenly perceiving its dangers.

*

*  *

The story of Marie-Anotinette presents us with the case of a relationship pertaining to a register analogous to that of syneisaktism: namely, the Platonic relationship that united the Queen and the Swedish Lieutenant General Count Fersen.[64] Based—in

---

[62] Syneisaktism refers, in the first centuries of the Church, to the cohabitation of women and men in the cadre of a brotherly and chaste relationship and in view of a reciprocal spiritual and social support. The women in question are sometimes denoted as *"mulieres adoptivae"*, *"agapetae"* and *"virgins subintroductae"*. It seems that this practice was relatively frequent, as testified by second century sources. It is interesting to note that most of the Fathers of the Church condemned syneisaktism very sharply. Elizabeth A. Clark has devoted an interesting article to the more nuanced, but nonetheless negative, position of Saint John Chrysostom in "John Chrysostom and the Subintroductae," *Church History*, vol. 46, no. 2, June 1977, pp. 171-85.

[63] Cf. "Syneisaktism: Spiritual Marriage," *Breaking Boundaries: Male/Female Friendship in Early Christian Communities*, p. 65.

[64] Count Hans Axel von Fersen was born in 1765. He distinguished himself

the case of Fersen—upon an aspect of service to the Lady that may pertain to an initiatory understanding of chivalry, the mysterious—and all too easily defamed—character of this relationship suggests, according to Massignon's vision, a truly sacrificial vocation of the Queen for the sake of the Kingdom. It is clear that Massignon understands the relation between the Queen and Fersen in terms of a spiritual surpassing of the concupiscent limitations of sexuality. The expressions that foster his hypothesis deserve closer scrutiny:

> A provocation to sanctity that invites danger, piercing through temptation to its ultimate truth; without any straying in one's intention, and any flickering of the eye?.... Sleeping under the same blanket, in perfect abandonment of non-violence with the elder, the adolescent reclining on his nape, the woman letting her hair down; in the dormant water of sleep; in no man's land, a sort of magnetic "torpedo" defuses the current in the other person, all carnal tension extinct. This exists, my testimony is direct.

This is an allusion to a genuine spiritual exercise that aims at surpassing the idolatrous potentiality of sexual desire. The risk is real, since it is a question of transcending that which naturally shuts the soul by enclosing it within the carnal limitations of its élan and its object. The "technique" in question does not seem to be of a "tantric" sort, at least not in the sense that it would aim at channelling and converting an energy flowing from a sexual origin. It appears that the aim of this practice is, rather, to put out the fire of sexual desire by a vigilant frequentation of its object. Nothing is neglected in order to introduce the context

---

with Rochambeau during the American War of Independence. History has left him with the reputation of having been the alleged lover of Queen Marie-Antoinette and the father of her son, Louis-Charles, known as Louis XVII. Contemporary historians and biographers of both Marie-Antoinette and Fersen have clearly rejected this claim. Massignon was convinced that the character of the two protagonists and the social and psychological context of the court of France at the time made it impossible to understand this relationship in any other way than a platonic one.

in which desire could be ignited; the loosening of the hair, the languid pose, everything appears to be combined to ensure that one "plays with fire". How should one understand this "ultimate truth" of temptation that one must "pierce through?" Should one think of it as a reference to its "nothingness", its lack of substantiality and being, as one reveals in full light the ontological levity of what until then was seen as good, or truly being? Or is it rather, more positively, a question of going back to the root of desire in order to find there the only Desire (this *'ishq* that Ibn 'Arabī defines as the highest pitch of love or its excess, *ifrāt al-mahabba*),[65] which is nothing but the thirst for the Absolute, the thirst for God? The reference to sleep and to a "non-violent" abandonment—at the same time as the image of a torpedo defusing the other's desire—could well suggest the "reverse" side of Union, that is, the great Peace, for which sleep is a dim, but very natural, image.

Whatever the spiritual and moral implications of this rather particular vocation may be, Massignon understands the relationship between Marie-Antoinette and Fersen as transcending the purely individual—and private—aspect of their love in a redemptive act pertaining to a collective, and even eschatological, function. For him, the two lovers are indubitably associated in a sacred service to the monarchy which, in the Queen's case, stands as the "substitutive" sacrifice of a *compatiente*. The Queen's destiny is even assimilated *mutatis mutandis* to Mary's: the two women were humiliated but also the victims of the disgraceful calumny that branded them as "strangers" in relation to those for whom they sacrificed themselves. In both cases, the "restoration" of the spiritual integrity of the Kingdom (France or Israel) presupposes a "rehabilitation" of the Virgin Queen who is also its spiritual Mother. For Massignon, any attempt at

---

[65] "Beside its limpidity in the attachment to a single being, this affection is properly speaking what is called original love (*hubb*), and besides its appearance in the seed of the heart (*habbat al-qalb*), which has also been called original love, it has the virtue of penetrating man entirely and making him blind to everything save the beloved." Ibn 'Arabī, *Traité de l'amour*, ed. Maurice Gloton, Paris, 1986, p. 123.

restoring monarchy that is not based on the prerequisite of a "revision" of the process of Marie-Antoinette is as misplaced and illegitimate as the restoration of a Jewish state that would not be accompanied, or even inaugurated, by a rejection of the suspicions weighing on the mother of Jesus.[66] In other words, in both cases, the accusation of being "mother of a bastard" lies at the centre of Massignon's argument.

One may understandably be puzzled by Massgnon's over-emphasis upon Queen Mary-Antoniette's function in the economy of collective salvation, and one may therefore deem his "mystico-political" demands as disproportionate, idealistic or even imbued with an unbridled mysticism. A deeper scrutiny of the spiritual significance of the rehabilitation of the Queen Mother might enable us to modify or qualify this first impression. It is first of all appropriate to stress that the spiritual reality of the queen, like that of woman in general, places her on a level that transcends the domain of the law, as well as that of the merely "carnal" nation. On a most immediate psychological plane, Marie-Antoinette "places herself above the laws", "she shows pride", she clashes violently with the conventions of the bourgeoisie: "The Queen of bees, in her nuptial flight, precedes from above

---

[66] Regarding the vision of the peasant Martin, calling into question the legitimacy of Louis XVIII, Massignon writes: "Martin brought to Louis XVIII, who had dishonoured the Queen Mother in order to oust his nephew Louis XVII, the conditional threat of a punishment, were he to have himself crowned in the place of his nephew, who was still alive. This message also showed Louis XVIII that he had lied in treating the Queen Mother as the mother of bastards. Herein is the essential point, for our present study, of Martin's message; the rehabilitation of Marie-Antoinette as a prerequisite to any legitimate restoration, a point that the 'survivalists' neglected." *Ibid.*, p. 675. Similarly, Massignon poses the rehabilitation of Mary as a prerequisite for peace in the Middle-East: "The world shall have no peace in justice neither in Palestine, nor elsewhere, as long as Israel will not revise the trial of the Mother of Jesus; at the end of this year, one must repeat it again; and all the efforts of righteous men like Jules Isaac and Sholem Asch, in order to recognise Jesus as a martyr in Israel, come up against this prerequisite question." "Nazareth et nous, Nazaréens, Nasara," *OM III*, pp. 492-93.

the flight of the swarm, on the way out of the abandoned hive."[67] As queen, she is identified with the archetype of woman who, according to Massignon, who follows Bloy on this point, "claims privileges and not justice".[68] These privileges arise from woman's "divine privilege" of revealing the Beauty and Mercy that she "receives" in her body and in her soul. Woman is "divine" insofar as she is "chosen" to manifest Truth and Beauty. For Massignon, woman "was made for" this privilege, and not for establishing justice in this world, which is a masculine vocation. It can be said that the Marian and Christic archetypes are the highest references of Massignon in this respect. Mary expresses the privilege of receiving the *fiat* and the conception of the Word, whereas Jesus is identified with the Truth and Justice of the Kingdom of His Father. The privilege of woman is precisely that of being the "seat" where the Man of Justice is conceived. According to the divine right consecrating the French monarchy, the Queen is the "sacred soil wherein the inheritor is conceived".[69] Similarly, the Virgin of Israel is the spiritual "seat" of the birth of the Man-God. Thus, the Virgin Queen and Mother lies at the very heart of the whole spiritual edifice, she is the "sacred hostage" that cannot be profaned without it collapsing completely. Her character of "stranger" (Marie-Antoinette was first of all for the French "the Austrian", hence becoming the catalyst for French republican nationalism) is the symbol of a higher spiritual affiliation, one that transcends the natural and "native" world. She is also, and more profoundly, a "stranger" in relation to the law—hence the suspicions of society upon her—through her special disposition to grace; and it is on this point that the Queen falls under the archetypical category of the Marian way.

Massignon has commented many times on the dimension of legal "scandal" that characterises Mary. The unconditional giving of herself to God, which is the essence of her being, places

---

[67] "Bi-centenaire de la naissance de Marie-Antoinette," (1955), *OM III*, p. 687.

[68] *Ibid.*, p. 686.

[69] *Ibid.*, p. 682.

her in a sphere upon which the law has no hold whatsoever. Her destiny as the "chosen among all women" "displaces" her radically, in such a way that she cannot even have a normative identity vis-à-vis the world of the law that surrounds her but cannot receive her; hence the tension between her spiritual mystery and its envisagement within legalist Judaism. Mary is the model of woman, precisely due to her perfect attention to the power of grace and her perfect conformity to its "exceptional" and "free" plans. Through her ontological proximity to the world of infancy, she also enjoys a more immediate, less abstract and notional, consciousness of the modes of the divine presence within souls.[70] This affinity with spiritual infancy is also related to the spiritual maternity that makes her carry in her own being the promise of sanctity found in every human being who comes to life. And yet, this affinity, or even this complicity, between woman and the domain of grace in its extra-legal dimension, reveals its eschatological dimension in the Marian presence in history. If it is true that history is the manifestation of the freedom of grace that reveals, from within, the truth of the forms that are its vehicles without containing it, the heightened presence of Mary in the world since the latter's entrance into the industrial era cannot but have a parallel spiritual meaning. Massignon strongly believes in this Marian presence, as testified by apparitions and messages such as those of La Salette (1846), Lourdes (1858), Pontmain (1871) and Fatima (1917). The presence of Mary is both the measure of, and the antidote to, the spiritual devastation of the modern world. She is also and above all the compassionate reminder "weeping" at the sight of the earthly Church's compromising of principles and reiterated betrayals, forgetful as it often is of its formidable privilege of being the "salt of the earth".[71] In

---

[70] "....woman has a secret instinct of the presence of God in innocent beings and infancy, since yet again it is in her that the infancy of Christ began." Unpublished text of *"Le front chrétien"* conference.

[71] "'The weeping one' already means the Immaculate Conception; she is the one who will heal in Lourdes, but who is anticipated, in the bitter solitude of her predestination, in her Priesthood of Virgin-Mother, in her "Soledad" of Calvary, that centuries of accumulated spiritual insipidity on

this context of the signs of the times, the Marian benediction, the rigour of mercy as it were, is the only one to clearly show a way out of the "gravity" of the modern world through "grace", to use the terms of Simone Weil's spiritual dialectics; and this is what leads Massignon to write: "There is something new; there is a new perspective: this lever of the world that should lift all the rest. There is an escape from mechanism."[72] It is this saving dimension which constitutes the last "virgin point" in the historical economy of the world.

\*

\* \*

We have already observed the extent to which femininity is envisaged in Massignon's work less in its dimension of aesthetic theophany—as is the case with Corbin—than in relation to a sacrificial and saving predestination. As for feminine beauty itself, it appears first of all as the object of a perception that is primarily characterised by a distrust toward its idolatrous potentialities. It is in the "Prayer for Sodom" that we can better grasp this reservation arising from an ascetic instinct of transcendence. In such a perspective, there is indeed a discontinuity between a natural sexual attraction, as resulting from an amorous glance, and the love of God. In a sense, and beyond its specifically homosexual character, uranism represents for Massignon the very type of an illusory liberation from the natural constraints of the flesh, and, on the other hand, an ignorance of the fundamental transcendence of the Beloved who cannot be approached through any surge of earthly desire. All platonic love that would postulate a vision of God on the face of the beloved ignores in this sense the post-lapsarian demands of the flesh. In such cases, the matter is a "refined paroxysm of exalted idolatry",[73] as was mentioned ear-

---

the part of the clergy and the lukewarmness of baptised nations forced to cry." *Parole donnée*, p. 171.

[72] Unpublished text of *"Le front chrétien"* conference.

[73] *Les trois prières d'Abraham*, Paris: Cerf, 1997, p. 56.

lier. Significantly, Massignon expresses himself here in terms of extremity and intensity, not in reference to metaphysical reality or contemplative assimilation.

The vocational originality of this approach, but also its limitations, can be better grasped in contrasting it, in a kind of spiritual dialogue, with Corbin's exposition of the notion of *amphiboly*[74] in the aesthetic contemplation of human beauty. In this comparative context, Massignon's perspective appears all the more "mystical" and jealous of the divine transcendence as it is contrasted with the gnostic and immanentist perception proposed by Corbin. Corbin conceives of the relationship between the created and the Uncreated, following Rūzbehan al-Baqlī, as a manifesting effusion—*tajallī*—of the latter in and through the former. The matter, therefore, is not as much a mystical sublimation of desire as it is a gnostic conversion of one's way of looking. "Amphiboly" is a term forged by Corbin to translate Rūzbehan's *iltibās*, an Arabic term that connotes both a "clothing" of Divine Reality and a resulting "ambiguity" of the signs that manifest the latter. The "entanglement" of the Divine within the theophanic forms may lead, for a contemplative soul on the spiritual path, to an immediate grasping of the Uncreated in the created, not so much as an intellective progression through the stages of a Platonic dialectics, but as a reading of the metaphysical message of beauty as self-knowledge in beauty itself, neither alongside it nor above it. We will quote here an extract of Corbin's translation of Rūzbehan's *Kitāb-e 'Abhar al-'āshiqīn* (The Book of the Jasmin of Lovers) that provides a clear sense of the spiritual horizon of such aesthetic contemplation by emphasising its fundamental non-dualism:

> The supreme beauty is joined to my love, because from the start my story proceeds from this origin in which love and beauty are joined. If we are not ourselves love, the lover and the beloved, then who is? All that is not this indivisible instant is but the world of duality. Meditate upon this oddity: it is

---

[74] The term "amphiboly", coined by Corbin to translate the concept of *iltibās*, refers to the intuitive grasping of divine Beauty in human beauty.

myself who, without myself, is the lover of myself. I do not cease to contemplate myself, without myself, in the mirror of the existence of the beloved. Then, who am *I*?[75]

In this experience of "amphiboly" and knowledge of Self in the mirror of the other's beauty, the ascetic perspective of the pious devotee is transcended, since it is none other than an error of metaphysical optics, a breach against *tawhīd*. Lest there be a misunderstanding on the inner conditions and requirements of this way, it must be added that Corbin does not ignore the prerequisite need for a purification of the heart and an exercise of the will that keeps the "faithful of Love" from the perils of instinctive sensuality; for he must first "traverse the bridge which overhangs the hell of carnal nature".[76] However, this asceticism is only preparatory: it is the condition of the possibility of an experience that takes us beyond all ascetic or penitential perspectives. As we have seen, the *shahīd* or contemplator recognises in the contemplated beauty what he is himself in his most profound reality, the unity of the contemplator and the contemplated, the unity of the lover, the beloved and love. This experience does not amount to an idolatry that would stop short at the obstacle of the created, since it presupposes a sort of contemplative tension between the nostalgia for the absent and the joy of presence, the "anguish before the impossibility of finding" and the "exultation of this discovery".[77] The beautiful form gives and takes away at the same time, without in any way abolishing transcendence in the name of an immanence that would be a mere pretext for worldly superficiality and ease. Although it escapes the scrupulous piety and the lowered gaze of the legalist believer, it cannot do without the oscillations and tensions that testify to the metaphysical subtleness of the relationship between the Real and its theophanic "clothes". This is why the love

---

[75] Cf. *Rūzbehan. Le Jasmin des Fidèles d'Amour*, trans. Henry Corbin, Verdier, 1991, p. 109.

[76] *En Islam iranien* III, p. 77, n. 78.

[77] *Rūzbehan. Le Jasmin des Fidèles d'Amour*, p. 170.

for beauty becomes in certain respects an asceticism of its own kind: it requires a metaphysical vigilance of the eye that prevents the contemplator, however exhilarated he may be by the ecstatic contemplation of the beloved, from dropping the prey for the shadow.

Massignon is averse to that type of contemplation, which he deems to be marred by carnal complacency, or at any rate incapable of providing a genuine access to the Divine. His criticism of Udhri, or courtly, love (*hubb 'udhri*) testifies to this. This type of love, to which historians tend to attribute a Bedouin origin, is content with a look, "with all its undisclosed weaknesses",[78] and seemed to him no less marked than uranism by a dangerous and illusory angelism. In this respect, Massignon seems to consider that Islam has been somewhat "contaminated" by the Udhri and Platonic point of view.[79] This evaluation seems to have been a result of the observations and experiences of the young Massignon in Iraq. It appears that his friend Luis de Cuadra, a convert to Islam, had initially invited the young Massignon to consider that one cannot understand the Islamic psyche without being initiated into uranism. "Consent to a morose delight", "deliberate renunciation to the glimpsed purity of the divine essence", platonic love ignores in any case the lordly inaccessibility of the true Beloved. In fact, even if the criticism of Massignon against the strategies of transposition or the spiritual sublimation of eroticism aims primarily—as we have indicated earlier—at homosexuality, Massignon's "uranism", the matter amounts in any case to a warning against the illusions of an erotic contemplativity that would be forgetful of the dimension of transcendence. It is the underestimation of the mystery of God's elevation "beyond all created things" which actually collides head on with the spir-

---

[78] *La Passion de Hallâj*, pp. 177-78.

[79] "At the third stage of virulence, and this is the post-Islamic Arab type with which all the Muslim world has been impregnated, the psychology of inversion becomes more complex; at this stage which is posterior to the Revelation and the Messiah, a profound, inextirpable faith in a revealed God intervenes, dictating an ambiguous attitude, implying a latent contradiction." *Ibid.*, p. 40.

ituality of Massignon. It is without any doubt in his *"Prière sur Sodome"* that one can find the most complete elucidation of his point of view on this subject. There, Massignon vilifies the quasi-Promethean efforts of the creature to climb to God through the intermediary of other creatures. For Massignon, this is a "ladder of illusory terms put up for climbing to the absolute and stealing away the real".[80] Only God bestows the gift of mystical union, and in the absence of grace all "power of oneself" is doomed to failure. The love of God is "transnatural", and therefore not commensurate with human love. It is "rapture", not "ascent". Since God is not a "usual object of love", it is He who defines the nature of the love directed to Him. Below this divine "definition" of love, it is clear that Massignon can only identify in platonic love an idolatrous sublimism that hides its complacencies and its sterility under the guise of refinement or aesthetics. As in Simone Weil's meditation on nature and grace, the origin and level of love can corrupt its spiritual potentiality: every love in the natural sense of the word is not convertible into an effusion of grace; "the flesh is dangerous insofar as it refuses to love God, but also insofar as it meddles in loving Him indiscreetly."[81] However, such a position does not imply in the least that one must favour over natural instinct a sort of allegorical flattening of love for didactic purposes, as in the mediaeval *Roman de la Rose*. In point of fact, Massignon envisages two perilous modes of the spiritualisation of *eros*, the first sinning through carnal complacency—it is aesthetic love which makes "a mute idol shining with a divine reflection"[82] out of the face of the beloved—and the second through philosophical fading—this is the philosophical utopia of the pure idea; and it appears that Massignon went so far as to include the masterly works of Ibn ʿArabī and Dante among erotic attempts arising from the latter.[83]

---

[80] *Les trois prières d'Abraham*, Paris: Cerf, 1997, p. 45.

[81] *La pesanteur et la grâce*, Paris, 1948, p. 62.

[82] "Influence musulmanes sur la chrétienté médiévale," *OM I*, p. 66.

[83] "In others, that which is commemorated from the form of the beloved is but her word, her persuasive diction, her echo: the marvelous voice of

Notwithstanding, as we have already suggested with regards to his relationship with Mary Kahil, Massignon seems to have been both fascinated and attracted by the concept and practice of syneisaktism, this spiritual discipline that consists in "sleeping under the same blanket"—metaphorically or literally speaking—in order to sublimate desire in a chaste going-beyond of temptation. Certainly, Massignon sees in this phenomenon a "perilous psychology"[84] situated in a zone of ambiguity, the literary manifestations of which bear witness most often to a "precarious compromise", or even a straightforward failure. However, at the end of a sinuous and complicated process that bears witness without doubt to the questions, uncertainties, and tensions experienced by Massignon on this complex issue, it appears that the final conception of woman presented in his work led to a resolution of the contradictions that had been at work in his life. "The chief intention which must brace our bow, like the arrow, towards its single goal, its supreme end"[85] ends up determining, not without oscillations, the spiritual trajectory of *eros*. This half-carnal, half-spiritual temptation that seems to have greatly solicited Massignon's attention is ultimately the object of a spiritual sublimation under the sign of maternity and predestination.

We are presented with this perspective in a text of 1961 dedicated to "the temptation of the ascetic Suka by the *apsara* Rambhâ."[86] It is significant that this late text was given by Massignon himself as the formulation of a response to the problem which the integration of *eros* into the spiritual life had represented for him. It is equally interesting to note that it is in the

---

the counseling angel, the inspiration of great thinkers: it is Diotima for Socrates, in the *Symposium*, the daughter of Ibn Rostom for Ibn 'Arabī, and Beatrice in Dante's work. And for Guillaume de Lorris, and especially for Jean de Meung, this is exactly the symbolical "Rose". The love poem thus dissolves into philosophical abstraction." *Ibid.*, p. 67.

[84] "La tentation de l'ascète Çuka par l'apsara Rambha: Sublimation de ce thème dans la devotion populaire," 1961, *OM III*, p. 727.

[85] "Influences musulmanes," *OM I*, p. 67.

[86] "La tentation de l'ascète Çuka par l'apsara Rambha: Sublimation de ce thème dans la devotion populaire," (1961), *OM III*, pp. 723-28.

climate of Hinduism, which in certain respects is considered reluctantly by Massignon,[87] that the dialectics of contemplative asceticism and erotic beauty is resolved. It is permissible to wonder about this coincidence. Let us first specify that the Massignonian perception of Hinduism tends to overemphasise the dimension of methodical asceticism on the one hand, and that of intellectuality on the other. Now Massignon marks these two aspects with a strong suspicion of spiritual sterility. It was probably through meditation on the Gandhian experience that Massignon engaged, at the end of his life, in a more positive re-evaluation of Hindu spirituality on the basis of an Abrahamic understanding of the latter. In fact, he did not hesitate to attribute an Abrahamic persuasion to *satyagraha* (non-violent resistance, literally "holding firm to truth") due to Muslim influence or interferences. The readily mental and hyper-technical dryness that Massignon deems to be dominant in large segments of Hinduism seems to him foreign to the fire of divine desire that he always assigns to a genuine spiritual impetus. In this respect, Hindu spirituality appears in a rather sterile and egocentric light.

From another viewpoint, the Hindu world is without doubt one of the spiritual universes wherein femininity is envisaged in as many different aspects as one can possibly conceive of. In this regard, the figure of Sītā[88] constitutes a central model in the Hindu vision. But woman is equally susceptible to seductive,

---

[87] We mean that Massignon remains largely impermeable to the highest forms of Hindu spirituality, which he seems to conceive as so many "impersonal" disciplines arising from the "natural mysticism" theorised by Louis Gardet.

[88] Sītā has been mainly "immortalised" by the Rāmāyana, but she is already a secondary goddess of the Hindu pantheon after Vālmiki. A consort goddess of the gods of rain and fecundity, her name—which means "furrow"—also indicates that she incarnates the purely maternal and virginal substance. In the Rāmāyana, she becomes the figure of the perfect spouse who places the support and love of her husband Rāmā above everything else, including her own life. Treated unjustly by Rāmā, who accuses her of having given herself to Rāvana who had made her a victim of public infamy, she returns to her motherland wherein she continued to live in purity. The sacrificial and virginal destiny of Sītā therefore makes her similar to the "*compatientes*" of the spiritual universe of Massignon.

dark or destructive depictions, as in the case of the evil-doing *dâkinis*. It is this juncture, the encounter of the respective ascetic and feminine dimensions and the resolution of their conflict in the history of the ascetic Suka and the *apsara* Rambha, that captures the mystical imagination of Massignon very strongly. Fundamentally related to the notions of *Māyā* and *Shakti*, Hindu femininity is envisaged as both the mysterious principle of the manifested universe, the divine power of creating worlds and beings that is readily associated with the cosmic dance of the gods, as well as the source of ignorance and false identification of the Self (*Atmā*) with that which is other than It in an illusory manner. Certainly, these two apparently contradictory aspects represent in a sense, as Frithjof Schuon has well demonstrated, the two authentic aspects of the feminine mystery of Eve and Mary. It remains nevertheless true that Hinduism emphasises perhaps even more the aspect of ambiguity which is inherent to the feminine reality in its most diverse aspects. This ambiguity in fact lies at the very heart of the metaphysical and cosmogonic unfolding and display that Woman suggests. The most essential inwardness, that Rambhā gives the ascetic Suka to "feel", is at once an infinite night and the merciful source of all the world's rivers and oceans. Massignon clearly presents herein the mystery of infinitude to which sexuality gives access through its most profound mystery. The images of the "churning of the sea", from which issues the story of the *apsara* and that of *amritā*—the beverage of immortality—and finally that of the "Aeschylean Oceanid", point to that immanent infinity and intoxication with the Divine that sexuality and femininity enable one to sense in the limitless expansion of their energy.[89] Furthermore, this mystery enables us to understand why it is unmistakably the theme of divine maternity which defuses the potentially subversive charge

---

[89] " .... The dazzling ascension of Suka to the heaven of asceticism makes the beautiful Rambhā "find" her predestination and her finality as *apsara* anew, born as she is from the churning of the sea, a dispenser of the *amrtā*, the ambrosia that inebriates with sanctifying immortality—not corrupted by a flesh vowed to putrefaction; but a soul of Aeschylean Oceanid, consoling a hero envied by the gods." "La tentation de l'ascète Çuka," *OM III*, p. 724.

of sexual practices with spiritual orientations. One is reminded of the figure of Ramakrishna who saw in the multiple reincarnations of Woman—including prostitutes and impure women[90]—so many epiphanies of the Divine Mother, and who worshipped his wife, Sarada Devi, as such.[91] The link between spiritual maternity is in this case connected to the "respiration of the heart's perfume", which seems to give access to an inner dimension of woman wherein man recognises himself as a son of the feminine Substance which he could have run the risk of treating as nothing but an object of concupiscence. Massignon's meditation on this mystery, starting from the history of Suka and Rambhā, dwells first upon the image and not upon the text.[92] And this is not without significance, for in fact it is the image itself, in a contemporary painting by Vasudeo H. Pandya, which allows one to take the full measure of a look, hence unveiling the spiritual truth of the scene. Massignon defines this "reciprocal gaze" as "open" and not as "fixed" or "closed". The two characters are not in a sexual face to face encounter, but in a sort of spiritual communion that is devoid of any tension. The ascetic perceives the young beauty as his Mother. It is remarkable that this reading of the scene results from a "popular sublimation" that is posterior to the classical theme of ascetic literature. Massignon meditated upon the link between this popular inspiration and the spiritual archetypes. The latter appeared to him to arise from a

---

[90] "I saw him in front of those women, wrote Vivekananda; he fell at their feet, wetting them with his tears: 'O Mother! It is Thou! Behind this form, Thou art here, on the street. Behind another form, Thou art the Universe. I greet Thee, O Mother, I greet Thee....'" quoted by Romain Roland, *La vie de Ramakrishna*, Paris, 1978, p. 106.

[91] "On a May night, having prepared the service, he had Saradevi sit on the seat of Kālī; and, as a priest, he performed the ritual ceremonies—the Shorashi Puja (tantric ceremony)—the worship of woman. They were both in a state of ecstasy and half-consciousness (or supra-consciousness). When he came to his senses, he saluted in his female companion the Holy Mother. She had been incarnated, in his view, in this living symbol of immaculate humanity." *La vie de Ramakrishna*, p. 106.

[92] The question pertains to a detail of a 1927 chromolithography and a *marathi* poem of Mukteshvar from the seventeenth century.

spiritual layer which is not limited to the collective unconscious of Jung but which expresses a true psycho-spiritual field, an, as it were, subjectively objective domain that Henry Corbin would categorise as *mundus imaginalis* in the light of his study of Iranian Sufism and Ibn ʿArabī. According to the vision stemming from these popular archetypes of the relation between the sexes, man perceives in woman, or rather, in the secret that she unveils for him, the "mother of his being", that is, his very essence, the primordial substance that orients his fate. When Suka addresses Rambhā as his mother, he envisages this relationship in the popular Hindu terms of transmigration: "And you shalt be my mother, and I shall have the unique honour to have a mother like you. About my past I no longer worry, and what gives me joy now is the thought that I shall have the privilege to be your Son in my new birth."[93] Massignon reads this future Motherhood in terms which clash with the transmigrationist context of Mukteshvar's poem and lead back to the central theme of "original predestination". Alluding to Christ's response to Nicodemus (*John*, 3:4-6) concerning the true return to his mother's bosom, that is, to a rebirth according to the Spirit and the entry into the Kingdom of God, Massignon dismisses the transmigrationist view in order to replace it with an inner, Christic eschatology. Thus, in the Gospel of Saint John, the doctor of Israel visits Christ at night, the pure night of inner truth—the Layla of the Sufis—in order to beg him to explain to him what the birth in the Spirit is. This return to the mother is not in the flesh, but rather a return to the Spirit, to the eternal fate that is the essence of mankind. It is necessary to keep in mind, in the context of spiritual motherhood, that the Arabic term *umm* (mother) also refers to the idea of the essential matrix, as well as being used as a superlative of perfection. In Massignon's thought it is, no doubt, a matter of a very profound intuition of the *Fitrah*, the original and normative substance that Islam considers as foundational and the very basis of the possibility of any spiritual restoration.

In exchange for this profound "recognition" from man, woman too, as she runs the risk of passionate desire, becomes

---

[93] "La tentation de....", *OM III*, p. 725.

aware, like Rambhā—the most beautiful of *apsaras* according to
the ascetic Suka—of her "'virginally' maternal predestination"[94]
*vis-à-vis* man. This predestination is also, in a sort of complementary way, that of the *apsara* who grasps, by the ascetic's
gaze open onto the sky that contemplates her, her most profound nature as pure source of Infinity, her "second beauty".
But this predestination can only be actualised insofar as a third
term converts the possibility of opposition between the two into
a genuine unity. Grace, Love and the spirit of Truth form this
third term that prevents the confrontation of the two human beings from closing in on itself. It is equally striking to note that
Massignon finds herein the Christian scheme of the inner life
of the divine tri-unity that "translates" the Hindu experience in
terms that exclude any monism. Massignon finds in this opening a completely satisfying solution to the problem of sexuality,
a solution that he considers as more "frank" and direct than that
of Christian syneisaktism, insofar as the latter still confined one
to the risks of an ascetic feat not disentangled from inner tensions, where it seems that the challenge consists in conquering
Peace through a hard fought battle rather than in identifying
oneself with it. Hence the relative instability of the phenomenon
of syneisaktism, which could only be perpetuated in the context
of an exceptional support by grace, rather than resulting from a
spiritual realisation rooted deeply in being (*sat*).[95]

*<br>* *

If Woman constitutes the virginal and maternal Substance
of all created beings, she also represents the original and fundamental Norm. At this point the two notions of *Fitrah* and *Fātir*
should be brought together, since they are closely related to the

---

[94] *Ibid.*, p. 724.

[95] From the fourth century onwards, the practice of syneisaktism was
condemned by the synods of Elvira and Ancyra, as well as the Council
of Nicaea. Cf. Rosemary Rader, "Syneisaktism: Spiritual Marriage," in
*Breaking Boundaries*, New York, 1983, pp. 67-68.

meditation of Massignon on Fātima, a major incarnation of the archetype of the *compatiente* in the spiritual universe of Islam. The two terms issue etymologically from the same root *fatara*, which means to slit, referring thereby to the idea of separation and, by extension, to that of origin. The thirty-fifth sūrah of the Qur'ān is called *Al-Fātir*, its first verse referring to the divine Name that can be translated as "The Originator." As for the term *Fitrah*, it refers to the idea of original perfection and to the primordial nature assigned to man by the Originator. These two concepts are therefore connected to the idea of a state of being and understanding that forms the very basis of the project of spiritual restoration of Islam. From this point of view, Islam will appear as a recovery both in the socio-political and the somatic meanings of the term.[96]

Massignon, in his commentary on the *ahādīth* of Jābir Ansārī, refers the term *Fātir* to the original Wisdom which Frithjof Schuon has described as the informal Wisdom which transcends the formal message of the Law. Massignon speaks of a "first Wisdom to have emanated from God" that is also identified with feminine Perfection. Fātima embodies this Wisdom in Islam, just as Mary embodies it in the Christian domain. If, as a daughter of Muhammad, she can also be designated by the name *Umm Abīha*, mother of her father, it is because, in her inner and archetypal reality, she is mother of all the prophets as "perfect Femininity" and "Substance of Prophecy". Here the daughter is mother by virtue of an inversion according to the Spirit: the daughter according to nature and the Law is mother according to the Spirit. Thus, for Massignon, femininity is in its deepest divine essence the principle of unity that is the prime intention of all divine words "made flesh".

The mystical inwardness manifested in and through woman is also related to the mystery of divine transcendence. The most intimate is paradoxically the most distant. The secret of woman is dissimulated and revealed at the same time in diverse forms that allude to it. This is the reason why the most profound in-

---

[96] Let us note that the Vietnamese refer to Islam by using the expression *Dao Hoi*, the second term of which means to recover from an illness.

wardness, just like the most absolute transcendence, can only be intimated, ineffable as it is, in the nakedness which is also a "sublimation" of colours into the "dazzling whiteness of ecstasy".[97] Here Massignon alludes to the undressing of Ishtar—mothergoddess, but also virgin warrior of Sumer and Akkad—during her descent to Hell. The goddess proceeds in her quest for her deceased lover, Tammuz; by descending more and more profoundly towards the innermost circle of the earth, she is forced to undress one article of her finery at each of the seven doors through which she must pass, until the final revelation of the most naked inwardness. The spiritual kinship between Ishtar and Esther suggested by Massignon is not without profundity: in view of the supplication of the king Assuerus for the salvation of his people, Esther goes through a sort of symbolic undressing in the humiliation of her body by abandoning her sumptuous clothes. In both cases, it appears that an element of suffering is present (at the innermost point of her quest, Ishtar is afflicted by Namtar, a hellish deity, with sixty illnesses). The revelation of the heart therefore implies an inner death which does not come about without sacrifice. In this connection, Massignon compares the myth of Ishtar with the *ihrām* of the Hajj, a cloth worn by the pilgrims which constitutes an approximation of primordial nudity, "gradually exteriorising the inner fire".[98] Analogically, feminine nudity embodies the innermost *haqīqah*, as Frithjof Schuon has clearly shown; but one must stress that, in Massignon's work, its consideration involves sacrificial connotations that refer it to the climate of Christian mysticism rather than that of intellective gnosis. In the direction of elevation and transcendence, which Islam envisages as being in relation to the masculine and the geometrical, this nudity is expressed through the de-individualising abstraction of Muslim art and, during the *mi'rāj*, through the abandoning, one by one, of the seven "essential layers" of the created prophetic nature at the seven gates of the seven heavens. But it is also expressed, in a sense which

---

[97] "Ishtar," (1958), *OM III*, p. 316.

[98] *Ibid.*, p. 316.

reminds us of the dimension of feminine infinitude, through the celestial blue of the domes and the flowery mosaics of heaven.[99]

*

\*   \*

The theme of Perfect Woman as the original matrix of all prophecies is distinctly associated by Massignon with the theme of the predestination of the elect; hence the question of the relationship between the two notions. For Massignon, predestination is rooted in the primordial layer of divine Wisdom. We find this principle both confirmed and illustrated in the very beautiful text dedicated by Massignon to his pilgrimage to Ise and in his meditation on the Shinto figure of Amaterasu-Omikami. In the founding myth of Shintoism, the solar goddess Amaterasu, who is an incorruptible and glorious goddess, hides in a cave in order to escape the pranks of her terrible and tempestuous brother, Susano-o-no-Mikoto. She comes out only after being attracted by a mirror placed in front of the cave by the gods. Thus the mirror "returns" the world to the Light of Truth by "inviting" the latter back into the realm of phenomenal outwardness. It is from a meditation on the spiritual function of the mirror in a number of religious and folkloric traditions from the Middle East and South-East Asia that Massignon draws a most profound mystical exegesis concerning the destinal role of the Virgin-Mother. Commenting upon the Persian custom of the "Mirror of Our Lady Mary" (*Ayine-i Bibi Maryam*), Massignon unveils what he conceives as a Marian archetype of predestination. In the Persian custom, the mirror is traditionally situated on one of the walls of the room where a couple engaged to be married contemplate each other for the first time. Each of them can see the other according to his or her "real" nature, which is the reverse of the

---

[99] "And as with painting, distilling the colour pigments, so dense and hard, into bright colours in the most diaphanous shades; just as the clattering of the blues in Iraqi earthenware triumphs in a celestial, asmāngūnī blue, the old treatise from the time of Ma'mūn in Baghdad entitled *sirr al-khalīqa* triumphs." "Ishtar," (1958), *OM III*, p. 316.

fallen nature to which they ordinarily have access. Massignon compares this custom with the image of the Shinto priest-woman leaving the sacred mirror next to a tree, and who—during an ablution—saw her own image redressed in the reflection of the mirror on the surface of the water. This "redressed" image suggests that the nature of the Virgin of Transcendence is like that of a mirror restoring human beings to their primordial norm. The Mirror of Mary is therefore identified with the inner vision of the elect souls that original Wisdom glimpses in and through the Word of God.[100] The maternal Wisdom is also, according to this mystery, both the Paradise that is promised from eternity to the elect and the Star that guides them in the night of their earthly journey.

It is by virtue of this Marian mystery of predestination that femininity is able to play a fundamental role with respect to the ultimate ends of humanity. The theme of the "final promotion of the feminine sex", to use Massignon's expression, is closely linked to that of the advent of Justice, or of the Judgment by divine fire. It is at this point that we encounter what might be called the dimension of the rigour of femininity, a dimension that Hindus perceive in the destructive and purifying figure of Kali. This aspect of avenging majesty is denoted as the "ultimate indignation of Woman that will burn the world".[101] Eschatologically, it expresses a spiritual reversal that leads inwardness and spiritual poverty to triumph *in fine*, thereby exteriorising the primacy of the love of God and charity. The end of history is in this sense the reverse of its unfolding. Massignon sees in Fātima, as spiritual mother of the Mahdi, the announcer of the establishment of a new Law that is none other than the inner Law of the heart. Fātima is understood by Massignon—following cer-

---

[100] "This mirror is named *Ayine-i Bibi Maryam*, Mirror of Our Lady Mary, probably because it is the "redressed" vision she enjoyed, as Primeval Virgin, before the creation of bodies, seeing all the Elects, from inside the heart of her shadow-body, in God's own Word." "Visite au bois sacré d'Isé," *OM III*, p. 719.

[101] "L'expérience musulmane de la compassion ordonnée à l'universel à propos de Fatima et de Hallâj," *OM III*, p. 647.

tain Shī'ite inspirations—as the "incarnation" of an awaiting for perfect Justice, a Justice that is only approximated by the Law brought by her father. Developing an intuition of Archbishop Fulton John Sheen,[102] Massignon draws a parallel between the historical function of Fātima and that which is assigned to Esther in the Bible. The latter is offered as a "substitute" to her husband King Assuerus for the salvation of the Jewish people. As a young Jewish woman with no *prima facie* spiritual vocation, she gradually becomes the feminine symbol of the spiritual truth of her people, thereby announcing—from a Christian point of view—the Jewish betrothed one *par excellence* that is Mary.

In the perspective of this inner oblation to God (*al-Bātul*) which Esther prefigures in the Old Testament, Fātima embodies for Massignon, if one may say so, the principle of a christianisation of Islam or, at least, a final revelation of the *'isawiyah* heart of the Islamic tradition. For Massignon as a Christian mystic, Fātima becomes the sign of the incompleteness of Islam as a Law.[103] It is a known fact that Massignon's attraction to Islam has always been qualified, and in a sense halted, by the legalist character of its common tradition. The profoundly Christian, and therefore essentially interior, sensibility of Massignon, is marked by reservations towards a tradition for which penitence is symbolically replaced by ablutions. On this account the "facilities" of Islam amount ultimately to nothing but this reduction of the Love of God to an obedience to His Law. According to the Shī'ite emphasis that informs Massignon's work in this respect, the difficult relationship, tense with oppositions, between the daughter of the Prophet and the future Caliph 'Umar, the

---

[102] "Just as Esther (before the First Coming) was a 'Marian figure' for Israel, Fatima can be 'a Marian figure' for Islam (before the Last Coming)." Quoted in the preliminary to "L'oratoire de Marie à l'Aqça, vue sous le voile de deuil de Fâtima," *OM I*, p. 592.

[103] "Above the law, bequeathed by the Prophet to be applied as such, why would Fātima entertain a foolish hope in a more perfect Justice, a grace of Ihda (*ihdinā* of the Fātiha, recited for the dead, and for the coming of the Mahdi) from Irshād, guiding the community towards a collective ideal unaccomplished by the founder of Islam, towards the secret of its heart (*sirr al-ikhlās*)?" *Ibid.*

"tragic dereliction" of her destiny, and the sacrificial character of her vocation, all bear witness, in their own suggestive way, to this duality between the inward and the outward. This polarity corresponds essentially to the distinction arising from the two versions of the *hadīth al-thaqalayn*—with respect to the two legacies of Muhammad—at the farewell pilgrimage. One of the versions identifies the legacy as being the Qur'ān and the *Sunnah*, whereas the Shī'a interpretation stresses the authority of the descendants of the Prophet.[104] Sunnism and Shī'ism acutely diverge on this point. It is both curious and telling that Massignon, for whom Sunni and Arab Islam had been the starting point, eventually felt so profoundly called by the world of Shī'ism and the Persian world with which it is identified to a large extent.[105] Massignon has indeed mentioned himself the fateful events that initiated him into the inner truth of Shī'ism. The suffering and decisive episodes of his archaeological mission of 1908 to the desert of Kerbela and Najaf opened for him a comprehension of the spiritual vision of extremist currents of Shī'ism threatened by the conspiring of the powerful of this world, and utterly dependent upon sacred hospitality and thirsty for eschatological justice. Massignon pointed to a direct correlation between this central personal experience of his on the way back to faith and the emergence of his academic interest in Shī'ism—particularly in the *Nusayris*. Inner and biographical experience was thus the "unconscious" seed of a subsequent intellectual vocation: the premises of the vow have blossomed in the Christian scholar's oath.[106]

In the wake of a Shī'ite vision of Fātima, which he interprets in a way dear to his heart, the "humiliation" of woman in Islam

---

[104] On this point one may refer to Kaj Öhrnberg's work, *The Offspring of Fatima, Dispersal and Ramification*, Helsinki, 1983, p. xv.

[105] Pierre Roclave has retraced the major stages of this affinity with the mystical themes of Shī'ism; cf. "Louis Massignon et Henry Corbin," *Luqmân*, Spring-Summer 1994, pp. 64-65.

[106] "A personal, aborted, secret experience which emerged consciously for me on the field of my scientific researches only twenty years later." "Les Nusayris" (1960), *OM I*, p. 623.

can be traced back, in Massignon's perspective, to the "humiliation" of the Spirit by the letter, of Grace by the Law, of the mystics by the doctors. In Islam, the spiritual and mystical elevation of woman runs parallel, as it were, to the social abasement of women,[107] and Massignon articulates these two apparently contradictory aspects by emphasising their hidden nexus. However, the "humiliation" of woman is in fact also the prefiguration and the symbol of a victory. Woman, through whom salvation takes place, is not only abased according to the world and the law, she is not just passive, she is also "the strong woman, who arouses the hesitant warriors, and who shakes out the cowards."[108] The Virgin-Mother is not only mercy and love, she is also and *a priori* purity and rigour. Thus, one can understand her deep connection with the eschatological impatience of the Judgment. The *compatiente* is impatient—if one may say so—precisely because she already carries in herself the truth of the advent. This purity is none other than that of the fire that cries vengeance against injustice precisely because it is the very element of the feminine perception of the "virgin heart" starting from which everything that is not real will be burned.[109] Even human love, when lived intensely without conceding its most extreme purity, has the virtue of purifying through tears, death and suffering. On this subject, Massignon has meditated upon the crystalline totality of Bedouin love that leaves the lover helpless before the beloved. For the desire—"the very veil of Attraction of Divine Desire,

---

[107] "We do not ignore the fact that this unexpected and paradoxical exaltation of woman in Islam, as symbol of the supreme paradisiacal ideal, was formed in antithesis to a very contemptuous conception of the ordinary woman." "Mystique et continence en Islam," in *Parole donnée*, Paris, 1962, p. 277.

[108] *Ibid.*, p. 649.

[109] "Only the Spouse 'without a spouse', the predestined Virgin ('they ran out of wine' in Cana), can discern the virgin heart that exists, at the battlefront and further on, in no man's land, in the heart of the comrade for the comrade of the last charge, be he the worst of outcasts." *Les trois prières d'Abraham*, p. 47.

and which kills"[110]—that is revealed therein in all its incorruptible radiance is nothing but the dynamic and mystical dimension of the virgin heart, or Meister Eckhart's "spark of the soul"
(*fünklein der Seele*). It is in this deepest core of the heart that
dwells the fundamental femininity of the soul, the pre-eternal
consent to divine Will and Love. This is the primordial Sanctity
which constitutes, as it were, the most deeply buried stratum of
the soul, the anti-lapsarian norm of human existence. If Massignon claims to be a representative of an archaeological vocation, this is so in two senses, the first of which, outwardly, is but
the circumstantial symbol of the second: for him, archaeological
and scientific research is just a path leading to the discovery of
a truth buried in the inmost depths of the soul, the only one
that finally matters.[111] Thus, the archaeological investigations
that would lead Massignon along the symbolic trajectory of his
destiny towards the discovery of the Passion of al-Hallāj appear,
therefore, like milestones of a demiurgic ruse that would take
him back to his true self.

The feminine inversion of religious values that presides over
this exhumation of the truth within the heart, this transposition of the inward to the outward, must be understood in an
altogether central relationship with the fundamental theme of
sacred hospitality. In fact, the host is received "inside", be this
interior that of the home or the land, or, more profoundly, that
of the heart. To receive in one's heart means to acquiesce to what
is imposed upon us by destiny or by the *fiat*. The stranger is
therefore the symbol, and also the manifestation, of transcendence and metaphysical and spiritual otherness. Herein lies the
key of the "technique" of spiritual de-centring advocated by
Massignon. The "*point vierge*" is precisely the place in the soul
where the welcoming of the Other may occur. With regards

---

[110] "Mystique and continence en Islam," in *Parole donnée*, p. 279.

[111] "….I am first of all an historian who has been occupied with archaeology
and diggings, who then dug into his personal psychology and the
psychology of others, in order to find a sort of initial spark, an ember that
glowed under the ashes of the years, and which I believe to be divine." "Le
vœu et le destin," (1957), *OM III*, p. 688.

to *amān*, sacred hospitality, Massignon can write thus: "....this Right of Asylum that any honourable man, especially an outcast, cannot betray; because it is his last *point vierge*, his honour as a man."[112]

Now, one may be led to think *prima facie* that woman is more "closed" than man to this welcoming of the stranger precisely because of her mysterious inviolability, as well as her more exclusive attachment to strictly natural bonds that keep and nurture the heart within the precinct of familiarity. There can even be a more or less natural egoic conservatism in woman that makes the acceptance of others outside the bonds of institutionalised love difficult for her. The matrimonial jealousy of woman arises from this limitation. To the avarice of man corresponds the jealousy of woman, which, far from bringing everything back to itself as in man's case, "builds a zone around herself, a zone of jealousy, which is her temptation".[113] As an illustration of this negative tendency, Massignon does not hesitate to highlight the potential opposition between natural and supernatural love through the typical example of a woman who could not accept the spiritual sentiments of her husband towards another woman, through a sort of natural instinct of exclusivism reticently resisting the freedom of grace.[114] Now, true love implies a sort of withdrawal before God which sometimes forces us not to be the single affective centre in the life of another human being:

I do not think that it is possible, when loving souls divinely,

---

[112] "Toute une vie avec un frère au désert: Foucauld," in *Parole donnée*, p. 71.

[113] "L'involution sémantique du symbole," (1960), *OM II*, p. 630.

[114] "I have a friend who has done much for the Church and who told me about a rather terrible moral dilemma that occurs quite often (I am speaking about an old man); he found himself having a purely spiritual affection for someone, and his wife did not understand. She told him: 'I would have liked much more that you live unhappily rather than there being a soul above me whom you prefer.' This is an absurd idea on this woman's part, and yet somewhat legitimate in consideration of the sacrament; she is right, like the Jews, not to forgive her husband for having let the door of his intimacy with God open." Unpublished text of "Le front chrétien" conference.

not to love them sometimes together with others that one has
not chosen and whom God has chosen for you.[115]

This truth is all the more the ordeal *par excellence* reserved for
woman that man, and especially spiritual man as a centre, will
have the tendency to realise in himself the plenitude of his creative receptivity to the feminine.

Notwithstanding these initial reservations that pertain to a
psycho-sociology of woman rather than to her spiritual essence,
woman is identified most profoundly with the inner instinct of
hospitality. This is so first of all in the sense that she receives the
other in herself through the conception and the transmission
of the lineage, just like she does at home, in the domestic space
wherein she reigns.[116] Fātima, the archetype of spiritual femininity in Islam, is not just "mother" of the family lineage of the
Prophet, she is also the protector of the "spiritual parenthood"
as indicated by the "role of the daughter of the Prophet shelter-
ing the poor non-Arab clients of the Prophet, like Salmān".[117]
Therefore, the distinction between the agnatic—through the male
stock—and cognatic—through marriage—lineages, introduces at
the very heart of Islam the possibility of a "welcoming" of the
stranger. Fātima is situated precisely at the point of convergence
of these two groups. It is she who introduces the "strangers" into
the family of the Prophet. The Massignonian understanding of
Shī'ism is thus clearly dependent on this double feminine vocation of Fātima. Massignon understands the Fātimid inspiration
as a way of "fulfilling" Islam, and at the same time as the spiritual
principle of a movement related to the "righter of wrongs" figure
of the Mahdi. This fulfilment takes place through the reception
and the integration of non-Arab converts; but its *sine qua non* re-

---

[115] *Ibid.*

[116] "Only the woman, mother, daughter or sister, [who is] perpetually mi-
nor under the old Law, is dedicated to hospitality, hence defending the
genealogical perpetuity of the race, of which she is the organ of transmission." "L'expérience musulmane de la compassion ordonnée à l'universel, à
propos de Fâtima, et de Hallâj," *OM III*, p. 644.

[117] *Ibid.*, p. 650.

sides paradoxically in the mystical bond of filial proximity to the Prophet. Hence the insistence of Fātima—and following her, the insistence of Shīʿites—on the quasi-sacramental presence of the Prophet, which guarantees the universal vocation of Islam that excludes political fragmentation and Arab tribal claims. Now, this presence presupposes a receptivity, a mode of emptiness and poverty, and even a sacrificial humiliation, to which Fātima Zahrā's fate bears witness. She was indeed characterised by her "occultation" and her "abasement". She remained concealed under the family relationships that weave, as it were, a five-fold veil hiding her truth, a concealment which is also reinforced by a destiny marked by frustrations, sacrifices and disappointments.[118] In other words, Fātima, as archetype of the humiliated woman, is "covered" by the iniquity of the world that the purity of her heart may remain the inner secret of perfect sanctity. In this context, the tension which places Fatima in a posture of confrontation vis-à-vis the first two Caliphs, Abu Bakr and ʿUmar, reflects in a certain manner that between the masculine and the feminine poles of the spiritual message of Islam. The former organises the life of the community and the rules of its functioning on the basis of election and jurisprudence, whereas the latter emphasises a family and mystical line on the basis of a spirituality with personalist tendencies that introduces, as Frithjof Schuon has shown, a Christian archetype within Islam.[119]

---

[118] "In the intertwining of destinies which concern us here, there is the strange case of Fātima. Embodying, according to unanimous tradition, the purest sanctity, she was put aside, frustrated and forgotten. On occasion she was treated in a hard way even by the Prophet her father. Herein is the whole drama of a celestial soul predestined to be the martyr of terrestrial life. Her abasement is, as it were, the shadow cast by her spiritual elevation, human individuals appearing in her destiny as the cosmic instruments of her painful alchemy." Frithjof Schuon, "Images d'Islam," in *Christianisme/Islam: Visions d'œcuménisme ésotérique*, Milan, 1981, p. 143.

[119] "In a certain way—and as an approximation only—Shīʿism is an "Islamic Christianity"; its fundamental theme is the "divine humanity" of its great saints, then the martyrdom of the uncomprehended light, and finally the sacramental presence of this light in the form of the Imamate." *Christianisme/Islam: Visions d'œcuménisme ésotérique*, Milan, 1981, p. 148.

It is on the basis of this interiorist vision that one can fathom why the holy war of women is the *hajj*. This idea, to which Massignon returns on several occasions, is not just a further illustration of the affinity between the feminine and the supererogatory that we mentioned earlier. Certainly, the *hajj* is incumbent upon the believers only in a conditional fashion when compared to other canonical obligations. It therefore presupposes the very possibility of an interiorisation, which the Sufis have most often conceived as an injunction to perform a pilgrimage to the Ka'ba of the heart. This appears in a most meaningful light when considering that, in Massignon's view, every pilgrimage is fundamentally a de-centring experience. Every pilgrimage presupposes that one leaves "oneself", or the horizon of one's immediate familiarity, henceforth consenting to make room for the divine Centre. To move means in a sense to accept to modify one's "ego-centred" vision in order to become oriented from a centre that "de-centres" us. Woman alludes *par excellence* to this capacity for *faqr*, this inner receptivity to the divine Word, and it is by virtue of this receptivity that she conceives Wisdom. For Massignon, woman does not "comprehend", she "conceives". She "makes room" in herself and with herself, she does not grasp, she does not embrace, she is not suitable for possessing and appropriating. Extrinsically exempt from stain through the virginal incorruptibility of her nature, woman can thus appear as a heroic warrior in the quest for the attainment of Wisdom. Her combating incorruptibility is the pledge of her virginity and her conception of Wisdom. On this point, Massignon calls on a universal and perennial folkloric and mythological treasure that "sublimates" a unique, exceptional woman as an archetypal model. Commenting upon the pioneering role of the Javanese Raden Adjeng Kartini in the domain of women's education in Muslim Indonesia, Massignon sees in the inspiration awakened by this young aristocratic lady an outward manifestation of this very spiritual phenomenon. Therein he reads "the resurgence ... of an ancient archetypal theme of humanity, the isolated apparition of a 'sublimated' exceptional person, of a woman 'masculinised into a hero', for the initiation of other women into a Knowledge which is normally reserved for men ...

137

and, beyond that, to the *conception* of Wisdom."[120] It is interesting to note that, in conformity to his perspective according to which the establishing of Justice is also a terrestrial and external eschatological phenomenon, Massignon reads some aspects and breakthroughs of the "cause" of women—especially in Islam—as an outward manifestation of the final "promotion" of Woman in sacred history. Still, we believe one should understand this promotion or this "cause" as a final compensation, or as a sort of re-equilibration that places the immediate psychological and social manifestations of the relationship between the sexes into perspective, without however implying any egalitarian flattening down of the profound prerogatives of each half of mankind. For Massignon, the promotion of woman is a matter of Justice in the deepest sense of the word, and not a calling into question of the metaphysical economy of the rapports between the male and the female, including their outward concomitances. Massignon points to the abuse, including the institutional abuse which is the ransom of contingency, not to the spiritual and psychological norm.

How can we understand "this ideal sublimation of woman above her sex" if not as a sort of spiritual reversal of the social order of things? The "exceptional" temporal character of this reversal is intrinsically connected to the mystery of the iniquity of this world and to the metaphysical inversion that converts the inward into the most outward and the higher into the lower. Massignon is well aware of the fact that feminists have but very little gratitude to him, when considering the most immediate level of social life, for his attributing to women an inner eminence that borders on mystical devotion. During a conference on women's education, he declared, with a full lucidity as regard the dialogue of the deaf opposing him to most modern women: "I went to preach to the feminists who received me very badly, because they said: you have a way of admiring us which shunts us aside."[121] In order to grasp the position of Massignon and

---

[120] "Preface aux lettres javanaises de Raden Adjeng Kartini," in *Parole donnée*, p. 392.

[121] Conference de Toumlinine, 1957.

to appreciate all its depth, we must understand—leaving for a moment the ground of social contingencies which may obscure the principles at play—the Christian spiritual economy of his thought, a traditional thought for which sex is not an external and, as it were, accidental reality, but rather a profound existential vocation. There is an inner, principial reality of the sexes which is expressed in the way of an inverse analogy. The highest according to the inner vision appears as the lowest according to the outward vision: "The first shall be last." However, this inverse analogy cannot be absolute without doing away with all communication between the orders. Thus, a woman of ancient China, although submitted to man according to the necessity of the world, had—as Massignon likes to remind his readers—the right to intercede before the Law in view of saving a person condemned to death. The inner privilege of woman can therefore also come to light within the world of outward justice. This is the reason why, in this domain as in others, the exception restores, so to speak, the principial order of things. The "*shahāda* Fatima" of some Indonesian Muslim spiritual schools mentioned by Massignon expresses this mystery in the most direct manner possible: "I bear witness that Fātima, the precious pearl [or essence] (*jawhar karīm*), the Woman, is the Light of Prophecy (*Nūr nubuwwatin*)—she, the daughter of Muhammad."[122] On this level, Fātima is "mother of her father" just like the Holy Virgin appears in her supreme function of Mother of all the prophets. The "feminine" religion overtakes the "masculine" religion—if one may use such provisional expressions so susceptible to psychological and social misinterpretations—in the sense that the supreme Prophecy is envisaged in its supra-formal dimension, which coincides with the divine intention in its most central and most universal dimension, but always in a more or less silent or concealed way, as befits its mysterious profundity.

---

[122] *Ibid.*, p. 400.

139

3

# UNIVERSALISM, RELIGIOUS DIVERSITY
# AND "ESSENTIAL DESIRE"

The concept of religious universalism is obviously not univocal. In the present context, we envisage it as referring
to a spiritual vision according to which religious particularity
eventually oversteps its own confessional limits in order to open
up to a universal truth and soteriology. Assuredly, a number of
major religions of our historical cycle—starting with Buddhism,
Christianity and Islam—are indeed characterised by a universal
vocation, at least inasmuch as they consider their apostolic mission as embracing *de jure* the totality of humanity. Nevertheless,
this does not mean that these "universal" religions are properly
speaking universalist, since they can claim, and in a sense cannot but claim, as formal belief systems, a more or less exclusive
privilege of truth. In the context of the main religions of our
world—leaving aside the non-traditional movements and doctrines which consider themselves independent of any confessional affiliation—the concept of universalism may take on at
least four meanings, two of them falling under a model of intrinsic universalism, whereas two others may be deemed to participate in a somewhat extrinsic model. Universalism may primarily
be defined—and we believe this is its highest level of manifestation—as a doctrine asserting that a single universal truth, transcending the diverse confessional worlds, reveals itself through
each of the traditional religions of the world while maintaining
a transcendent independence with respect to their exclusive
claims. In other words, there is a universal truth which the diverse religious languages seek to evoke and awaken in us, but
which, in itself, transcends the limitations of the various creeds.

141

A second type of intrinsic universalism also admits the universality of an essential truth, but it reserves its access to spiritual approaches that necessarily proceed through the mediation of that particular form by intensifying or interiorising it. In other words, the first type of universalism proceeds from the universal essence in order to comprehend and love the particular form in and through its universal content, whereas the second approach discovers and realises the universal essence through plumbing the depth of the very life of that particular form. It goes without saying that these two comprehensions of spiritual universalism, although profoundly different in their modes of apprehending the truth, can combine in variable proportions, since they are not incompatible on the plane of their concrete methodical modalities.

Extrinsic religious universalism—referring to religious positions in which the universalist and supra-confessional essence is not at all inherent—may also be apprehended in two forms. It reveals itself first of all in the various religious perspectives that, although they presuppose the intrinsic spiritual superiority of a given confession, nevertheless envisage the other religious worlds as susceptible to being "accomplished" or "completed" through the mediation of the religious faith that the former convey and profess. The modes of this "accomplishment" cover a wide range, but at any rate such a position presupposes that foreign confessions can serve as a support for that goal. In this sense, the particular religious form is somehow universalised beyond its strict terrestrial boundaries. The second type of extrinsic universalism differs from the first in that it envisages the said accomplishment not as a phenomenon which is based on what is valid in the foreign forms, but, on the contrary, as an end that is realised in spite of these forms. This type of universalism underlines the impossibility of fixing boundaries for divine mercy, and presents this mystery as an inclusive principle of religious universality, without affirming any less clearly the exclusive truth of its *credo*.

\*

\* \*

To speak about universalism in the work of Massignon may sound like an exaggeration or misstatement if universalism is understood as being founded upon the principle of a unity of essence among all the forms of the Spirit. More precisely, if one means by "universalism" the idea—introduced by René Guénon and magisterially explicated by Frithjof Schuon—according to which a single and universal Truth underlies all the religious forms that make up the spiritual patrimony of humanity, one may not apply this term without abuse to Massignon.[1] Independently from this aspect of the question that will be developed in the coming pages, it is appropriate to emphasise, in this context, that the esoteric and universalist perspective, better known in the English-speaking world as the "Perennialist School," does not claim in the least to bypass or abolish the diversity of the great religious traditions of mankind on the plane of their formal expressions and their specific means of grace. For Frithjof Schuon, for example, while it is true that the transcendent and universal unity is accessible from the vantage point of any particular orthodox tradition in its innermost and secret heart, the fact remains that the differential particularity is also necessarily manifested more clearly at the periphery of this tradition. In this sense, universality is synonymous with inwardness: the heart is the summit, the point from where one can contemplate the integral breadth of diverse religious landscapes from the perspective of their transcendent unity. This presupposes not only a very high degree of spiritual realisation, whether actual or virtual, but also a keen and supple metaphysical and spiritual intuition as well as sufficient infor-

---

[1] The universalist position to which we allude here is that of the esoteric current known as the *Perennialist School* in the United States. This school appeared at the beginning of the 1920s with the work of René Guénon and Ananda K. Coomaraswamy. The universality of symbols and the metaphysical and esoteric character of their significance form two key concepts of this doctrinal corpus which, starting from the 1950s, was prolonged and deepened by the work of Frithjof Schuon, who laid open the esoteric thesis of the transcendent unity of religions. One must also mention within this movement the works of Titus Burckhardt, Marco Pallis, Martin Lings and Seyyed Hossein Nasr.

mation concerning other creeds. This explains why a plenary recognition of the "transcendent unity of religions" has rarely been afforded to religious figures of the past. Be that as it may, this unity can never be realised but inwardly, and not in the domain of forms that are necessarily diverse by virtue of the infinity of Divine Possibility. For his part, René Guénon has underlined the distinction that should be drawn between a universal "synthesis", which starts from the essence in order to interpret the manifold religious phenomena, and a "syncretism"—often criticised by Massignon—which most often amounts to nothing more than a spiritual mosaic bereft of any rigorous inner unity.

In contrast to the spiritual synthesis provided by the doctrine of "the transcendent unity of religions",[2] Massignon's approach presupposes a religious and vocational multiplicity that is not reducible to any objective transcendent unity whatsoever, besides, of course, the intrinsic unity of God. In this respect, it could be argued that Massignon's point of view is, in fact, less intellective than mystical, less doctrinal than methodical. Founded upon a "science of compassion" and an inner hospitality towards the Other, Massignon's spirituality implies the irreducible reality of otherness, in both the form of the divine Other and that of the neighbour. Massignon's mystical thought seems, as it were, "pulled" between the imperative demands of otherness and the unifying dynamics of Love. Indeed, as Amira El-Zein has remarked, there exists an often implicit but nonetheless real tension[3] between the notion of the other, whether it be apprehended in terms of understanding or love, and the mystical ideal of union that Massignon expresses so well, though not without a particular inflexion of the original text, in his beautiful rendering of Hallāj's verses into French:

---

[2] This is the title of Frithjof Schuon's first work to have appeared in French.

[3] "I and you join together in 'an East in the metaphysical sense of the word,' at the centre 'of a spiritual world,' *'alām qudsī.*" Amira El-Zein, "L'autre dans la spiritualité massignonienne," in *Louis Massignon au cœur de notre temps*, ed. Jacques Keryell, 1999, p. 43.

*Entre moi et Toi (il traine) un "c'est moi" (qui) me tourmente...*
*Ah! Enlève, de grâce, ce "c'est moi" d'entre nous deux!*[4]

The inclusion of the notion of "torment" (*me tourmente*) and
the introduction of an expression referring directly and explicitly to divine grace (*de grâce*) may be deemed to give an interpretation of Hallāj's text that "Christianises" it, while deflecting
the pure issue of metaphysical and spiritual identity that lies at
its core. In a sense, Massignon's translation, by introducing a
notion that is not explicitly present in the Arabic *fārfa' binnaka*,
highlights the tension to which we have just referred in resolving
the question of identity and otherness through the intervention
of divine grace. In contrast, Martin Lings' English translation of
the same verses remains closer to the literal meaning as well as to
the crux of the ontological question of identity:

*Twixt Thee and me an "I am" is, o'ercrowding me:*
*Take, by thine own "I am", mine from between us.*[5]

Notwithstanding the reservations one may have about Massignon's interpretation of Hallāj's perspective, it is in the aforementioned tension between the "need" for the Other and the desire for union that Massignon's work draws perhaps its essential
spiritual dynamic. From our current point of view, the spiritual
desire that animates this tension can be taken as the principle
of a religious universalism in the sense of a convergence or triumph, while not for all that being synonymous with an intrinsic
universalism of the first type,[6] the uniqueness of the Christian
Revelation constituting for Massignon too central an element to
be transcended in the Mystery of supreme Unity.

---

[4] *La passion de Hallâj III*, Paris, 1975, p. 55.

[5] *Sufi Poems: A Mediaeval Anthology*, compiled and translated by Martin
Lings, Cambridge, The Islamic Texts Society, 2004, p.28.

[6] And neither of the second type, given Massignon's clear reservations
towards non-personal and non-theistic forms of spirituality, and his relative
lack of perspicacity in their regard.

\*

\* \*

One would therefore not do justice to Massignon's thought if one did not situate it within a Christian, and more particularly Catholic, range of issues, which gives it all its meaning. On a first, still elementary and passive level, this spiritual and psychological rooting of Massignon in Christianity is "psychically" identified, by virtue of its terrestrial and physical characteristics, to his explicit and reiterated attachment to his country, France, from which his openness towards the other and his love of the "stranger" could not in any way sever him.[7] For him, there is a profound truth in the physical and geographical immediateness that constitutes a sort of "premonitory sign" of the spiritual. Thus, for example, Massignon does not hesitate to connect himself spiritually to some of the aesthetic and psychic choices and characteristics of his father, the sculptor Fernand Massignon, *alias* Pierre Roche. He meditates on everything that, in connection with his father's thought and work, can be symbolically enriching in the virginal and nurturing soil of France, primarily through its most profound folkloric and moral aspects.[8] For

---

[7] "One must stress here a point dear to his heart and which he would tackle repeatedly with those close to him: he was horrified to be taken, because of his love for the Arabs, for a countriless person, or a cosmopolitan without a homeland. Quite the opposite; he saw himself as an ardent Frenchman, profoundly rooted in his land and its dead. And he had wanted to devote a scholarly study to his old parish, in Labbeville-en-Vexin. Besides, can one imagine a Massignon that had another nationality than ours?" Vincent Monteil, *Mémorial Louis Massignon*, Cairo, 1962, p. 95.

[8] Massignon finds some prefigurations of his spiritual vocation in the aesthetic intuitions of his father: "My father was a sculptor who had taken the name Pierre Roche ... the youngest son of peasants, who were labourers until the Revolution of 1789 in the French Vexin ... my father had remained permeable to the 'charm' of the simple life of the farmer, sensitive to the pure mystery hidden behind the naïve harshness of nature. He had ceased to believe in God, but he kept his faith in the miraculous birth of France in the fifteenth century, in the virginal apparitions that Jeanne d'Arc had glimpsed through the trees, after the candles she offered to Our Lady of Bermont in the forest; and he had made a solitary pilgrimage to Domrémy,

the collective "flesh" is also, if one may say, the terrain in which archetypical truths are rooted, in a way that is more or less unconscious for most but always potentially available to the discerning: this is the most precious gift that the cultural psyche may offer us in a passive but virtually fertile manner. Massignon does not conceive these archetypal truths like Jung, who reduces them to mere strata of the "collective unconscious" that bear no ontological relationship with transcendence; he understands them, rather, as converging "signs", as much on the individual plane as on the collective level—thereby linking the two—that shape configurations prefiguring and "constructing" the spiritual reality of every community and every human being.[9] Massignon's thought presents us, on this point, with a remarkable convergence with the reflections presented by Simone Weil in her work *L'Enracinement* ("The Need for Roots"). For both of them, the collective cultural field is like the nurturing soil of the individual spiritual vocation. It is by feeding on the rich substance of the latter that spiritual man finds himself able to draw and put to use the resources necessary to transcend the particularity that has nurtured him. All genuine and integral cultures, whether they be regional or national, provide their participants with the means of surpassing their particularity, and herein lies, in fact, their highest legitimacy. Every traditional civilisation offers, among all the vocational possibilities that it proposes to those included in its area of expansion and its common representations, that of escaping the natural cycle of terrestrial existence.

---

in silence, in 1889. The marvelous artistic paradox of an inviolate Virginity blessing the tools, the seeds, the harvest, the cattle, was dear to his mind." "Méditation d'un passant aux bois sacrés d'Isé," *Parole donnée*, Paris, 1962, p. 412.

[9] "This is how the definitive, supra-historical physiognomy of every person, city, and group is constructed; through a series of unforeseen findings, converging "surprises" and "recognitions", which the most judicious of Freudians, Jung, from Zürich, minimises by reducing them to cyclical reappearances of natural archetypes." "Le mirage byzantine dans le miroir bagdadien d'il ya mille ans," *OM I*, p. 128.

While truly "de-centred" in the Islamic world in order to be able to rediscover his hidden spiritual filiation, Massignon had also intended to "re-centre" himself by returning to the religious and psychic milieu which prepared "from afar" the forming of his spiritual identity. Spirituality is not just a matter of individual vocation; it is also the result of a religious interiorisation of the past generations, those of which we have often lost sight, but to which we are "genealogically" and subtly attached, knowingly or not. This is the way Massignon, towards the end of his life, worked towards connecting himself to the parish of his family by delving into a socio-religious study of the "premonitory signs" of his own vocation. In the 1959 article that he devoted to the parish of Labbeville—the origin of the paternal branch of his family—the Islamicist engages in a particularly instructive reflection on the relationships between the parish, the local spiritual terrain, as it were, and the ecclesial and apostolic universal which it is called to serve. Christian parishes are defined by Massignon as "shelters wherein God, this stranger Host, this displaced Person *par excellence*, has come to seek hospitality."[10] The parish, centred upon the church which is the sanctuary of the Presence of the divine Other, is also the natural cadre wherein this other stranger, the priest, is received, and whose spiritual exile and sacrificial "strangeness" was magnificently described by Bernanos in his *Journal d'un curé de champagne* ("Diary of a Country Priest"), published in 1936. There is in the figure of the Western European priest an aspect of indelible solitude that comes out precisely in this "foreign" otherness further reinforced by the tough discipline of celibacy, which makes him both a necessary and dreaded "asocial" presence in the community. It is through the encounter of the psycho-social milieu and this priestly stranger that the gifts of the Spirit can ripen within society and fertilise the local soil throught the universal seeds of the Word of God. The highest function of the priest is therefore to make the "visitation of grace" flourish and fructify, a visitation that Massignon suggestively characterises as a sort of "spir-

---

[10] "Labbeville: sa vie parossiale de la ferme abbatiale du Bec à la dernière lettre d'Altamura," (1959) *OM III*, p. 321.

itual exogamy".[11] By encouraging and supporting the religious vows that may emerge in the parish, the priestly host contributes to revealing some contemplative souls to themselves, thereby allowing them to be freed from the limiting boundaries of their parish in order to leave the world behind them: "because these vocations, which are the Christian flower of the parochial territory, leave it and are often transported far away."[12] Leaving the parish means here finding it on another plane, that of the mystical Body of the Church, and therefore giving life and force to it by interceding for it. One is not among one's own, but by abandoning them one rediscovers them in the Spirit, and this is an inescapable spiritual truth against which all cautious familial deference and passionate nationalism can do nothing.

It is according to an analogous spiritual "logic" that a "Muslim expatriation" enabled Massignon to return to his place of origin in order to awaken the spark of universality that slept buried within. It is first necessary to emerge from a spiritual particularity in order to be able to recover it in all its richness, a richness that is intimately linked to its universal vocation. "Happy is he who, like Ulysses, has returned successful from his travels":[13] the spiritual journey is, moreover, a return to one's own terrestrial roots, or more precisely, towards what is best and most real in them. Returning to the places of the parish of his forefathers, Massignon finds there a number of vestiges and signs which he can interpret *a posteriori* as the distant seeds of various aspects of his vocation and work. How can one not be struck, for example, by the profound sense of destiny highlighted by Massignon's ancestors, forced as they were to leave their home in Vexin to settle in Paris "for having sheltered Cadoudal",[14] "the last spear" of the avengers of the monarchy and Marie-Antoinette? The religious fidelity illustrated by this episode in the life of Massignon's forebears finds a remote echo in the pages filled with mysti-

---

[11] *OM III*, p. 321.

[12] *Ibid.*

[13] Joachim du Bellay, Les Regrets, sonnet XXXI, 1558.

[14] *OM III*, p. 331.

cal profundity that he devotes to the much maligned Queen of France whose life was ended by decapitation. Another revealing "premonitory sign" lies in Abbot Mésières, priest of Labbeville from 1896 to 1927, who in 1904 confided his concerns over the fate of the Church in France to Mélanie Calvat, the visionary of La Salette whom Massignon places among his "*compatientes*".[15] Here, too, the lesson of the premonitory sign is that of faithfulness and inwardness, the ultimate message of the Seven Sleepers of Ephesus that Massignon will peruse as his viaticum.

\*

\*  \*

Notwithstanding the aforementioned meaningful links between the particular and the universal, the personal and the collective, then considered now from an angle that breaks away from any natural limitation, blood kinship—the most elementary source of identity—appears as a reality definitely better transcended. This is so precisely inasmuch as one renounces oneself in order to offer one's being to the other, "substituting" oneself for them and tearing oneself away from the illusion of being the centre. This is the reason why the notion of universality appears most commonly in Massignon's work in connection with the themes of compassion and human brotherhood. Love is indeed the principle of universalisation *par excellence*. Here, it is not just a matter of Aristotelian *philia*, this natural and spontaneous predisposition to human benevolence towards others, a kind of psychological *material prima* of all civic life. For Massignon, there is, beyond this ethical and social sphere, a spiritual reality that animates, strengthens and purifies the natural inclination that is no more than its often ambiguous trace; for human souls, this

---

[15] "She draws to La Salette those who are concerned, heavy with secret tears, to pray for the fallen privileged, the bad Priests. Her last letter, dating from the night of her death, to the priest of Labbeville (the old parish of the Massignon family), who thought of exiling himself amidst the very crisis of the Church of France (14th-15th December 1904), is a cry of piercing faith: *faire la morte et rester fidèle*—to lie dead and remain faithful." Vincent Monteil, *Parole donnée*, p. 39.

is a "call to come out of themselves towards others, to love in a brotherly fashion outside of their milieu and their kin in the time and space of the here-below, in a brotherhood that is oriented towards the universal."[16] The true identity, which is "oriented towards the universal", is therefore only reached on the basis of a de-centring that can also be described as a change of level. On this plane, the natural bonds of blood can even become an obstacle: does not the Christic message—just like Islam, but with a greater insistence than the latter—emphasise the tension between the familial and the spiritual? The episode of the Temple included in the Gospel of Luke presents us with the young Jesus ignoring his mother, who is worried by his disappearance, in the name of the unconditional primacy of the Spirit.[17] A number of powerful words present in the predication of Jesus have the same meaning, especially the formula, *Mater mea et fratres mei hi sunt, qui verbum Dei audiunt et faciunt* (My mother and my brothers are those who hear the word of God, and do it. Luke, 8:21), not to mention the famous warning, *Si quis venit ad me, et non odit patrem sum, et matrem, et uxorem, et filios, et fraters, et sorores, adhuc autem et animam suam, non potest meus esse discipulus* (If any man come to me, and hate not his father, and mother, and wife, and children, and brothers, and sisters, yes, and his own life also, he cannot be my disciple. Luke, 14:26). In the same spiritual perspective, studying Massignon's life one clearly senses that the relationships between his universalist vocation of compassion and familial and local demands have often been difficult for him to negotiate. The weight of "carnal" imperatives naturally makes the access to the universality of human experience arduous, not to say impossible. First among all, carnal nationalism is characterised by a relationship of opposition with any spiritual recognition of man's highest vocation. As for the family as a natural entity, its gravity and its more or less unconscious resistance to the Spirit results from a tendency to close in upon itself, to enjoy

---

[16] *Parole donnée*, Paris, 1962, p. 65.

[17] "*Et dixit mater ejus ad illum: Fili, quid fecisti nobis sic? Ecce pater tuus et ego dolentes quaerebamus te. Et ait ad illos: Quid est quod me quaerebatis? Nesciebatis quia in his quae Patris mei sunt, oportet me esse?*" Luke, 2:48-49.

an all too human comfort within the limits of its illusory self-sufficiency. *A contrario*, it is very clear that for Massignon, the most real community is not that which is based on the proximate evidence of blood and place. The true community is the result of a choice, not of an arbitrary election founded on purely individualist criteria of taste and affinity, but on a divine choice that brings together the scattered members of the invisible Church: "It is through the saintly friendship established between determined and predestined persons that the eternal Community is built."[18] Moreover, these friendships acquire a meaning only on the basis of what Massignon eloquently designates as the "great disturbance" of human engagements and sufferings. In this sense, the true friend is a "disturber" who is also *a priori* "disturbed". In other words, the natural order must be "disturbed", called into question, even shattered, by the interferences of evil within existence so that a change of level may make way for the formation of a spiritual crest line gathering all those who have accepted to make of their suffering a holocaust "oriented to the divine universal". Thus, the literality of terrestrial lives is sometimes raised up to the plane of a supernatural life which makes its deepest truth come to light.[19]

In this perspective, the drama of Israel is conceived by Massignon as the most direct example of the deadly limitation of any cultural or national identity that would lose sight of the universal horizon which alone gives full meaning to its principles. This tension and the potentiality of conflict are all the clearer in the case of the Jewish people, as the latter is marked by a privilege of "super-naturalisation" by vocation and destiny, a predestination which should protect it from a "carnal" and temporal temptation leading it to withdraw and "curl up" in its purely terrestrial

---

[18] *Parole donnée*, Paris: 1962, p. 96.

[19] "It is through the saintly friendship established between determined and predestined persons that the eternal Community is built: so that it may appear therein, in the mode of all beauty and truth, projected from our lifelines on the fundamental liturgical cycle, the diverse forms of deifying intimacy realised in the 'great disturbance' of our sufferings and our works—in union with the creative will." *Parole donnée*, p. 96.

identity.[20] As we have suggested earlier, Massignon sees a symptom of this carnal temptation of the Jewish people in the Judaic attitude towards Mary. For him, what many early Jews actually reproach Mary for is her welcoming the stranger unto herself, her having opened herself to the hosting of transcendence, the Holy Spirit.[21] According to this vision of things that evidently arises from a Christian archetype, if the Jews have refused Mary it is because of their incapacity to open up to the Stranger who alone can orient their vocation to the universal. The people of the elect can only be defined and perpetuated "upwards", and all betrayal of this supernatural vocation is a negation of its own nature. Similarly, although less directly than in the case of Israel, every terrestrial collectivity can "betray" its archetype by letting the principle of universality that it carries in its bosom decline. This is why Massignon, who has remained faithful to a Christian and universalist vision of France, conceives of his endeavour in this respect as a reminder and a manifestation of the universal essence of the "Elder Daughter of the Church". On a less directly religious plane, Massignon does not hesitate to define a universal mission of France that would be related to its double vocation of justice and rational clarity.[22] Thus the reference to Joan of Arc in the context of the French colonial presence in Islamic lands reveals this "place" wherein the particularity of France "is subordinated to the universal" in the very motion of its affirmation. Massignon has often been misunderstood on

---

[20] "Indeed, with a strange continuity, through all the crises of mankind, social pain resorts to the obscure symbols of the prophets of the small people of Israel, our universal prefiguration, when we suffer; why should its faith weaken at this time in the universality of this promise, and believe that a material and perishable possession could consume it?" *Ibid.*, p. 127.

[21] "What Israel does not pardon this Jewish virgin, who is the flower of Israel, the whole consummation of Israel's fate, the consummation of Abraham's vocation, is that she accepted a stranger as a host; she is the wife of the stranger." Unpublished text of "Le front chrétien" conference.

[22] "The supreme international vocation of France ... is just as much to prescribe an ideal in accordance with justice and to spread a clear language, that its lack of musicality saves from ambiguity and pathos." "L'Occident devant l'Orient, primauté d'une solution culturelle," (1952), *OM I*, p. 212.

this point, no doubt due to many of his analysts remaining prisoners of a very circumstantial and superficial vision predicated on a crucial contradiction between an abstract universal and a jealous, even aggressive, identity. For him, as for any genuinely spiritual person, the universal is not a juridical abstraction to be engraved onto the world, willingly or not, nor is identity an arrogant self-satisfaction feeding the contempt or hatred of the other, such that *tout ce qui est national est nôtre*, "right or wrong my country". The contemporary world might learn today from the profound convergence of identity and universality in Massignon's work. The principle of universality is indeed the "virgin heart" of the nation wherein "its essence is epiphanised". The "purest" place of identity is also that which escapes identity as a limit and illusion. This is just as true for a person as it is for a country; not that this "place" is envisaged by Massignon in terms of a universal Substance, simultaneously immanent and transcendent to the particular subject, who would be "nothing" without It—or Her—in the likeness of *Atman*, the transpersonal Subject of non-dualistic Hinduism. In Massignon's work this essence of the soul that escapes the limitations of the soul is rather envisaged, mystically, as a motion, as the desire of the Divine which is inherent in man. Moreover, in Massignon's work, this desire, ever determined by the dynamics of otherness, informs a clear tendency to interpret non-dualism in terms of a static and flat monism. It is well known that the ways of Massignon and his student Corbin part on this point, as we are reminded by Pierre Rocalve and Jean Moncelon,[23] Massignon favouring a form of

---

[23] Cf. "*La divergence fondamentale—irréductible—portait sur leur conception du rapport de la créature au Dieu transcendent.*" ("The fundamental and irreducible divergence between them lay in their respective concepts of the relationship between the creature and the transcendent God.") Pierre Rocalve, "Louis Massignon et Henry Corbin," *Luqmân*, Paris, printemps-été 1994, p. 82. Massignon's lack of interest for later Sufism, and especially his caution vis-à-vis Muhyi al-Dīn Ibn 'Arabī, was another motive of surprise for Henry Corbin: "*Il y a parfois dans l'œuvre scientifique de Massignon, des affirmations qui étonnent, des thèses auxquelles on ne peut se rallier, voire des jugements dont la partialité est tout près de nous scandaliser.*" ("There are sometimes in Massignon's scholarly work affirmations that

*wahdat al-shuhūd* (unity of witnessing or of testifying) over the strict unity of being (*wahdat al-wujūd*) of the Akbari School informed by the teachings of Ibn ʿArabī.

\*

\* \*

On the level of the life of nations and civilisations, the "virgin heart" is also *mutatis mutandis* the locus wherein the desire of the universal emerges. Some predestined figures embody this essential point. Joan of Arc is one of these figures in the spiritual history of France. In actuality, she does not defend the identity of France by sacrificing herself for it if not on the basis of a love of God that universalises the spiritual function of the nation. We can understand, therefore, how profoundly Massignon could be shocked by the condemnation of a Moroccan Shaykh to eighteen months in prison, in 1956, for having invoked the name of the *pucelle* in the context of the events in Morocco.[24] This decision of French administration and justice betrayed the principle of universality: it monopolised and "carnalised" the saint, making her an instrument of a colonial policy without horizon; "loving one's country does not consist in becoming the complacent puppets of those who buy and sell the host: he is sacred." And this is an even more reprehensible error since it frustrates the other from accessing the universal which our identity should guarantee him, and which it does guarantee him in truth and spirit. It is clear that this is a matter that transcends a political rhetoric based on the universal vocation of France as constructed by the ideologues of the French Revolution. In reality, what

surprise, theses we cannot accept, even judgments the partiality of which comes close to outrage us.") Jean Moncelon, "Louis Massignon et Henry Corbin," *Luqmân*, Paris, automne-hiver 1996-7, p. 35.

[24] "Remember the Moroccan Shaykh Abd al-Wāhid b. ʿAbd Allāh, who invoked thee in a mosque, at the Suaika of Rabat, against a regime of deportations and tortures? He was condemned, of course, despite an appeal from the Pope, to eighteen months in prison. Motive: usurpation of the name of a saint reserved for the use of the good French master." "Jean d'Arc et l'Algérie," *OM III*, p. 604.

Massignon has in mind—more profoundly than any humanitarianism of hospitality, however praiseworthy it may be—is a vision of the other as "messenger from God": the imperative of this envoy carries a spiritual necessity that must open one's own self to the universal. Moreover, this is how the most central Mystery of Christianity, charity as love of God in and through the love of the neighbour, is found crystallised in Massignon's thought through the mediation of the "good Samaritan", the Muslim brother.

*

* *

In Massignon's case, it is plain the question of religious universality cannot be envisaged independently from the problem of the confrontation between Christianity and Islam. The last two important religions that have appeared in human history, both universal in their own respective views, are at once kin to a common mythological climate of Biblical origin, and yet profoundly different in their respective spiritual economies. Massignon's Islam has been written about a great deal, some going so far as to suspect that he rallied this faith by pushing his opening onto the other to the limit of spiritual identification. On the opposite side, others accuse him of having betrayed Islam by infiltrating it through a pure apostolic technique of conversion. It is therefore not out of place to ponder the issue of Massignon's actual position on Islam.

In this respect, the "second prayer of Abraham" presents us with a synthesis, at once dense and nuanced, of the Massignonian vision of Islam. This second prayer is focused upon Ishmael and the Muslim world that issued from him. As situated within this Ishmaelite lineage, Muhammad is first of all the Prophet of "temporal involution" as a "return to the farthest past".[25] Herein lies the core meaning of the return to Abraham that Massignon describes in incomparable terms of profundity and sensibility, and that he prescribes as a response to the crisis of Christian

---

[25] *Les trois prières d'Abraham*, p. 110.

consciousness: "This contemplation in the hand of God, this silent, immaterial and sacred premonition of a pure, omnipresent divine transcendence, wherein a Christian who knows the gift of God recognises, in its simplicity, the patriarchal worship of God of the earliest times."[26]

While Abrahamic in his love of Islam and his debt towards its spiritual reminder, Massignon remains nevertheless fundamentally Christian. He rejects Muslim "transcendentism" in its diverse manifestations. Downstream, Islam seems to him, first of all, to "block" the communication between God and the terrestrial realm through the "suspensive clause of natural causality" that Massignon reads in the Qur'ān. Massignon downplays the immanent "divinity" of the Book and its correlative capacity to function as a spiritual bridge between God and mankind. In doing so, Massignon is in no way unfaithful to the Islamic overemphasis upon God's transcendence, but he tends to omit or underestimate the theurgic and transformative dimension of the Qur'ān in Islamic life and practice and its immanent divinity within the soul. Massignon is keen to introduce the Qur'ān in terms of its exalted transcendence and supreme incomparability—*i'jāz al-Qur'ān*—not only because of the Islamic insistence upon these aspects of the Book, but also because he preserves thereby the exclusiveness of the sacramental economy of Christ's Redemption. The paradox is that Massignon's reading of the Qur'ān may bar any sense of sacramental union by highlighting its emphasis on the transcendence of the Divine, while elevating the Book to the selfsame forbidding realm as God himself. In this view, the Qur'ān draws its transcendent divinity from its function as an inspiring but prohibitive gateway to Divinity. And more generally, Massignon's Islam, curiously disconnected from Sufi theophanic immanentism, is characterised by a relentless emphasis on the ontological gap between the Divine and the terrestrial, as illustrated in Massignon's view by the extreme occasionalism of Islam in its obsessive negation of secondary causes. Notwithstanding this clear-cut delineation between the Divine and the human, Massignon understands

---

[26] *Ibid.*, p. 110.

Islam as nevertheless having reaffirmed "what inviolable seal, forever virginal, encloses the mystery of the Incarnation."[27] In other words, Massignon's Islam opens up to the mystery of the Incarnation through the privilege of virginity that it grants to Mary, thereby implicitly but clearly distinguishing Christianity from the human, terrestrial, material idolatry and divinising worship of pagan religions. Upstream, however, Muhammad "declines the mystical engagement"[28] by stopping at the threshold of the divine precinct. The Prophet remains at a distance from the burning essence of Divine Life, which can only be understood, for Massignon, in its dimension of internal, interpersonal love. Muhammad is therefore not initiated into the personal life of God, the door to which can be opened only by the Mystery of the Trinity. Nevertheless, Massignon maintains that the Qur'ān does not refute the Trinity. For him, Sūrah 112 (*al-Ikhlās*) affirms the unity of the Essence (*Huwa Allāhu Ahad*) and not "the divine unipersonality". In other words, Unity is not envisaged on the plane of the divine Person, but on the level of the Deity or the hyper-luminous Darkness of the Essence. On this plane, Unity neither begets nor is it begotten. Hence, there seems to be in Massignon, at least implicitly and theoretically, a recognition of two planes, namely that of the divine Essence—which is incommunicable and ineffable, and whose transcendence is underlined by Islam—and that of the divine and trinitarian Life, which is a "constant communication between the Speaker, the Spoken to and the Spoken of".[29] In contrast, the interpretations of the Christian Trinity offered by al-Ghazzālī affirm that the Christian Trinity is situated at the level of the divine essence, a conclusion that would paradoxically concur with the views of the most extreme Trinitarians among Christian theologians.[30] Without

---

[27] *Ibid.*, p. 97.

[28] *Ibid.*, p. 71.

[29] "L'involution sémantique du symbole," *OM II*, p. 631.

[30] Cf. "Le Christ dans les Evangiles, selon al-Ghazali," (1933), *OM II*, p. 529.

entering into the details of Massignon's theological position, we will content ourselves with noting that his reading of the Qur'ān manifests all the inner logic and value—but also the limitations—of the theological and mystical point of view that it reflects.

For Massignon, just as for Pascal in the seventeenth century, the sense of the absolute akin to the Christian sensibility rejects the "Arabism" of Islam as an incapacity to grasp the Passion as something other than "God's defeat". This is the "protestation of the carnal nature of man" in its withdrawal from, and even rejection of, deification. In this realm, Islam is also coloured by an instinct of elementary religious "commerce", the spiritual "mercenariness" vilified by some Christian mystics, that sacrifices the transcending flight of the spirit to the imperatives of social equilibrium. This carnal "horizontalism" has equally been connected with the legalistic outwardness of Islam that was such a source of discomfort for Massignon. For him, Islam is "ill-equipped against hypocrisy",[31] unless it be the case of the Islam of the "expelled and the voluntarily exiled", the "veritable" Islam of 'Isa ibn Maryam which finds in Arabic the language of Peace and that of the "promulgation of the Second Coming". This, of course, is also the Islam of al-Hallāj, the "witnessing monism" through which God enunciates the one essential Desire. As such, or as the unshakeable faith in the God of Abraham, Massignon's Islam remains above all "the angelic spear throw that has stigmatised Christendom".[32] In this sense, Islam is also "a kind of rhyme with Christianity, which came about when the measure was met."[33] This rhyme implies an assonant Abrahamic harmony even though, moreover, the content of the verse it concludes differs from the preceding one in its substance.

*
* *

---

[31] *Ibid.*, p. 100.

[32] *Ibid.*, p. 112.

[33] "L'involution sémantique du symbole," *OM II*, p. 633.

As a Christian Islamicist, Massignon has very often opted for objects of study that simultaneously manifest and problematise his double vocation as a mystic on the lookout for living sources of spiritual inspiration and a Catholic interpreter of the world of Islam. Massignon's living spirituality did not predispose him to undertake a study of speculative and theosophical mysticism, a domain that would become an object of study favoured by his student Henry Corbin. Massignon was much more interested in spiritual destinies and supernatural events than in metaphysical doctrines as such. Indeed, these destinies and episodes shed light on Massignon's vision of the relationships between Islam and Christianity. The characters and events of this cross-religious spiritual universe are characterised by three terms which, we believe, describe quite well the Islamo-Christian odyssey of Massignon: *compatient* (or spiritual substitution), ordeal and exception—an instance that does not adhere to the rule.

The *compatient* substitution which we have already mentioned on several occasions constitutes a mode of presence within the other through the presence of the other within oneself. It would be possible to refer to this "substitutive compassion" as a universalism through reciprocal participation according to the sacred logic of hospitality. This is the way in which Massignon considered himself the spiritual host of Muslims, who were themselves in return the sacred guests of his soul. The French word *hôte*, used to refer to both a guest and a host, indeed does justice to the important notion of reciprocity connoted by the term. It is the same in Latin with the term *hospes*, and in Greek with the term *xenos*. Thus, hospitality had a sacred character in Western Antiquity, so much so that "the obligation due to the guest prevails in times of war and peace over the duty towards the state," as Pierre Souyris rightly remarks.[34] The bond between one human being and another is more important than collective obedience, as it arises from a more absolute necessity and a more profound layer of humanity. The host is identified with the Divine or the Intellect that readily assumes the forms of wandering and poverty. In this highly spiritual sense, the soul must receive

---

[34] Pierre Souyris, "De l'hospitalité," *Nouvelles de l'Arche*, no. 4, 1988, p. 29.

the Spirit by virtue of an inner hospitality that is the gateway to wisdom. This is how the narration of Ulysses' return to Ithaca presents us with the hero in the semblance of an old vagabond in rags[35] who has come to reclaim his kingdom. Joseph de Maistre has also remarked, in his essays on sacrifice,[36] that the notion of the guest goes back to the Latin *hostis*, a term referring in Rome both to the public enemy and to the stranger. It seems that the origin of this terminological paradox must be sought in the fact that the notion of *hostis* could refer to the idea of a juridical equality given to some foreigners, who were thus considered as "guests" from within. Pierre Souyris compares this notion of equalisation with that of compensation, which is central in the practice of the sacrifice of *hostia*, the compensatory victim.[37] As for Maistre, he relates this practice to the principle of the sacred hostage, the enemy or the other who is sacralised through and in the sacrifice. The wafer (*hostia*) of the Eucharistic sacrament equates with the divine lamb sacrificed in the holocaust of the Passion in view of the Redemption. The substitution consists in definitively becoming "other", in substituting oneself for the other as "sacred hostage". This is how a solidarity—a sodality, *badaliya*—which is the very movement of love in its universal vocation becomes implemented. Universality is thus conceived on

---

[35] "....one finds, in the mythology and folklore of almost all peoples, the theme of the royal hero who returns to his own kingdom under the guise of a poor stranger, or even of a juggler or a beggar, in order, after many trials, to reconquer the property which legitimately is his and of which a usurper had dispossessed him." Titus Burckhardt, *Symboles*, Milan, 1980, p. 39.

[36] "Maistre, to continue our exposition, identifies the Latin *hostis* with the French hote or visitor—*the stranger who is victimised*. 'The *hostis* being thus an enemy or a *stranger, and under this double regard* subject to sacrifice, the man, and thus by analogy the immolated animal, was called *hostie*. One knows how much this word has been both denatured and ennobled in our Christian languages [ie, hote, Eucharistic host]' (Maistre, "Eclaircissement" 310n)." Owen Bradley, *A modern Maistre: the social and political thought of Joseph de thought of Joseph de Maistre*, Lincoln: University of Nebraska Press, 1999, p.47.

[37] Souyris, *op. cit.*, p. 44.

the model of the mystical body of the Church, which is "catholicised" beyond its strictly dogmatic definition.

The ordeal, or test of truth, situates us on different grounds— at least apparently, since it does not seem implausible to interpret "substitution" as a manner of spiritual ordeal. Be that as it may, it is clear that Massignon envisages the "dialogue" among religions in the mode of an ordeal. He shows little interest in discussions that might only touch upon the surface of the respective spiritual economies for the sake of a facile inner comfort or a courtesy of compromise.[38] *Prima facie*, the universalist dimension of the ordeal seems rather paradoxical, since the trial is supposed to decide on a question—that of the Incarnation, for example—by excluding one of the possibilities put forward. The episode of the *mubāhala*, like that of the fire ordeal of Saint Francis in Damietta,[39] inspires Massignon's thought in two directions which are divergent and complementary at the same time. On the one hand, it is a question of stigmatising the Christians' tepidness and weakness.[40] On this subject, Massignon sometimes expresses a lively impatience with regard to the compromises and procrastinations of Christendom. He even goes so far as to postulate an inadequacy of Christians in proportion to Jewish and Muslim faithfulness.[41] Due to the extra-Christian develop-

---

[38] In his Memorandum read in English at the World Congress of Faiths held in London in 1936, Massignon rejects all facility and mediocrity in dialogue: "Let us offer all our best, entirely, even if it hurts, not in tiresome discussions, but living it, most compromisingly, even if love ends in a personal 'Chestertonian' duel, in a medieval 'ordeal.'"

[39] "(The sultan) wanted to test the Christian faith of this ardent 'missionary.' Tradition, portrayed with zeal by the painters, has it that he had invited Francis to walk through a brazier." Julien Green, *Frère François*, Paris, 1983, p. 238.

[40] Regarding the ordeal between the Prophet and the Christians of Najran, he writes: "Just what the Muslim Prophet offered the Christians of Najran (but, getting weak, they declined)." *Memorandum*, World Fellowship, London, 7th July, 1936.

[41] "Perhaps Muslims and Jews will be those who will bear witness to the God of Abraham, whereas Christians will continue the petty combinations with the people of the age, the Taylorisms and the techniques...." Unpublished talk from "Le front chrétien" lecture.

ment of the Western world, and its mundane fever for technological activism, Christians actually find themselves in a delicate
situation from where many think they can escape from below,
that is, by "Christianising" the idolatry of the world. Massignon
has little sympathy for this expedient apostolate, which does not
even manage to make good friends. On the other hand, and on a
more positive note, it is a question of stressing the fact that one
cannot try God. Indeed, Christianity cannot set the question of
the ordeal in the same terms as does Islam. For Christians, in
fact, "thc Light shines in the darkness, and the darkness comprehends it not"; in other terms, a Christian—unlike a Muslim,
for whom the status of man as *khalīfah*, or representative of God,
guarantees a terrestrial intelligibility of His messages, or *āyāt*—
cannot rely on a terrestrial verification of the Truth, at least not
before the Judgment and the final Parousia. In this sense, the
failure of the ordeal is the highest sign of the victory of Christ,
while it is also the most difficult to decipher. The ordeal therefore refers each of the participating sides to its own truth: the
Muslim to his glory of warrior of *al-Haqq*, the Christian to his
glory of witness of Christ. This is the reason why, quite paradoxically, it would not seem impossible for the ordeal to be understood ultimately as a figure of reciprocal injunction towards the
Good, a sort of "ecumenism of emulation", if one may use such
an expression. This is, for example, one of the possible meanings of Christianity's "stigmatisation" by Islam. The true holy
struggle (*al-jihād al-akbar*) is not a war directed against others;
it is rather—on the occasion of the spiritual challenge that the
other imposes upon us through his efforts towards sanctity—a
re-centring of our spiritual personality around the axis of our
faith. Thus, when Massignon refers to a "Christian front", this
expression points to an inner attitude of faithfulness to the supernatural centre of the Christian inspiration; not to a stcrilc
war of positions aimed at "converting" the other:

> Therefore one has to go through a kind of renunciation, of spir-
> itual poverty, and not try to defend the Christian front with the
> things one has snatched from the enemy, with the spoils taken
> on the barbed wire against the opposite side, but in a com-

pletely axial manner one must try to find within oneself the source of essential grace.[42]

It is also in this sense that, for Massignon, the *"compatient"* presence of Christians at the heart of Islam constitutes an inner challenge to the latter, much more so than all external attempts at conversion. The example of Charles de Foucauld must be understood according to such an evangelical logic of universality, his presence among Muslim Tuareg in the Sahara, in Tamanghasset, being martyrdom in the most essential, and etymological, sense. The universalism of the ordeal amounts thereby ultimately to a rejection of all flattening of religious diversity on the level of a natural religiousness or a rational religion. In this sense, Massignon seems to have reached an intuition of the dangers raised by a hasty and misled pseudo-esoterism that does nothing by reducing artificially the diversity of dogmas and religious practices to a unity without substance by ignoring the reality of the divine aspects and human perspectives, and confusing all levels and dimensions into a vague sentimental "wholeness".[43]

As for the exception (*istithnā*), the third central element of our reading of Massignon's "science of religions", it bears witness to transcendence at the very heart of the order of things, by "abolishing" that which "*is*" in the name of God, who alone is and is truly.[44] Indeed, it is also true that the *istithnā* emphasises

---

[42] *Ibid.*

[43] This capital distinction has been borrowed from Frithjof Schuon. It rejects *a priori* all reduction of the religious diversity to the level of subjectivist relativism. Schuon's plenary esoterism is no facile universalism, since it implies, and demands, an awareness of the aspects or faces of the Divine with respect to man as much as an awareness of the diversity of the human perspectives on the Absolute. On the one hand, it is not the same things that are talked about, and on the other hand, one speaks about the same things, but differently.

[44] It is also the principle of the method of authority: "It is extremely shocking for us to see this way of reasoning in which the affirmative particularity transcends the negative universal." "La syntaxe intérieure des langues sémitiques et le monde de recueillement qu'elles inspirent," (1949), *OM II*, p. 572.

and confirms the rule, the identity, through difference; but in doing so, it also annihilates it in its presumption of absoluteness. As Louis Arnaldez suggestively expresses it:

> This exception consists in saying "God willing." It means that at every moment the transcendent intervention of God can reduce human projects to *nihil*.[45]

The model of this exception is grammatical: it goes back to the syntactical structure of the *istithnā*, which is typified by the first part of the Shahādah: *lā ilāha illa 'Llāh*. The matter regards the juxtaposition of a proposition having a universal nature with a second proposition that immediately negates the former: "The general formula of the *istithnā* is: 'There is no *y*, but (= except) *W*.'"[46] According to this model, universality is envisaged negatively. Verse 18 of Sūrah 68 in the Qur'ān, *al-Qalam* ("The Pen"), announces the very principle of this exception: it refers to "the owners of the garden who had vowed that they would pick its fruits the next morning" and had "made no exception" (*wa lā yastathnūna*). And yet, in the morning, the garden was entirely razed. A "relative universality" is therefore negated by an absolute exception: God—the transcendent exception—reduces the creation—an immanent universality—to nothingness. The exception is therefore a direct manifestation of the *fiat*.[47] Theologically, it enunciates the non-reality of secondary causes. Thus, in a certain way, *istithnā* also does away with the Law, the Necessity, by affirming the Freedom of the Infinite. Massignon interprets this fundamental structure as a paradoxical sign of the hope for a final abrogation of the Law: "It is a discreet hope that, ultimately,

---

[45] Roger Arnaldez, "La pensée et l'œuvre de Louis Massignon, comme clés pour l'étude de la civilisation musulmane" in *Louis Massignon au cœur de notre temps*, Paris, 1999, Jacques Keryell, p. 310.

[46] *La Passion de Hallâj III*, Paris, 1975, p. 99.

[47] "(The term *istithnā*) lays out this unpredictable and sovereign exception, which threatens at every instant to interrupt the normal order of events, natural laws or canonical rules—for those who believe in divine omnipotence." *La Passion de Hallâj III*, p. 100.

God is good; that He will consent one day, in person, to free the believer from the heavy prescriptions of the revealed Law."[48] Some of the renderings of the Qur'anic expression *lā yastathnūna* as "would not set aside a portion (for the poor)"[49] can be considered to amount to a moral, or even a socio-political, flattening of the scriptural expression. It is however intriguing to note that this somewhat reductionist interpretation of the verbal form *yastathnūna* paves the way for a spiritual import of the *istithnā* that brings us closer to the Massignonian inspiration, that is, the spiritual meaning of sharing as an opening to the other. The relationship between hospitality and the exception as expressive of All-Possibility points in the direction of an imperative of transcendence. For the guest, or the other, is a messenger of transcendence who pierces through the veil of opacity of our ego, thereby de-centring us. The metaphysical "revolution" of *istithnā* that de-centres our small world by uprooting it from its temporary or fictitious coherence results in a spiritual "revolution" that undoes the inborn egoism of the subject. Thus the exception is the extreme case that coincides with what lies beyond the law. This principle connotes a heroism which leads us into taking the risk of precipitating ourselves towards God in all faith, to dare listening to the first movement of the impulse (a motion that Junayd recommended in following in the Path), because it is an opening to grace without egoic restraint.[50]

On the basis of such a concept of the "exception", could it be said that, with Massignon, Christianity is the *istithnā par excellence*? This interpretation can be based on a series of fundamental characteristics of this religion: not only its claim to the privilege of historical and eschatological uniqueness and its vo-

---

[48] *La Passion de Hallâj III*, p. 101.

[49] Such is the case in the English version of Maulana Muhammad Ali, *The Holy Qur'ān*, Lahore, 1995, p. 1088.

[50] "There is in this pursuit of the extreme case, beyond the law, a kind of instinct of grace that makes us not fear the trial, and understand in this pressure of war and enmity of the world that penetrates to our innermost self, in an unimaginably beautiful manner, a kind of considerate attention from grace." Unpublished text of "Le front chrétien" lecture.

cation as the simultaneous accomplishment and abrogation of the Law, but also its dimension of metaphysical "scandal", since it appears to overthrow the Law and the order of things by having God "abased" at the level of the created by the redemptive Incarnation. Ultimately, if *istithnā* is a figure of universality, it is not so much under the negative form of a suspension of everything as it is as an inversion of the inversion that obstructs the horizon of the universal.

We noted that Massignon's universalism remained intimately linked to a meditation on the widest horizon of various fundamental spiritual realities of Christianity. In fact, Christianity seems to assume for Massignon the function of a norm in matters of universality. It is quite clear that the question of the universal is defined by him within the limits of a range of possibilities extending from a defect to an excess, which are terms that he tried to avoid. On the one hand, we have a tense, heightened particularism that runs the risk of betraying the original vocation of its universal inspiration; on the other hand, we have a universalism that is too abstract, or too conceptual, and which does not do justice to the supernatural, "exceptional" inspiration of the religious. Now, it sometimes happens that Massignon comes to define Islam in terms of the latter, or in a way that appear to minimise its supernatural vocation. Commenting upon the metaphysical "poverty" of the Islamic dogma, the Christian Islamicist tended to define the latter, especially in his earlier years, as "the natural religion revived by a prophetic revelation often confused by the normal exercise of reason."[51] In certain respects, the privilege that Massignon assigns in contrast to Christianity is that of realising a balance between a monotheistic form that is too national—this could be the case with Israel—and a monotheism that is too elementary, schematic and static—and this could be the case with Islam. It is clear that for Massignon, the pitfall of Judaism is an ethnic huddling up, and that of Islam is the all too high degree of abstraction of its central concept. Massignon did intimate that Islam lends itself better than any other religion to the inclusion in its bosom of a maximally universalist per-

---

[51] "Les sources arabes utilisées par les Scolastiques," (1924), *OM II*, p. 488.

spective. The Qur'ān already shows the path of such a principle of universalist inclusion when underlining that all the terrestrial "hues" depend on the singular water of grace:

> Hast thou not seen that God causeth water to fall from the sky,
> and We produce therewith fruit of diverse hues;
> and among the hills are streaks white and red, of diverse hues,
> and raven-black;
> And of men and beasts and cattle, in like manner, diverse hues?[52]

One may well wonder whether Massignon, suspecting that this universality erases the supernatural exception, considered Islam—on the same line as Pascal, but without going as far as he did—to be ill-equipped against deism. It will be recalled *a contrario* that it is precisely this aspect of Islam—a "natural" and "rationalist" Islam, yet without doubt truncated—that could seduce a Voltaire. Against that which he tends to conceive as too immediate a universalism—and one not without platitude or facility, precisely because it is too natural and too rational—Massignon propounds a gradual universalism which he sees as the progressive inclusion and integration of all men of good will into the bosom of the universal Church.[53]

Contrariwise, Islam is readily associated by him to the universalist perspective as expressed in the works of Guénon. It is noteworthy that the latter, who was born a Catholic and had moved about in various occultist and theosophist circles during his youth, spent the end of his life in Cairo under the name of Shaykh 'Abd al-Wāhid Yahyā. For Guénon and his followers, Islam did indeed provide the most appropriate traditional framework

---

[52] *Qur'ān*, 35:27-28.

[53] "If we take, for example, the three 'Abrahamic' religions, Israel, Christianity, Islam, we realise that between Israel's jealous segregation and Islam's open easiness (and readiness to evolve universalism, simple and clear worship), room remains for Christians to elaborate the gradual incorporation of all men, through good will and good works, into the 'Church's soul'." *Memorandum*, World Fellowship, London, 7th July, 1936.

for the manifestation of a universalist esoterism. Massignon perceived very keenly and clearly that Islam could be interpreted and lived in this perspective. He even saw in original Islam a "conceptual syncretism".[54] In his speech at the Toumlinine conference in 1957, he mentioned explicitly "the school of Guénon", which according to him introduces many disciples to a vision of Islam as a "secret doctrine". Massignon tends to interpret this esoteric vision of Islam in terms of Hellenistic infiltrations. He links it to the doctrine of the *Ikhwān as-Safā'* (the Brethren of Purity), the occult school of the tenth century that originated probably in Basra and contributed to the integration of the Pythagorean and Hermetic doctrines into the intellectual corpus of Islam.[55] It is undeniable that Guénon's thought, through its mathematical and geometrical dimension, has an affinity with the works of the Brethren of Purity who "emphasised the metaphysical and symbolical aspect of arithmetic and geometry".[56] The conclusion of Massignon, who sees in this metaphysical doctrine the origin of the contemporary esoteric and perennialist movement, is nevertheless far-fetched. In fact, the secret doctrine of the *Ikhwān as-Safā'* constitutes an intellectual synthesis

---

[54] "It is not a contemporary phenomenon that Muslims began to see in Islam the universalist religion which will unite the unitarian forms of deism under a lay and egalitarian form, making the gestures of prayer uniform, at a fixed time. Universalism, which was prohibited to Israel by the Mosaic law, is not conceivable for a Jew except in the bastardised form of 'Noachism', and it is conceivable in Christianity as an incorporation into the soul of the Church through the baptism of desire;—but it comes through from the beginning of Islam under the form of a conceptual syncretism: the Qur'ān teaches that monotheisms are reducible and should rally to Islam, through a simple transposition and rectification of terms. Disarmed by its simplicity against theosophical gnosis, Islam soon made room to Manichean infiltrations (*zanādiqa, qaramatiyya*) in its guilds, which probably gave birth to Freemasonry through the Templars. In our day and age still, Islam is not capable of defending itself against syncretism, whether it is the case of the Scottish Rite or of the Grand-Orient, of positivists or Bahaïs." *Les trois prières d'Abraham*, p. 104.

[55] On the "Brethren of Purity," see Seyyed Hossein Nasr, *Science and Civilization in Islam*, Cambridge: ITS, 1989, pp. 152-57.

[56] Nasr, p. 153.

of a philosophical character rather than an initiatic school in the proper sense of Sufism. What makes Massignon profoundly ill at ease in such contexts is the idea that Islam and Christianity might be identified purely and simply with a secret doctrine. In point of fact, however, Guénon never affirmed such an identity for Islam, since he emphasised the double—both esoteric and exoteric—character of this spiritual tradition. Yet from another angle, he also affirmed that the essence of Islam, or essential Islam, is to be found in fact in its esoterism,[57] which can give some legitimacy to Massignon's analysis. As for Christianity, it is certain that Guénon—but not Schuon—considered the original, pre-Constantinian Christianity as an esoteric doctrine and an initiatic institution having lost, at a certain moment in history, this initiatic character. Massignon contests this point of view insofar as the conception it entails calls into question the very core of the universal and apostolic vocation of Christianity. To suppose that Christianity constitutes exclusively an initiatic doctrine means basically that one negates the universal message, in principle addressed to all, of the Christic predication. Notwthstanding, Massignon does not deny that Christianity as a spiritual education contains a "part of initiation", as the notion of "*catechumen*" (one instructed in the "catechism" of the Church in view of and in preparation for baptism) strongly indicates. What he fears, however, is that such a vision may give rise, as in some Guénonian circles, to a facile and basically pretentious élitism that overlooks or despises genuine evangelic simplicity. On the other hand, as far as Islam is concerned, Massignon sees in the figure of the Sufi *murshid*, that is, the spiritual master, a potential idol who, under the pretext of "filtering the light" of the Divine for the disciple, may in fact stand as a veil and give rise, from a certain limited or abusive point of view, to a sort of *shirk*. In fact, it seems that there is here a sort of compensatory interplay between the two religions. The emphasis on the person

---

[57] Guénon does not differ in this from Sufi masters such as Shaykh Ahmad al-'Alawī, for whom the "doctrine" (esoterism) lies beyond "religion" (exoterism). Cf. Martin Lings, *A Sufi Saint of the Twentieth Century*, Louisville: Fons Vitae, 1993, p. 25.

of Christ lessens the scope and impact of spiritual mastership to the point of reducing it to the function of a mere "director of conscience", since there is only one Master in Christ; it contrast, the extreme reduction of human mediation in regard to the Divine transcendence and omnipotence gives rise in Islam, as if by compensation, to the possibility of a veneration of the Shaykh as a divine epiphany.[58] It goes without saying that such adulation for the master in the climate of Sufism sounds as problematic to the Christian ear as does the worship of the *avatāra* in Hinduism.

\*

\*  \*

As indicated earlier, Massignon's universalism is centred upon spiritual figures and events that resemble exceptional points of convergence of various "tendencies" of God's will. In this context of "competing" Divine possibilities, and as far as religious universalism is concerned, it is appropriate first of all to comment on the cardinal role played by Salmān Pak[59] in the "universalist" vision of Massignon. In his introduction to *Parole donnée*, Vincent Monteil confirms that, starting from 1927, Salmān began to play the hermeneutical role of "substitute" that was initially—since 1908—that of al-Hallāj in the spiritual econ-

---

[58] "Herein lies the great danger in the Islam of congregations, where you are simply told that it is better to see one's *murshid* than to see God. It is rather abominable that one's spiritual director be superior to God. Because, say they, God could but blind us, whereas the *murshid* can filter the light of the teaching for the soul that listens." Toumlinine lecture, 1957.

[59] "Born in Persia, where as a young man he is led to Christianity through a pronounced ascetic vocation, he goes from master to master, and from town to town, exposing himself to exile and slavery; not just for finding a stricter rule of life and the rigorous monotheism sought by the other *hānif*, but to join a Messenger of God, who had been described to him, and whom he found in Muhammad. Admitted into his close circle, Salmān advises him at the battle of the Trench, and after his death remains the faithful friend of his family, that is, of the 'Alids, and the defender of their legitimate and unrecognised rights; until his death, in Madain, Mesopotamia." "Salman Pak et les prémisses spirituelles de l'islam iranien," (1934), *OM I*, p. 446.

omy of Massignon's thought.[60] While being one of the first four non-Arab converts, Salmān was both a "director of conscience" for the Prophet's descendants—that is, his nephews—as well as a representative and a protector of non-Arab converts. Hailing from a Zoroastrian background, Salmān had been in quest of the pure Abrahamic monotheism of the hunafā', and he joined at first the Christian communities of Syria before being "oriented" towards the Prophet by a Christian hermit. The plurality of his religious experience and his search for an underlying primordiality "opens" his Islam both in width and depth; the latter leanings making him clearly a spiritual figure akin to Fātima. This "opening" is therefore not a sort of extrinsic addition that would only include non-native elements in the *Ummah* by virtue of a kind of imperialist "assimilation". Quite the opposite, it is from the very heart of the "flesh" of the Prophet, if one may say so, that is, from his very family, that the inner principle of welcoming non-Arab clients and ultimately fostering the religious and cultural universality of Islam radiated. This universalising aspect of Salmān's function appeared symbolically in an episode of the Battle of the Trench (*al-Khandaq*). Having convinced the Prophet to dig a defensive trench around Medina and working himself on this task, Salmān tries to excavate a rock which he could not break. The Prophet seizes an axe and makes a spark spring forth from the stone three times. He then explains that each of the sparks has given him a vision of the area of expansion that would be opened to Islam: the South towards Yemen, the Maghreb and the West. Salmān thus became the symbolic initiator of the universalisation of Islam.

We wish to make an important digression in order to distinguish the role of Bedouin Arab culture from that of Arabic as a spiritual vector for Islam. Indeed, if the universalisation of Islam can *a priori* appear hindered by the tribalism of the Bedouins and what can be very approximately referred to as a

---

[60] "Louis Massignon m'a expliqué dernièrement comment Salmân lui est devenu, aussi, un intercesseur. Non pas en 1908, mais à partir de 1927. [Louis Massignon explained to me recently how Salmân became, also, an intercessor for him. Not so in 1908, but from 1927 on.]" *Parole donnée*, p. 31.

sort of Arab "protectionism", this universalisation seems however already present, at least in its seed, in the Arabic language as a vehicle of Revelation. Although the Arab tribes constituted in a certain sense an obstacle to the universalisation of Islam, due to what may appear at times as an excessive intensity and inordinate passion in the defence and affirmation of the prerogatives of their identity, the Arabic language appears on the contrary as a factor of spiritual opening. Massignon dedicated himself passionately to the defence and illustration of this thesis, and it is in fact on it that he based his vision of Arabic as the language of a civilisation with a universal vocation, reaching even beyond the limits of the Muslim world. Comparing the role of Arabic to that of Latin in the Western, European world, Massignon emphasises its civilising value, a value that is all the more powerful and influential in that it embraces both the spiritual and temporal realms.[61] Such a conviction is not only based on the historical evidence of the crucial role of Arabic in the propagation of philosophical and scientific learning in the Middle Ages. It is also founded upon a spiritual interpretation of the fundamental characteristics of Semitic languages, characteristics which—according to Massignon—Arabic has been able to preserve and illustrate in an eminent fashion. Two aspects of the Arabic language must be particularly emphasised in this regard: on the one hand, the three consonant root, and on the other, the tri-vocalic "animation". Massignon compares the tri-literation of Arabic roots to the fixed stars of a grand linguistic constellation. The comparison is not merely poetic: it emphasises the archetypal permanence of roots on the background of the divine infinity of the Night of the Essence (*dhāt*). This is how the "role of condensation and of hardening into abstraction[62] which befell

---

[61] "Indeed, for the converted Muslims, Arabic plays a civilising role comparable to that of Latin for the Christians of the West and that of Greek for the Christians of the East; even more so since it is their instructor not just in spiritual but also in temporal [matters]." "Comment ramener à une base commune l'étude de deux cultures: l'arabe et la gréco-latine," *Parole donnée*, p. 311.

[62] *Ibid.*, p. 303.

Arabic" was crystallised. Such a "hardening" is that of granite, which endures and bears witness in spite of, and against, time. It is in this linguistic trait that we must look for the secret of Arabic as a "language of analytical and atomistic, scientific, nominalist and detribalising culture".[63] The "analytical" independence and the almost hierarchic fixity of the roots evoke an abstraction and a transcendence that orients intellectuality to the universal and protects the language from any local monopolising through dialectical hybridisation. As for the second characteristic, namely the triple vocalic "animation" of consonants, it no longer relates to a reliance upon archetypes but to their "existentiation" by means of the voice and blood. The vowel is nothing but the vocalisation: it animates the fixed consonant through a sort of *kun*, or an individual projection into existence. Massignon also shows how the inscription of the three vowels in red ink on the silent "score" of the fixed consonants symbolically evokes blood, the bodily vehicle of the soul that can seal a brotherly alliance into an indelible union. In a certain manner, vocalisation can appear on a first level as an "individuation", since it is as if "suspended" on the breath of the individual; but in reality, it signifies above all, for Massignon, a witnessing by and through the voice, thereby sharing in the essence of the Semitic soul, the oral witnessing of God and to God, the *shahādah*. In this sense, Arabic appears like the universal language of the Divine promise; being primordial it is also charged with an eschatological mission. To these two characteristics a third can be added, which Massignon only mentions without pausing much on it, namely the "absolute" value of grammatical tenses in Arabic.[64] Arabic "absolutises" the action of the verb without subjecting it to a given subjective or circumstantial context. Thus, it situates the action "from the point of view of God" in the eternal present that is also its "principle". It therefore universalises verbal occurrences. The Qur'ān

---

[63] *Ibid.*, p. 303.

[64] "Verbal tenses are absolute; they have to do with the pure act; the word order is lyrical, jerked and disruptive." *Ibid.*, p. 312.

is entirely impregnated by this sort of non-temporal instantaneity that saps the idolatry of time as if from within.
The universal function of Arabic is all the more important in Massignon's thought as it partly results from an evolution of his thought, as the latter was initially determined by unenlightened Christian apostolic reflexes. In a letter written in 1951 to Rev. Father Denis, superior of the Toumlinine monastery, Louis Massignon defended the universal vocation of Arabic against any illusory temptation of a Christian apostolate in North Africa that would be based on cultural support of the Berber cause. Massignon could thus write:

> The Berber language is not and never will be a language of civilisation.... It needs the influence, at least indirectly consented to, of a language like Arabic, consubstantial to a revealed Book (the Qur'ān, or an edition of the Bible for the descendants of Ishmael).[65]

In fact, even beyond the question of Islam, Massignon considers that Arabic must be the language of Christian liturgy in the Middle East, precisely because among all the Semitic languages of which one could make use (Hebrew, Aramaic), it is the only one being situated on the "universal horizon".[66]

---

[65] Letter of 9th November, 1951. In this letter, Massignon confides that, for a time, he had been a more enthusiastic than discerning convert to the cause of a Christianisation of Berberism, under the influence of Charles de Foucauld: "Like all conquerors and beginners, I had been very sympathetic to this thesis; I had believed in the French and Christian assimilation of Kabylia by this revolving movement of Berberism (this has remained the plan of some administrators, especially those of the Hoggar), but then I saw that their de-islamisation of the Kabyles would turn into a Masonic laicism (and then into a xenophobic North African nationalism), and that there was no means of aligning the Berber dialects into a standard dialect which would be susceptible of becoming the language of a civilisation, nor to decently codify the Berber customs which, however much P. Letellier dislikes it, are morally a thousand feet below the Qur'anic code (especially for women)."

[66] Aramaic had initially been conceived by Massignon as a tool in view of the "final reconciliation with Israel". But the latter recognises only classical

*

\*    \*

In Louis Massignon's spiritual universe, Salmān may be understood as an interference of the Christian archetype in Islam, in the sense that he universalises Islam from the vantage point of the mystery of inwardness. In his important text dedicated to the *mubāhala* of Medina,[67] the ordeal between Christians and Muslims, the recourse to God in order to decide on the question of the Incarnation, Massignon emphasises—based on Shī'ite sources—the spiritually central and mediating role of Salmān. The Qur'anic reference is Sūrah 3, *Āl-'Imrān* (The Family of 'Imrān), particularly verse 61: *And whoso disputeth with thee concerning him, after the knowledge which hath come unto thee, say (unto him): Come! Let us summon our sons and your sons, and our women and your women, and ourselves and yourselves, then let us pray humbly (to our Lord) and (solemnly) invoke the curse of God upon those who lie.*

This passage appears in the context of the Qur'anic opposition to any form of "association", more particularly illustrated— in the encounter with Christians—by the insistence on the created character of Jesus. Massignon is particularly interested by the fact that, in the Shī'ite liturgy of the *mubāhala*, Salmān appears as a mediatory figure between the Christians and Muslims. He is both a "disciple of Christ", listed with the first three among the *mawālī* (the non-Arab clients converted to Islam), and a stranger adopted by the Prophet into his family, among the *Ahl al-Bayt*. Salmān is situated between the five members of the family of Muhammad and the group of Christians: he explains to the other *mawālī* the meaning of the scene. Massignon describes the hermeneutical and intermediary function of Salmān in the following terms:

---

Hebrew as a sacred language. As for a translation into Hebrew of the Latin liturgy, it was rejected by Rome on several occasions. Cf. the letter cited above.

[67] It regards the proposition of ordeal made by the Prophet Muhammad to the Balhārith Christians of Najran in the year 10/631, in Medina.

Disciple of Christ, Salmān's mission is to recognise in this glorification of Muhammad and his family, in this theophany, a new manifestation of the same Divine Spirit which has anointed the Messiah for the kingdom.[68]

In a certain way, by laying the stress on the identification between Jesus and the Spirit of God in the context of the rejection of the Incarnation, Salmān shows the path of a "double perspective" on Christ, at times envisaged in the perspective of his ontological status as a creature—in the manner of Adam—while at other times considered from the standpoint of his divine eminence (*Rūh Allāh*). *Mutatis mutandis*, the Salmānian function—at least in the way it is understood and presented by Massignon—is not unrelated to the double vocation of Massignon as interpreter of Islam for the sake of Christians and witness of Christianity before Muslims. Salmān "demonstrates" the spiritual validity of Islam from the starting point of a Christian desire for Abrahamic purity shaped by the anagogic asceticism of the Gospels. As for the function of "witness" that befalls Salmān, it is expressed in his "legitimist" faithfulness to the family of the Prophet, in a devotion that is both personal and mystical, and that Massignon tends to read in terms of an eschatological expectation of Justice.[69] Salmān, therefore, remains faithful, in a certain sense, to his original Christianity, by taking the side of those who are marked by the Spirit to the point of being defeated and humiliated in this world.

Massignon's Christian point of view appears precisely in everything that touches upon the vision of a humiliated incarnation of Justice. The world is not the realm in which the victory of the Spirit could prevail; the world is the domain of the Cross. On this point, Massignon virtually emulates the Jansenist position of a Pascal for whom the terrestrial defeat of Christ was the

---

[68] "La Mubâhala de Médine et l'hyperdulie de Fatima," *OM I*, p. 561.

[69] "Let there be, by the energetic faith of Muhammad in his Abrahamic lineage and in his vocation as warner (*nadhīr*), the desire of justice of an ascetic, anxiously awaiting the victory of a Qāyim, a Judge guided by the Spirit, who would finally extirpate simony and penetrate hypocritical hearts."

measure of the truth he incarnated in conformity to the Spirit, and thereby the exact opposite of the "theocratic" and "imperialist" terrestrial victory of Islam. Terrestrial failure "proves" the divine truth of the message, success demonstrates *a contrario* the falseness or the incompleteness of the inspiration. Deep down, the concept of ordeal or *mubāhala* which recurs so often in Massignon has no other meaning. The withdrawal of the group of Christians and the stigmatising of Saint Francis following the ordeal of Damietta,[70] testify indeed to the distance between the flesh and the Spirit, the world and the Kingdom. Here too, the apparent shortcoming is an inner sign of spiritual eminence. This paradoxical mystery is fundamentally that which led Massignon to identify, through his "science of compassion", with all the Muslim currents and sensibilities, like Fatimid Shīʿism, the Nusayrīs or ʿAlawīs and others, in and for whom terrestrial defeat is the very test and spiritual evidence of eschatological and celestial victory. Thus, Massignon likes to refer to the spiritual goals of Khasībī, inspirer of the Nusayrī,[71] for whom the divine cannot appear in this world except in the form of misery, illness and death. In this sense, these persecuted segments of marginal Shīʿism are the suffering and sacrificial avant-garde of the armies of Justice. It is they who, along with Fātima, Salmān and Hallāj, bring Islam to its completion by actualising both its pre-eminence and culmination in Love. Massignon's "Islam" therefore completes and perfects the Islam of the mullas, without abolishing it, reproducing thereby the spiritual mission of the Christic inspiration which has come to perfect, but not to destroy, the Law in and by Love.

---

[70] On this remarkable encounter, see *Crusader Art in the Holy Land, From the Third Crusade to the Fall of Acre,* Jaroslav Folda, University of North Carolina Press, Chapel Hill, 2005, pp. 113-14.

71 The Nusayrī or ʿAlawī are followers of the teachings of Muhammad ibn Nusayr an-Namīrī, a ninth century contemporary of the tenth Shīʿite imam. The Nusayrī community was primarily established by Husayn ibn Hamdān al-Khasībī under the Hamdānid dynasty (905-1004 A.D.). Contemporary ʿAlawī, who still count in the millions, live in Syria, Lebanon and Turkey.

Another important figure of the spiritual universe of Massignon, who was called to play an important role in his meditation on the relations between Islam and Christianity, is that of the Prophet Elias. Through his study of the "trans-historical role" of Elias in the Islamic tradition, Massignon paved the way to what could be deemed to be, on a spiritual plane, the most authentically and fruitfully universalist vein of this thought. It is no exaggeration to say that Massignon discovered in the Eliatic archetype as "configured" in Islam a fundamental dimension of his comprehension of Christianity that no doubt constitutes his most profound "catholicity". We are here introduced to the fact that Elias is identified with the freedom of the Spirit, which transcends the univocality of forms and the conventional intelligibility of events and actions. One particular sentence summarises better than any other this "esoteric", and at the same time fundamentally Christian, dimension of the Massignonian path:

> Above the Law lies the very freedom of God that spiritual affiliation offers to us, with the sense of our predestination to love; His love.[72]

In this regard, the encounter between Elias and Moses on Mount Tabor illustrates in a symbolic way the conjunction of the legalistic domain and the purely inner aspect of religion. Jesus "converses" with both characters, participating in the trans-historical and esoteric reality through Elias and in the historical and exoteric reality represented by Moses. The relationship between these two dimensions is analogous to the Massignonian complementarity between the "vow" and the "oath", or, from a slightly different point of view, the correlation between the spiritual guide and the institutional authority. The latter corresponds to the traditional lineage as a "provisional guarantee", whereas the former has its source in the discontinuous revelation of the Spirit, by virtue of its spiritual ubiquity. It can therefore be said that on Mount Tabor, Jesus is "consecrated" both as the

---

[72] "Elie et son rôle transhistorique, khadiriya, en Islam," (1955), *UM 1*, p. 142.

"Master" of inwardness and as the "founder" of the terrestrial Church. As a complement to what proceedes, a striking remark of Massignon is in order here: the Eliatic archetype is present at two events in the terrestrial "career" of Christ: at the baptism by Saint John and at the Cross. In the first case, the dove of the Holy Spirit appears as a direct consecration by a wandering and "primitive" prophet (*nabi*) identified with the "foolishness" of direct inspiration. As a spiritual ancestor of all the "fools for Christ's sake", Saint John the Baptist introduces a vertical blessing that is, in a certain way, the counterpoint to the "traditional" genealogy of Jesus that follows immediately after him in the Gospel of Luke and links him to David, Abraham and Adam. However, Massignon compares this encounter between the exoteric and esoteric dimensions in the Gospel (Luke, 9:28-36) to the Qur'anic account in the Chapter of the Cave. In Sūrah 18—the "Apocalypse of Islam" according to Massignon[73]—Moses is not on an equal footing with his mysterious interlocutor (Elias is not named, since he is properly speaking "unnamable" insofar as he is identified with the Name of God),[74] who, quite the contrary, assumes the function of spiritual guide with regard to Moses, the Prophet of the Law. In verse 65 of this Sūrah, Elias—who is often identified with the secret initiator *al-Khidr*, the Verdant—is introduced as an anonymous servant (*'abd*) of God having received a science (*'ilm*) from Him. Moses asks to be taught his mysterious companion's ways, which al-Khidr accepts to do reluctantly, provided that Moses offers perfect obedience without protestation. Let us note that Moses is thereby in quest of a "right science" (*'ullimta rushdan*) that might link him "directly" to God. The three episodes that follow each illustrate the staging of apparently unintelligible and reprehensible actions according to ordinary moral logic. In the first case, the Eliatic servant opens a breach in a boat and sinks it. This apparently destructive action may reveal a highly symbolic meaning, since

---

[73] No doubt in the sense that this chapter "uncovers" or exteriorises the most profound spiritual finality of Islam.

[74] "Because Elias is firstly a Name, which is secretly divinising and paternal: 'Yahweh is my God': he who has nothing but his God." "Elie," p. 143.

opening up the hole implies enabling a communication between two orders of reality which were heretofore rigorously separated. The second episode relates the travelers' encounter with a young man whom Moses' mysterious guide does not hesitate to kill without the least explanation. This new transgression is nothing short of an infraction of the Decalogue, and thereby an attack against the Law *par excellence*. The third episode presents us with a counterpoint of the first when, outside a city wherein Moses and his companion have just been refused hospitality, the "servant" repairs a wall just about to fall. Like the "destruction" of the first episode, the "construction" of the third appears all the more incongruous and unintelligible, as it ends positively in a rather "gratuitous" manner. It bears stressing that Moses, identified as he is with the plane of the common religious mentality, is particularly surprised by the fact that the Eliatic character does not ask for any payment for his work. This clearly indicates that the perspective of the mysterious companion is not one of merit and reward, as would befit a moral and legal vantage point, nor one of spiritual "bargaining" or wager, but pertains, on a much more profound level, to a "knowledge" directly received from the "Lord of both worlds". The voluntarist and religious perspective on the one hand, and the esoteric and sapiential point of view on the other, are very clearly illustrated by the two attitudes of Moses and al-Khidr respectively. The essential lesson of this series of episodes is nonetheless revealed to us only at the end of the journey: each and every one of the seemingly scandalous actions of the mysterious companion of Moses arose, in fact, from a capacity to situate the various characters, situations and events within the overall perspective of their providential significance. What is "wrong" on the social and moral planes proves to be "true" in terms of the nature of things and "reality as it is", beyond the concealing veils of *a priori* biases and prejudices. The boat in the first episode would have been confiscated by a king had it not been damaged and sunk; the young man who was killed would have led his believing parents into disbelief; and the repaired wall hid a treasure that was only to be discovered by the orphans, its owners, in their adulthood. In each case, therefore, the immediate evidence hid a secret truth that could only be grasped from a point of view transcending ordinarily conditioned human responses, external religious codification and the accompanying moral absolutisation of "literal" acts. Moreover, al-Khidr's actions were in no way the fruit of an initiative of his own: they arose, rather, from a direct intuition, a kind of divine "magic" that fathoms the intentions and ultimate meanings of the world and life. In such a perspective, wisdom consists in apprehending realities in the context of Reality, thereby "things as they are". This manner of perceiving the world proves to be very often unsettling when considered from the overwhelmingly "normative" standpoint of conventions and social mores lived without metaphysical transparency. The Eliatic "scandal" is but the product of the transcendence of the Spirit "forcing" the soul to "receive" a reality that is foreign to its habits and choices. God "scandalises" man by sending him what he does not expect, or what he has not chosen himself by virtue of his own vision of things, his prejudgments and his conditioned ways of acting. The latter can adjust indeed to a "literal observance" of traditional forms, but grace and its demands transcend the logic of these forms. In a way, grace drags the soul out of its horizontal psychic security and its "contracts" with Heaven in order to restore its primordial integrity, by virtue of an abrupt and violent decentring of the ego, along the vertical axis of direct inspiration:

> Divine friendship is not the fruit of literal observance, but of unconditional hospitality in which the soul receives the passer-by, the stranger, in the name of the invisible God, who sends him to her; often not without scandalising her: like Khadir scandalised Moses, according to Sūrah 18.[75]

This vertical inspiration that constrains and determines the soul by shattering its terrestrial balance in order to establish a new and higher one on the ruins of the former, is akin to gnosis insofar as the latter reveals its independence *vis-à-vis* the forms and attitudes that most often are its conditional and temporary vehicles. The image of the Eliatic "flash", which repeatedly ap-

---

[75] *Ibid.*, p. 159.

pears in Massignon's work, connotes the notion of a sudden and immediate consciousness that evokes the union or identification through heart-knowledge.[76] In *The Passion of al-Hallāj*, Massignon distinguishes carefully three types of religious knowledge that, we believe, form a kind of triangle of knowledge in Islam. At the base, on the left, the "traditionalist" practice of *dhikr* as recollection and a reminder that arises from passive reception and memorising—a symbolically feminine and conservative knowledge; on the right, "rational" learning that actualises the intelligence of consequences, inferences and deductions—a symbolically masculine and creative mode; and finally, at the summit of the triangle, we reach a direct accession to the divine mystery (*al-ghayb*), which is both feminine and masculine (or neither, since it essentially transcends this polarity), or considered as feminine in content (matricial, essential: *umm*) and masculine in its mode (instantaneous, discontinuous: *kun*). We summarise this triad in the following figure:

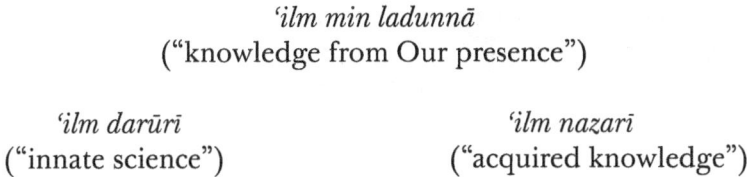

*'ilm min ladunnā*
("knowledge from Our presence")

*'ilm darūrī*           *'ilm nazarī*
("innate science")         ("acquired knowledge")

As Massignon rightly notes, the first two types of learning are of a natural order, whereas the "third path" is strictly supernatural. All three base their legitimacy on the Qur'anic message. The first type of learning is based on the *fitra*, the primordial norm which every child receives "naturally" engraved in him or her, but which is above all confirmed and, as it were, "awakened" by the different prophetic revelations, and in particular by the reading of the Qur'ān. It corresponds, in the scripture, to the divine injunction of "remembering" (*dhākirūn*). This refers to the actualisation or conservation of a synthetic awareness

---

[76] "The prophetic charisma, especially in Elias, is not limited to the serene unveiling of future landscapes, [rather] it explodes the present, axially, in a 'flash'." *Ibid.*, p. 161.

of "that which always is", and is ever available to a "listening" heart. The second type of knowledge, which is more prospective than receptive, is discursive, indirect and argumentative at the same time. It is related to examination and research. In Qur'anic language, it corresponds to the divine injunction of "reflecting" (*nadhirūn*). More analytic than '*ilm darūrī*, it constitutes in a sense a kind of logical and outward de-multiplication of the latter; it is, so to speak, the hammer of the discourse that hits the anvil of prophetic tradition. The third type of knowledge—for which the term *ma'rifah* is sometimes reserved—does not arise from a natural gift, but from a vertical grace. And it is precisely this knowledge that the Qur'ān connects to the *khadiriyyah* inspiration of Elias.[77] The reader has already intimated that the modes of relationship between these three types of knowing and the horizon of universality vary in degrees, even though all three of them are in principle open to the latter. The "natural" character of the first two types of knowledge presupposes indeed a dimension of universality: the *fitra* is universal as much as the rational and discursive capacity is. However, these two modes of knowing are *de facto* dependent upon traditional data that one of them conserves and the other applies. Reason is universal but dependent upon a set of information that necessarily restricts this universality. As for the *fitra*, the restriction of its sphere of universality is not substantial but accidental, in the sense that its "rekindling" is in fact—but not in principle—contingent upon Qur'anic audition. Only the vertical and supernatural science is not limited in any sense in its sphere of universality. It is actually pure grace from God, an inspiration that is independent of the other two paths, while confirming their essential content. This is the "ultimate science" that Hallāj highlights as supreme wisdom:

---

[77] "In brief, the account of the meeting between Moses and an anonymous character (al-Khidr), confident of the most secret intentions of God, implies the existence of a third path, purely and constantly supernatural, giving access to the divine mystery (*ghayb*): 'the knowledge from Our presence', '*ilm min ladunnā*." *La Passion de Hallāj*, p. 64.

This is the ultimate knowledge giving us, at the very instant of their actualisation, the simple understanding of the real relationships between perishable things, their divine Propriety; linking us constantly, through the weft of events, to God's coherent design by participation in His essential life. It is unique, it stems from divine Unity itself, the simple principle of all determinations.[78]

*
*  *

The importance and centrality of this Eliatic "science" must lead us to attempt to ponder Massignon's position in regard to what has often been conveniently, and not unpolemically, called "gnosis". Let us first of all specify that, when using this loaded term, we are referring to the traditional idea of a "spiritual knowledge" that could give access to the "mysteries" of the Kingdom of God, and this quite independent of any allusion to the currents going by the name of Gnosticism in the early Christian era. In this respect, the term gnosis (from the Greek *gnôsis*) should not be a source of excessive wariness for any Christian theologian fully aware of his or her tradition. Saint Paul uses the term in the sense of a "heart knowledge" that is in fact identified with the perfection of faith. This gnosis (*gnôsis tou Theou, scientia Dei*, Romans, 11:33)[79] to which Saint Paul refers consists, as Jean Borella has shown, "not solely in acquiring restricted doctrines....but also (in) comprehending in a new light the unsuspected depth of the faith of the Church".[80] The difficulties and concerns surrounding this term result in particular from the fact that it is readily associated, especially in our age of the questioning of faith, to the often diffuse and almost always polemical notion of an extraordinary knowledge reserved to a small secret

---

[78] *La Passion de Hallāj*, p. 68.

[79] A reference to which one may add *2 Cor.*, 11:6, where Saint Paul contrasts eloquence with "gnosis" (*gnôsis, scientia*).

[80] Jean Borella, *Esotérisme guénonien et mystère chrétien*, Lausanne, 1997, p. 202.

185

élite that is the holder of the "keys" of the Kingdom. Thus, the term almost unavoidably connotes a contempt for "faith", a pretention to rise above all devotion and all moral imperatives, as well as an explicit or implicit recognition of essential differences in nature among the spiritual capacities of men. Massignon rejects this notion rather vehemently, just as he most often rejects, or marks with a pejorative nuance, the term theosophy, which equally connotes some sort of heterodoxy and the pretentions of human intelligence. The ambiguities of this term are therefore at the origin of confusions and a dialogue of the deaf that is sometimes exploited by those who think they have a religious or spiritual interest in doing so.

In a contemporary context, and leaving aside for now the specifically Christian and Pauline references, orthodox gnosis is almost by definition in solidarity with a universalist vision, since supreme spiritual knowledge is in principle accessible starting from any genuine confessional form, of which it is actually and ultimately the transcendent heart. This is the notion of a "transcendent unity of religions", as articulated by Frithjof Schuon in his classic and seminal *De l'unité transcendante des religions*, first published in 1948. It is on this level that gnostic universality meets with some fundamental aspects of comparative mysticism in which Massignon had become interested as a Christian Islamicist. The main texts that Massignon composed to engage in comparative analyses are instructive in this respect. In his essay *Textes musulmans pouvant concerner la nuit de l'esprit* ("Muslim texts that may concern the night of the soul," 1938), Massignon compares a few of the writings of Hallāj, Bastāmī and Qushayrī to the "second mystical night" of Saint John of the Cross, starting from the idea that "it is not forbidden to think that beyond the boundaries of the visible Church, the Holy Spirit can sometimes elevate souls of good will to very high places."[81] It would therefore appear rather clearly on the basis of such premises that what can be called Massignon's universalism is primarily founded upon a distinction between the visible Church and the

---

[81] "Textes musulmans pouvant concerner la nuit de l'esprit," (1938), *OM II*, p. 397.

invisible Church. In other words, the latter brings together souls who do not necessarily participate in the sacramental life of the terrestrial Church and are actually situated outside its sacred precinct. By virtue of their virtuous intent and profound quest for the Spirit, these souls can gain access to genuine grace on a level that indeed transcends the purely natural order. In a certain sense it cannot be otherwise, since in themselves sacraments are but provisional means of access to grace and cannot therefore in any sense limit the latter. As a consequence, it would appear that these souls do not attain a veritable mystical experience except "despite" the limitations of their spiritual tradition. It is also appropriate to add that this experience does not seem to be considered by Massignon as belonging to an order as elevated as that arising from Christian mysticism. An extra-ecclesial, and extra-Christian, mystical life can only attain the supernatural order in the mode of spiritual death; it cannot enter the divine life since the latter requires a participation in the sacraments of the Church:

> Outside the Church, in which the sacraments give access to a life "partly linked" with God here below, the true mystical vocation can only give a response of death to the divine desire that the soul senses, death becoming the triumphant issue of a sort of inner duel between the amorous soul and a hiding God.[82]

As expressed in the preceding paragraph, Massignon's Christian vision paints a picture in which grace can only bestow a desire for God on those who do not belong to the Church while falling short of making them full participants in the divine life, since the latter presupposes the Trinity. Indeed the Trinity *is* the divine life, an understanding that is readily opposed—in a Christian context—to the presumed "abstraction" of Unity. Accordingly, Massignon sees in the ascension of the Prophet stop-

---

[82] *Ibid.*, p. 400.

ping at the threshold of the "precinct of Union"[83] a rather direct illustration of this Christian truth. In a certain manner, the Prophet merely recovers the injunction of transcendence given to the Hebrews, but it is not part of the mystical life of the Unity of the three Persons.[84] Hence, in such a "personalist" and Trinitarian perspective, Islam may be considered to forbid access to the most profound reality of mystical life. By virtue of the spiritual logic of its relation to the Divine, Islam condemns to death every mystic who would overstep the "lotus of the limit". But, at the same time, the paradox of this "limitation" is that it arouses, or can arouse, among Muslims a desire of mystical "transgression". In other terms, the spiritual "reserve" and restrictions of Islam may actually fuel a desire for union which, according to Massignon's analysis, is manifested most powerfully in Sufism.[85] The relative and conditional "exclusion" of Sufis from ordinary Islam is explained by Massignon on account of this mystery of an inner desire fed by the metaphysical and spiritual gap highlighted by the Law. Under the sanction of the Law, such a desire can therefore only be consummated fully in death.

The figure of Hallāj constitutes the touchstone of this mystical and Christian vision of Islam. From 1909, Massignon became passionately interested in the figure of this martyr saint of Baghdad, who seemed to provide the French islamicist with the keys to his own spiritual destiny and the secret personification of his very original understanding of the relationship between Islam and Christianity. The mystical martyr of Islam was condemned to death, "martyred" and put on a cross in Bagdad in 922. His greatest crime was to utter anā'l-Haqq ("I am the Truth," or "I

---

[83] "L'Hégire d'Ismaël," in Les trois prières d'Abraham, Paris, 1997, p. 70.

[84] "If he finds engraved in his memory the tablet of the creative decree enjoining worship to everybody, he [nonetheless] does not give the ultimate meaning of the precept; his will does not dare to adhere to the counsel of perfect life; he declines the mystical betrothal, whose enigma he keeps silent, at the risk of death, to all Muslims of the future." Ibid., p. 71.

[85] "Its exclusion from divine union, like the exclusion of Moses from the promised land, may have prepared an access to it for others by making them desire the supreme hegira." Ibid., p. 70.

the Truth"). In 1912, Massignon devoted an important article to the different interpretations of this "theopathic locution".[86] His analysis of these interpretations enables us to grasp a number of specific and defining traits of his conception of al-Hallāj, although the article in question does not attempt to provide any final answer regarding the case. Looking into the various types of condemnation, absolutisation and suspension of judgement regarding this verbal "jaculation" or *shath*, Massignon tends to reassess and question what he calls the "monist" interpretation of the locution, particularly that of Ibn ʿArabī. This interpretation is based on the central concept of the Unity of Existence, or *wahdāt al-wūjūd*, that asserts a universal unity of essence and thereby ultimately denies the essentiality of "otherness" or *siwa' Llāh*, "other than God". It is clear that, for Massignon, such an understanding of Hallāj, insofar as it "refuses to separate the Absolute from the contingent", cannot basically account for the *Anā* ("I") that it must abolish in a sort of extinction akin to the spiritual climate of non-dualistic Hinduism. Massignon cannot accept this reduction of Hallājian spirituality to a "mere transposition into Arabic of the *Tat tvam asi* of the Gītā, or the *Aham Brahmāsmi* of the Vedantists".[87] Yet nonetheless, this mystical inclination seems to predispose in itself to what Massignon refers to quite pejoratively as a "syncretist universalism". The distinction, inherent to mysticism—at least in Islam—between the outward reality (*sharīʿah*) and the inner truth (*haqīqah*) can in fact lead, as Massignon is obliged to point out, to a sort of antithesis within a religious tradition. This antithesis between the shell and the kernel is only reducible on the basis of a monism—we prefer to call it a non-dualism because of its affinity with an apophatic metaphysics—"asserting the *identity of the opposites*, and leading to the *annihilation* of thought in the impersonality of the pure idea".[88] In other words, according to this vision—also shared by

---

[86] "Ana al-Haqq: etudes historique et critique sur une formule dogmatique de théologie mystique, d'après les sources islamiques," (1912), *OM II*, pp. 31-39.

[87] *Ibid.*, p. 32.

[88] *La Passion de Hallâj III*, Paris, 1975, p. 257.

Ibn 'Arabī—the duality which mysticism introduces at the heart of religious life through its surpassing of common understanding and practice reveals its illusory character from the point of view of the unity that constitutes its end. This is expressed in the most profound and unsettlingly paradoxical manner by Ibn 'Arabī's teaching according to which "the *haqīqah* is the *sharī'ah* and the *sharī'ah* is the *haqīqah*." *A contrario*, Massignon cannot see Hallāj pulled into this non-dualist realm without apprehending that the desire (*'ishq*) that animates his quest be overlooked or by-passed, thereby blurring the distinction between Lord and servant that is its condition *sine qua non*. In contrast, *hulūl*, the "divine informing of the heart of the saint"—hence identification, according to Massignon, with the Perfection of divine immanence which is Christ—is for him a much more appealing and satisfying interpretation of Hallājian mysticism. In this sense, there is little doubt that, for Massignon, the case of al-Hallāj constitutes a vibrant, if indirect, testimony of Islam's shortcoming and Christianity's perfection. In fact, Massignon conceives Hallāj as a "substitute" for the Prophet, sacrificially overstepping the limit marked by the Law to invite Muhammad to mystical union, to the consummation of the "mystical moth" in the divine Fire.[89] Like Fātima, who is like the secret conscience of the early Muslim community, Hallāj shows the path of a fulfilment of Islam through its inner "other": *tasawwuf* or mysticism. The "universalism of Hallāj"—and these words are actually used by Massignon[90]—consists in a penetration of diverse theological and confessional forms that are *a priori* foreign to him, but which he prolongs and surpasses along the way on his own divine ascension. We can measure the extent of Massignon's identification with Hallāj when reading that the inner method of the latter lies

---

[89] "During his nocturnal ascension, *al-mi'rāj*, Muhammad stopped at the divine threshold without daring to 'become' the burning Bush of Moses; al-Hallāj, who was his substitute through love, exhorts him to move forward, to enter into the fire of divine desire until he dies therein, like the mystical moth, and to 'consume himself in his Object'." *Parole donnée*, p. 82.

[90] Massignon defines the inner approach of Hallāj as "a method of universalist mystical introspection," *Parole donnée*, p. 76.

in entering "the confessional necessity of the other".[91] Is it not what Massignon advocates himself when referring to the need for decentring oneself in the other? Massignon revels in quoting Sufyān ibn 'Uyaynah, an early foremost authority in *hadīth* and Qur'anic exegesis, according to whom "those from among our doctors of the law (*'ulamā*) who have gone wrong became like the Jews, and those from among our ascetics (*'ubbād*) who have gone wrong became like the Christians."[92] In this sense the mystic of Baghdad participates in the movement of the completion of the Law of Islam by passing into the Law of Love. In the same vein, Massignon does not hesitate to see in the martyred nephew of the Prophet, Husayn, and Husayn Mansūr al-Hallāj two figures—one an imperfect forerunner, the other a consummate culmination—of this fulfilment. Thus, the martyr of a personalist mysticism that forms one of the fundamental tenets of the Shī'ite inspiration joins the martyr of divine Life. According to this vision, "voluntary death" would appear, in Islam, as a spiritual overcompensation for Islam's incompleteness through a mystical participation in the Christic mystery. Consequently, in the same way as the doctors of the Mosaic Law had to condemn Christ to die on the cross, the *fuqahā'* can only crucify and martyr him who utters the mystery of divine immanence, thus confirming the Law in its simultaneous want and need. Let us take note in this context that Massignon establishes a very suggestive symbolic distinction between "crucifixion", "martyrdom" and "stigmatisation". For him, in spiritual history it is not Judaism, but Islam, that provoked, the appearance of stigmatisation in Christianity. Islam "stigmatises" Christianity in both a literal and a metaphorical sense. In a sense, Muslims stigmatise Christianity by reminding Christians of a shortcoming in faithfulness to the call of divine transcendence. Islam, in its absolute demand of its affirmation of transcendence, points out the resulting shortcomings of a religious "bargaining" with the world that constitutes the deadly flaw and deviation of the Church.

---

[91] *Ibid.*

[92] *Ibid.*, p. 258.

Islam thus "judges" Christianity by the yardstick of its Abra-hamic filiation. This should help us understand why Massignon is so particularly sensitive to the sin against the Spirit that he perceives in simony, the commerce of religious and ecclesiasti-cal offices, a powerful symbol of the betrayal of the religious demand for justice. Contrary to these unworthy "compositions" and compromises with the world, Islam restores the purity of the "patriarchal worship of the earliest times".[93] At the same time, on the historical and geopolitical plane, Islam is "the thrust of the angelic spear that has stigmatised Christianity" by denying it ac-cess to the Holy Land and to the routes of an apostolate to the South and the East. At the same time, Islam is also and above all the catalyst of a mystical stigmatisation that is epitomised by Saint Francis of Assisi's mark of sanctity. The seventh chapter of *Vita Sancti Francisi* by the thirteenth century historian Julian of Speyer relates the episode of the encounter of Saint Francis and the Sultan Malik al-Kamil, and the failure of the Saint to convert the latter, by referring it to the ordeal. The story ends with the following sentence:

> But in all these things the saintly man did not see his desire fulfilled; for the Lord had blessedly reserved to him the privi-lege of a unique grace: carrying the emblem of the wounds of Christ.[94]

The last words refer to the stigmatisation at La Verna, which occurred about five years later and two years before the death of Saint Francis, a miracle that was induced by the vision of a cruci-fied six-winged seraphim.[95] In the context of this sort of confron-

---

[93] *Ibid.*, p. 112.

[94] *Francis of Assisi: Early Documents, Volume I: The Saint*, eds. R.J. Armstrong, J.A.W. Hellman and W.J. Short, Hyde Park, New York: New City Press, 1999, p. 395.

[95] *Ibid.*, p. 410. "The essential of the current version is reduced to the following: on 14th of September, the day of the Exaltation of the Holy Cross, at night, a seraphim with wings of fire—coming straight from Isaiah (6:2)—carrying the image of the crucifix, fell from the sky upon Francis

tation between Christianity and Islam, Massignon deciphers the spiritual meaning of stigmatisation as the concrete mark of a terrestrial incapacity transmuted into celestial grace, it is the "wound" inflicted by a world that remains closed to the Spirit, hence the most profound Christ-like witnessing to the Truth.

\*

\* \*

We now wish to focus, in a more directly critical perspective, on two aforementioned aspects of Hallāj's Sufism as understood by Massignon: firstly, the question of the completion of Islam through the Hallājian path of substitution, and secondly, and in a more general manner, the problem of the reduction of mysticism to a path of "death" in Islam. To begin with, it is important to evaluate the extent to which the Massignonian vision of Hallāj "christianises" in an abusive way the figure of the mystic from Baghdad, particularly by restricting the scope of his universalism. Undeniably, the "logic" of the Hallājian inspiration partakes in a Christic archetype[96] and therefore in an inward emphasis that transcends ordinary Muslim faith and practice, but one may nevertheless wonder whether, in his case, it is more a matter of "returning to a [common] Base"[97] than of fulfilling an incomplete revelation. Indeed, Massignon may appear to make a maximal, and perhaps excessive, hermeneutic use of the Hallājian mystical practice that consists in making use of the

---

who was in contemplation outside of his grotto and imprinted the marks of the torture as well as the ecstasy of the spear on his right side. A fact which seems indubitable is that all the population of the surrounding area saw the summit of La Verna wrapped in light as if the sun had already risen." Julien Green, *Frère François*, p. 293.

[96] "Hallāj represents within Sufism the special grace of Christ as it manifests itself in the Islamic universe. He is a Christic Sufi, if we can use such a term, that is, he manifests *al-barakat al-ʿisawiyyah* as it is said in Arabic, within him." Seyyed Hossein Nasr, "In Commemoration of Louis Massignon: Catholic, Scholar, Islamicist and Mystic," *Présence de Louis Massignon*, Paris, 1987, p. 51.

[97] *Parole donnée*, p. 76.

vocabulary of religious schools that are foreign to him in order to "correct and sublimate it". It would be appropriate first of all to distinguish between the terminology, the concepts and the inner experience, since the relationship between these three elements is necessarily somewhat fluid and diffuse. Terminological "otherness", for example, is of a completely different order than confessional otherness. One should also determine the exact meaning and import of the "correction" and "sublimation" in question. Is it a matter of rectifying a biased perspective, or even a metaphysical error, or is it rather a question of opening the spiritual range of a given point of view by unfolding its latent implications? Correcting and redressing presuppose the pre-existence of a negative "curve"—implying a straightening of what goes askew—or else merely the presence of a limitation, in which case one must unfold the whole "measure"—just like straightening up after having crouched. The hypothesis of a "sublimation" would seem parallel to the second interpretation, unless one understands it as a "passing beyond" that makes the "sublimated" position moot.

If one examines—based on Massignon's studies—the mystical viewpoint of Hallāj, it appears that the essential aspect of the path that stems from it consists in aiming at the consummation of the human subject in the divine Object[98] in a way that unveils the divine Subject who Alone is, and who Alone can testify that Reality is One. This amounts to saying that the individual subject cannot become the universal Subject, but it can pass away into the Object, who being most profoundly the Only Subject and the Only Reality, "objectivises" the human subject. It is this Divine Subject that constitutes the "base" or root of all consciousness and all understanding; it is the universal Substance of all prophecy and all sanctity, as beautifully expressed in Hallāj's verses:

---

[98] Thus, Massignon explains that the "capital fact" of al-Hallāj's "doctrine" is the ecstatic consummation of the subject into the Object, which is accompanied by a "sudden (and amorous) transposition of the roles between the subject and the Object". *La Passion de Hallâj III*, p. 360. This transposition means that the Object is in fact the only Subject there is.

Earnest for truth, I thought on the religions:
They are, I found, one root with many a branch.
Therefore impose on no man a religion,
Lest it would bar him from the firm-set root (asl).
Let the root claim him, a root wherein all heights
And meanings are made clear, for him to grasp.[99]

It flows from these lines that Hallāgian universalism need not be interpreted as a mere horizon of universal hope, a prefiguration of the ultimate fulfilment and sublimation of all truths issuing from "good wills". Exceeding such a confessional reading that falls short of accounting for its full meaning, Hallāj's universal vocation is founded upon a recognition of the ultimate "language of the Self"[100] that is the very root or etymon of all authentic religious languages and dialects.

Some earlier considerations have led us to conclude that Massignon—as it appears particularly from his 1938 essay on "the night of the spirit"—seemed to consider death as the only spiritual outcome of Muslim mysticism, a somewhat surprising conclusion founded on a sense that the Prophet, as the archetype of mystical life in Islam, "did not attempt to enter into the personal life of God".[101] It may very well be that Massignon's scholarly emphasis on early Sufism results from this "life-denying" and "ascetic" vision of Muslim mysticism, while also probably contributing in return to reinforce this view. There is no doubt that Massignon overemphasises the Muslim idea of divine inaccessibility, seeing therein the theological source of a mysticism of "aridity" which can but "consume itself, indiscriminately, before the glory of the inaccessible divine Unity";[102] hence, also, his definite insistence on the rigorous and exclusive virtues of *faqr*

---

[99] *Sufi Poems: A Mediaeval Anthology*, compiled and translated by Martin Lings, Cambridge: Islamic Texts Society, 2004, p. 34.

[100] This is the title of one of Frithjof Schuon's books in English. Cf. *Language of the Self*, Bloomington, 1999.

[101] "Textes musulmans pouvant concerner la nuit de l'esprit," p. 399.

[102] "L'aridité spirituelle selon les auteurs musulmans," (1937), *OM II*, p. 389.

(poverty, *vacare Deo*) and of *sabr* (endurance, patience). However, Massignon's reader can hardly understand what a spiritual "death" could be that is not concomitant with a "life" in God. Did not Hallāj write "My death is in my life, and my life is in my death"? And did not Ibn 'Arabī see this mystical formulation as related to verse 153 of the Sūrah of the Cow, *And call not those who are slain in the way of God "dead". Nay, they are living, only ye perceive not*[103]? Along the same lines, one can call into question the validity of Massignon's interpretation when acknowledging that classical Sufi spirituality is based upon the fundamental distinction between the two complementary realities of *fanā'* and *baqā'*, extinction and subsistence or permanence. The first corresponds to a spiritual death consummated in obedience (*'ubudiyah*) and the annihilation of one's will (in volitive terms) or in the dispelling of the illusion of separative existence (in intellective terms), whereas the second goes back to a realisation of the self, or a "recovering" of one's identity according to the divine intention and the most profound meaning of one's life within the providential design. This amounts to the recognition of two "layers" of subjectivity within mankind, of which one has to die so that the other may live, a distinction analogous to Saint Paul's duality of the "old man" and the "new man". It bears mentioning in this very context that Massignon provides in fact one of the spiritual keys to make sense of this distinction through his enlightening analysis of the idea of the spirit in Islam. The classical distinction between *nafs* and *rūh*—commonly translated as "soul" and "spirit", respectively—corresponds in part to the spiritual duality in question. The term *nafs* refers most often to an instinctive, passionate or tenebrous inner zone that is associated with the breath "coming from the bowels" and linked to digestion.[104]

---

[103] *Traité de l'amour*, p. 222.

[104] "*Nafs*, the soul. In this inner and secret hollow are accumulated—through the digestion which takes place therein—sensations and actions, different residues: an incoherent and obscure mass of floating illusions, thoughts and desires, which have nothing in common except this perpetual fickleness, this particular swinging to and fro which the individual oscillation of the heart, *taqlīb*, precarious life, imprints on them: this is the soul, the 'self'."

The "precarious life" of the self lies precisely on this level, which makes it plain why the main work of the *nafs* is to submit and die in order to clear the ground for the Spirit. In highlighting the fact that the very term *nafs* is associated with the expiration of the breath coming from the belly and the mouth, Massignon invites us to meditate upon its symbolic and operative relationship with death, rejection and annihilation. The *nafs ammarah* (the soul in its aspect of dark concupiscence) must "die" in order for the *rūh*, the spirit, to live and be affirmed. The translation and semantic range of this word is extremely vast since *rūh* may refer to the Holy Spirit, to God Himself or to an angel. In all cases, however, *rūh* is associated with inspiring (as opposed to expiring); in contrast to the "carnal" character of the *nafs*, *rūh* is "spiritual" and proceeds from the forehead and the brain through the nostrils. It is therefore more "subtle" and "fresh" than the breath that is expired; it is thus related to "perfumes", or the spiritual qualities and associations of things that are so important in Islamic spirituality. It "brings to life" and "inspires". The Qur'anic association of the *Rūh* with Jesus indicates a profound connection between Spirit and Life. It is on this point that the Massignonian interpretation of mystical life in Islam as the exclusive abandonment to a death "warning" from God can seem unilateral and marred with confessional partiality. In fact, the *nafs* itself, when regenerated and restored to its normative characteristics that are then transparent to the light of divine intentions, can be transfigured by the Spirit and, once wedded to it, participate in its very life.

Whatever might be the extent to which Massignon tends to "christianise" some areas of Islamic mysticism, he appears to leave the question of the extra-ecclesiastical intervention of the grace of Christ in the framework of Islam somewhat in suspension, perhaps as much due to prudence as to indecision. However, he hints at—and sometimes even affirms—its presence in such "transparent" cases as that of al-Hallāj. It may well be that he also intimates its efficiency when referring to the "theologi-

---

*La Passion de Hallâj*, p. 19.

cal, Abrahamic faith of Hallāj",[105] an expression implying a supernatural inspiration by the grace of the Holy Spirit. In the logic of the questionable distinction, established by Louis Gardet, between "natural mysticism" and "supernatural mysticism", Muslim mysticism partakes undeniably, for Massignon, in the latter, unlike Hindu and Buddhist mysticisms. It may therefore be allowable to think that Massignon's reduction of Islamic mysticism to the status of an experience of spiritual death short of a true fulfilment in the life of Divine Love is but an indication of a definite theological prudence on his part—or perhaps even a pious reticence bound to the imperatives of a confessional context—and not the expression of a conviction deeply anchored in the soul of a faithful son of Abraham who did not hesitate to state:

> I believe in the same God of Abraham as the Muslims and as Maryam in her Magnificat.... I believe in the imminent, personal God of Abraham.[106]

From another point of view, it is difficult to ignore Massignon's seeming attribution of the pre-eminence of Christianity to an affirmation of the Christian privilege of unveiling the full meaning of charity. It is this privilege that confers upon Christianity the gift of perfect realisation of the mystical vocation, since it is through it that the soul of the Christian mystic enters into the intimate life of God. For Massignon, it is clear that if Islam is nonetheless a Reminder (*dhikr*) that brings us back to even before the "special pact of alliance" of Judaism, it neither "establishes a *vital* communication between the Creator and humanity" nor explicitly dispenses the "counsels of perfect life" that culminate in Union.[107]

---

[105] "Let us assess the legacy of my work on the Badaliya: 1. The defence of the acting out of the theological, Abrahamic faith of Hallāj that made me find God." In *L'Hospitalité sacrée*, ed. Jacques Keryell, p. 323.

[106] Quoted by Pierre Rocalve, "Louis Massignon and Abraham," *Luqmân*, XIII, 2, Summer 1997, p. 33.

[107] Cf. *Les trois prières d'Abraham*, p. 92.

\*

\* \*

As we have just suggested with regard to the case of al-Hallāj, if there be a domain wherein the universalist tendencies of Massignon's might come into full light and be brought to complete fruition, it would certainly be that of the study and approach of mystical phenomenon. It is clear that the only desire which burns in every soul that sincerely listens to its divine vocation is for God. However, this would in no way mean that mystical experiences and their modes are univocal and reducible to identity. In fact, Massignon proves to be particularly attentive to the diversity of the points of departure of the human subject with respect to the experience of the Divine. He also engages in comparative studies that aim at a better definition of these models by relating them to cultural categories arising, through formal affinities, from the specificity of different types of "artistic inventions". Massignon thus seems to suppose that these various cultural models are partly akin to the plurality of the modes of mystical experience; in this vein, the modes of the relationship with God might be correlated with a spectrum of modalities of artistic and intellectual expression. This does not mean that Massignon subscribes to a "constructivist" model that would make of the mystical journey a pure relativity or a mere cultural "construction". In fact, the structures he draws out are neither necessarily nor exclusively associated with a particular context; interactions and borrowings can complicate the picture.

The way he has laid it out for us, Massignon's categorisation corresponds essentially to the comparative typology of Semitic, Indo-European and Finnish-Hungarian languages that he develops along broad lines. In the first linguistic group, argumentation proceeds from isolation and separation, abrupt jumps and contrasts; the languages of the second group are presented to us as being logical—syllogistic, analytical and oblique. As for the third category, agglutinative in structure, they are concatenated, synthetic and encompassing at the same time. Massignon compares these systems of linguistic approach to artistic representations such as the art of the garden, cartography and calligraphy, but we will restrict ourselves, in this context, to an examination of these systems in their relation to mystical life. We believe, moreover, that it is fruitful to relate these various "modes of argumentation" sketched by Massignon with the major structures of the *imaginal* that have been characterised and studied by the anthropologist Gilbert Durand, namely the ternary of the schizomorphic-heroic (diurnal) systems, synthetic-dramatic and mystical-ironic (nocturnal) structures.

The first model is introduced as "a linear duel (with the object) through an approach from a bird's eye view". It amounts to an "objectivising" mode of approach that hardens the oppositions through contrasts and segmentations. In the spiritual domain, this objectivising contemplation is expressed by a "full detachment *vis-à-vis* things that are transitory".[108] It is intimated that this model, which is parallel to the mode of argumentation of the Semitic languages, has also an affinity with Muslim transcendentism and the exclusive asceticism of early Sufism. This model is also fundamentally polemical, and as such it appears to correspond quite accurately to the "diurnal" and "diairetic" or separative imagination pointed out by Gilbert Durand.[109] This structure of imagination is actually characterised by a marked distinction between the terms (hence its "diurnal" and differentiating character) as well as by its oppositional, or even polemical and heroic connotations. In mysticism, these are the great hyperbolic alternatives like paradise and hell, the here-below and the hereafter, and so on, that are particularly representative of the Semitic sensibility. In this type of symbolic configuration, the idea emerges from a kind of violent confrontation akin to the sparks gushing forth from the contact of two flints. In this symbolic register the matter is to distinguish and separate in the way the *furqān* does, thus a discriminating mode of apprehension, the spiritual archetype of which is manifested in and by the Qur'ān and the *Shahādah*.

---

[108] *Parole donnée*, p. 315.

[109] Cf. *Les structures anthropologiques de l'imaginaire*, Paris, 1969.

The second model reveals a clear affinity with Graeco-Latin thought, which is based on "the logical breach produced in the object by an invasive discursive reason".[110] The "oblique" character that Massignon attributes to this intellectual *modus operandi* refers to a sort of rational, thinking outwardness that results from the introduction of a third term, the *triton ti* of the Greeks, which places the two terms of a dialectical antagonism in relationship with each other. This approach is therefore based on the number three, just like the first approach is based on the number two under its aspect of oppositional binarity. In the present case, the restoring of unity takes place through a setting in perspective of reality from the vantage point of the rational subject. The "gardens, the water parterres and the pruned thickets (*ars toparia*) extending all the way to the horizon with the Medicis and in Versailles" illustrate this model in the domain of the organisation of space. This process of ordered systematisation starting from a geometrical or logical centre translates, in mysticism, into "the hierarchic, gradually purifying search for the highest perfection".[111] An appropriate, and quasi-archetypical, illustration of this model lies in the type of spiritual and intellectual approach arising from Platonism and its structures of progressive elevation towards the Good, the *Agathon*. This generic approach may be deemed to parallel, to some extent at least, the "synthetic structure" of imagination[112] pointed out by Gilbert Durand. This latter is indeed characterised by an insistence on the reconciliation of opposites by referring to a cause or a goal that orders them in the framework of an historical or logical development of the type of the Great Chain of Being. The mystical quest of

---

[110] *Parole donnée*, p. 315.

[111] *Ibid.*

[112] One could object to this rapprochement that Gilbert Durand envisages more readily this synthetic mode with respect to time than in reference to space or the logos. It seems to us, however, that this point of view is transposable both "logically" and "spatially" insofar as the synthesis may depend on a logical cause or a spatial "end". In all of these cases, the matter is to "recover" and "gather" multiplicity from the vantage point that transcends it *a priori* or *a posteriori*.

the "highest perfection" is nothing but a search enabling one to read the totality of existence starting from the standpoint of a principial cause or a fundamental goal.

The third model of positioning, which arises from an "inner" and no longer "outward" approach of the object, responds to a mode of consciousness in which "we not only want to delimit and know (the object), but (also) to understand it, to savour it within us and to identify ourselves with it, in its very centre, where our thought is collecting it."[113] On the mystical plane, one could refer to this way as to a method proceeding from a sort of "enstasis" that leads multiplicity back to an immanent unity which dissolves the former as if from within:

> Like the transfiguration of colours by golden red backgrounds in byzantine iconography; in mysticism this corresponds to the typical inhibition of reflection in ecstasy: when all discursive meditation is abandoned.[114]

This inward mode corresponds fully, in the imaginary typology traced out by Gilbert Durand, to the mystical and nocturnal register of imagination, which proceeds through inclusion, penetration, descent, assimilation or digestion.[115] Durand moreover reserves the qualifier "mystical" for this type of structure insofar as the accent is placed on the "fusional" nature of the experience.

Despite their differences, which delineate a genuine typology of "strategies of thinking", it is appropriate to emphasise—and this is the point that Massignon wants to highlight—that these three modes can be found within a single language, or even the same cultural or artistic realm. This is especially so when, as is apparent in the domain of Arabic thought and literature, "the

---

[113] *Parole donnée*, p. 316.

[114] *Ibid.*

[115] Very significantly, Gibert Durand places this structure under the feminodule epigraph of Lao-Tse: "The spirit of depths is imperishable; it is called the mysterious Female...." in *Les Structures anthropologiques de l'imaginaire*, 1984, p. 225.

geographical and historical conditions of the expansion" of such cultures "have led them to reflect for us these tendencies and distinctions in images of characteristic contours, whose study is made possible and, in terms of the comparison of cultures, essential."[116] For example, one could have no trouble in finding the three modes of approach to the objective mentioned earlier in different sectors of Islamic mysticism. Let us mention as an example the affinity of the first mode with the abrupt hyperbolism of the manifestations of Sufism in the first centuries of Islam, particularly with figures such as Ja'far al-Sādiq (second/eighth century) or Sari al-Saqati (third/ninth century), such tendencies being illustrated by the following two passages from Farid al-Dīn 'Attār's *Memorial of the Saints*:

> To remember God truly is only possible on condition of forgetting all things beside Him (Ja'far al-Sādiq).[117]

> Whoever wishes his faith to remain intact and aspires to the happiness of the next life must stay away from people (Sari al-Saqati).[118]

The second mode highlighted by Massignon is illustrated, in the mystical theology of Islam, by figures profoundly influenced by Neo-Platonism, such as the great sage of the fifth/eleventh century Ibn Sīnā (Avicenna). In such cases, thought rises from the sensory plane to the angelic and intelligible planes, up to the King who "among them all ... is the most withdrawn into that (His) solitude."[119] As Seyyed Hossein Nasr indicates: "In the *Visionary Narratives*, Avicenna, the natural historian, scientist, and philosopher, becomes a navigator of cosmic oceans, and a way-

---

[116] *Parole donnée*, p. 316.

[117] *Le Mémorial des saints*, tr. A. Pavet de Courteille, Paris, 1976, p. 26.

[118] *Ibid.*, p. 242.

[119] *Science and Civilization in Islam*, second edition, Cambridge: Islamic Texts Society, 2003, p. 303.

farer from the world of gross forms to the Divine Principle."[120] Through a synthetic progression, the mystic-philosopher reaches the supreme plane of the "highest perfection". As for the third mode analysed earlier, it seems to us to be best characterised in and by the "science" of the professed, or confessed, Love within the realm of a mysticism with non-dualistic leanings such as Rūmī's or Ibn ʿArabī's. In this case, the "self" is extinguished in the divine Presence by realising its "non-existence", being thereby absorbed and drowned in the divine Subject.

Thus Massignon envisages universalisable models of approaches to the divine Object, which can be combined in varying degrees in accordance with the interplay of historical and geographical determinations. In this respect, he appears to account for the existence of a plurality of mystical paths somewhat independently from any reference to an exclusive—namely Christian—criterion of the supernatural.

\*

\* \*

Aside from such a science of the structural universality of mystical ways, there also exist comparative approaches based, in various respects, on ideals of universality that are more or less fictitious or partial. The outcome of these types of enquiry is often limited to the aggregation of disparate borrowings whose diversity is combined in a more or less accidental unity that does not result from any central and truly synthetic point of view. Thus critics are not unlikely to express an interest in exchanges and "crossover" texts that would seem to bear witness to a common literary and cultural language. More specifically, the question of imitation turns out to be of a somewhat more than negligible importance in the examination of the relationships between distinct religious universes. Independent of any relationship with a foreign culture, and in a most general sense, it must be acknowledged that imitation is a fundamental recourse in all kinds of literary apprenticeship and religious socialisation.

---

[120] *Ibid.*, p. 299.

There is indeed no religious learning, nor any socialisation, that does not entail imitation. In the case of inter-religious or inter-cultural imitation, the phenomenon of borrowing presents us with a more delicate difficulty inasmuch as it raises the question of its motivations and modalities as well as that of the *rapport de force* between the two terms of the imitation. Literary and religious imitation seems to be comprised of three instances: the first is that of occasional encounter—this is the "chance happening" of destiny that connects the two terms; the second instance—that settles the encounter into duration—consists in the discovery of a *"certain* analogy of *intellectual* method"; and the third—the very condition for the fruitful character of the imitation—lies in a common purpose. Accordingly, one could refer to these three phases as presenting a respective analogy with the material cause, the efficient cause and the final cause. The latter highlights the epitome of imitation insofar as it can only fully unfold and fructify on the basis of a common spiritual desire.[121] In this sense imitation both presupposes and avers a profound spiritual convergence, so that it could in no way be reduced to the status of a more or less circumstantial or gratuitous borrowing.

Notwithstanding this highest manifestation of imitation, the latter is also a key concept in the historicising hermeneutics exclusively engaged in an evaluation of the "commerce" of literary and imaginal forms relating two particular traditions.[122] Against this reductionist and outward concept of imitation, Massignon develops a critical argument that may be deemed to situate him between two poles—though no doubt not at an equidistant location from the two—on the question of the interpretation of the

---

[121] *Parole donnée*, p. 69.

[122] Massignon presents his ideas on the matter in the context of the interpretation of the Divine Comedy proposed by Miguel Asin Palacios in *La escatología musulmana en la Divina Comedia* (Madrid, 1919). In this work, Asin Palacios examines in great detail the material borrowings from Islam which he deems fundamental for the literary formulation of Dante's eschatology. Cf. "Les recherches d'Asin Palacios sur Dante. Le problème des influences musulmanes sur la chretienté médiévale et les lois de l'imitation littéraire," *OM I*, pp. 57-81.

conceptual and symbolic intersections between traditions. As a matter of fact, he engaged primarily, and vigorously, in a critique of the scholarly interpretation of "influences" and borrowings developed by the celebrated Spanish Islamicist Asin Palacios by emphasising his eminent colleague's exclusively quantitative, fragmentary and abstract character. In other words, the matter is not only to identify common elements and speculate on a more or less documented basis on their modes of emergence, one must also, and above all, be able to situate them within a spiritual dynamics of the religious soul and an inner purpose that only bestow real meaning to them.[123] Massignon's methodology, unlike that of most of his contemporaries, presupposes indeed a "sympathetic" penetration of the structures, modes of thinking and mystical experiences that are its objects of study; such an approach prefigures the "phenomenological" method of his student Corbin, for whom the phenomenologist of religion has no legitimate and satisfactory way to proceed than that which consists in letting the object "appear" (appearance = phenomenon) as it appears in the consciousness of the religious subject conceiving or experiencing it. This "phenomenology" is clearly akin to the posture of imitation advocated by Massignon in the approach of the other. The imitation in question is not just an outward and artificial representation, in the manner of the *phantasmata* of Plato's cave, but rather a psychic "entry" into the very movement of the other's life through "sympathy". Thus Massignon reproaches Asin Palacios for having not dared to engage in this "integral imitation of his object that a perfect critic must mimic". There is a sort of hermeneutical "magic" in the capacity to make one's own the motions and finality of the spiritual life of the other. To the objection that such a mimicking method might be in principle contrary to objectivity, Massignon's thought suggests that, quite the contrary, it constitutes objectivity *par excellence* since it is discharged of itself, at least temporarily, in order

---

[123] "Between the eschatological architectony of Dante and that of Saint Hildegard of Bingen, even though they are so parallel, I do not see a line of real borrowing, but the mark of an analogous mental activity, provided with the same materials and directed to a common intent." *Ibid.*, p. 61.

to let itself be "visited" by the foreign meaning. In contrast, the truth is that the much glorified bias of scientific objectivity, by treating the object as a plane surface, makes abstractions of the inner and spiritual configurations without which it is but a dead letter. Such a pretension of objectivity is in reality nothing but a cold subjectivism that gives itself away through the exclusiveness of its formal and quantitative method. Far from this *a priori* rejection of phenomenological meaning lies a spiritual approach that is entirely situated within a mystical "logic" of decentring. It is at this juncture, so we think, that the scientific activity of Louis Massignon reveals itself as totally inseparable from the religious foundations of his vocation. Be that as it may, this decentring presupposes a duality, namely that of myself and the other, hence limiting the horizon of universality to that of a participation, and perhaps even that of a convergence, without reaching the fold of an essential identity in the sense of the non-dualism of the *wahdāt al-wujūd*. Notwithstanding, this "imitation" cannot be merely reduced to the status of a technique primarily intended to secure a deeper access to "exotic" literary texts and documents; beyond such a technical thrust it is first and foremost a way of living one's own existence. On this point, Massignon has been quite unfairly suspected of seeking to "appropriate" and convert the other by mingling with him. A number of Muslim scholars have not eschewed understanding the meaning of his study of, and love for, Islam in such terms. Even if we cannot subscribe to this reductionist vision of Massignon's thought—at least because far from ever "seeking to convert" anybody, he flayed those who wanted to reduce Father de Foucauld's apostolate to an indirect colonialist enterprise of conversion—we must recognise, as demonstrated earlier, that Massignonian imitation may presuppose a sense of incompleteness of the one imitated, whose spiritual motion and destiny must be fulfilled and perfected in and through one's imitation of him. This spiritual model is not without analogy with the Evangelic mission that, while not inviting to the destruction of the Mosaic Law, calls for its "consummation" through the parturition of its ultimate truth. In this respect Massignon jeers at the practice and treatment of conversion as "a transit certificate that we label onto the conscience of others."[124] Contrariwise, the Christian Islamicist conceives of genuine conversion as a deepening of one's own faith through the mediating catalyst of the faith of others. No doubt, there is in every Christian—and probably among most other believers—a kind of "mask" or "dissimulation"—the "being all things to all men" of Saint Paul (*I Cor.*, 9:22)—that enables the apostle not just to speak the language of the other—a commercial strategy without nobility or any spirit of truth—but also to transfer himself to the heart of other believers in order to lead them to the discovery of "that which is best in their present religious loyalty".[125] Massignon uncovers a convincing example of this mode of apostolic presence in the case of Charles de Foucauld:

> There have been apostles who, through a certain superior abnegation of love, became purposeful imitators of the souls they wanted to "save"; and who, by assuming their language, their rhythm, their syntax, and their whole personality, sought to complete until the ultimate conclusions and the total truth, the works they had undertaken, and which death had interrupted.[126]

Certainly the incompleteness of the lives mentioned here pertains to the limitations of human existence as circumscribed by death; however, it is clear that this type of assumption by imitation also applies, *a fortiori*, to the limitations of non-Christian religions insofar as the latter are conceived as mere prefigurations of the total truth of the Gospel. On this point, there is little doubt that the perspective of Massignon implies, albeit discretely so, a superiority of the imitator in relation to the one imitated. When Massignon advocates, in the context of North Africa, a Christian architecture that would "imitate" the forms and the style of Islamic architecture, he shows the way to an "assimila-

---

[124] *Parole donnée*, p. 295.

[125] *Ibid.*

[126] *Ibid.*, p. 78.

tion" and a penetration that are also in their own ways modes of welcoming of the other, with no other purpose than to testify to the integral truth in the language of the other, while aiming to perfect the ultimately incomplete lesson of the latter. On this plane, imitation does not correspond to the model of social communications that sees "the inferior imitate the superior".[127] The borrowing is not so much a "taking" as it is a "giving".

If imitation through sympathy, which constitutes the background to Massignon's substitutive approach, rejects the fictitious presuppositions of a scientific objectivity that unavoidably "constructs" its object of study from the vantage point of a preliminary comprehension of what constitutes literature, culture and religion, it does not mean, as suggested above, that for that matter it joins with the integral universalism of gnosis. However, this universalism appears to be present in the background of Massignon's thought as an intellectual reality that haunts his mental universe without ever convincing wholly of its objective validity. It even happens that he gives voice to this perspective, as when he anticipates the objections of "some Hindu Gnostic" to Asin Palacios' external study of influences and borrowings. From the former point of view, coincidences and similarities do not arise from the plagiaristic techniques of authors; quite the contrary, they indicate that the visions which set them into place apply to the same reality, that everybody "has *seen* the same supernatural world".[128] Massignon does not explicitly reject the

---

[127] This law is part of a series of four rules formulated by Ribera in his *Origenes del justicia de Aragon*, rules that are discussed by Massignon in the already cited essay: "1. Imitation operates in direct proportion to the ease in communication; 2. The desire to imitate grows in direct proportion to the perfection of the model and the appetite of the subject; 3. The perfection and the quantity of the imitations are in direct proportion to the simplicity of the model and the intelligence of the agent; 4. The inferior imitates the superior." *Ibid.*, p. 70.

[128] "Here, some Hindu gnostic could object: why don't you ask Asin, together with us, to admit that if there is an often troubling concordance between many different descriptions of the abodes beyond the grave, this is not because their authors, who were mostly illiterate, met and copied from each other. These were not novels—these base productions of our times—

universalist conclusions of such a gnostic assessment; he simply judges them out of place in the context of a "positive science", which, in other words, is unable to assert or reject the supernatural events that are at the foundation of the analogies and convergences among traditional forms of mysticism. In fact, such a "positive science" cannot even address, properly speaking, the individual experience that founds this analogy, since this experience cannot be the object of a quantitative reading.[129] Massignon's perspective is therefore in full consonance with the gnostic critique of modern quantitative and scientistic ventures into the realm of mystical studies. In spite of this shared outlook, and from another angle, gnosis appears to Massignon in the form of a mere speculative philosophy, that is, an ideal theorisation that does not directly touch upon supernatural experience itself, nor *a fortiori* upon its impact on the will. The supernatural occurrence and the eschatological concordances that it may reveal in relation to such or such a form are observable only for the historian or the sociologist who studies their psychological and social effect on given mentalities. Thus, one notes a very clear tendency in Massignon's work to interpret gnosis as a philosophical outlook which reconstructs *a posteriori* a number of data of the mystical experience. In his view, there is a kind of "irreality" to the idea, be it a gnostic one, an assessment that betrays the fundamentally mystical, and not intellectual, character of his approach. In regard to this point, which we deem very significant, Father Laugier de Beaurecueil reminds us that "Massignon loathed 'philosophical' gnosis, however brilliant it may be, in

---

they made up, these were sincere visions. What the concordance of their visions proves is simply that everybody, Muslim and Christian, has actually seen the same supernatural world, a world that they try to describe to us by stammering; taken away from this sensory world, projected into a serene and glorious transcendence, thanks to a kind of fourth dimension of space that is only accessible in space." *Ibid.*, p. 80.

[129] "Positive science necessarily ignores the supernatural event, which is not even a ninth decimal for it, since, by definition, it could not, if it intervened therein, leave a perceivable trace in any statistics, being an exception." *Ibid.*, p. 80.

which he saw an escape from the human condition."[130] It appears, therefore, quite clearly that the kind of "gnosis" rejected by Massignon has little in common, if anything, with the living mystical path (*tarīqah*) of the Sufis.[131] Whatever the case of this terminological ambiguity with often unfortunate consequences may be, Massignon's comparative approach does not seem to reach a universalist horizon aside from the confrontation and the comparison of the inner experiences "finalised" by the same desire for God. It is at this juncture that we discover the essential concept of "baptism of desire", a truly universalist opening in the economy of Christianity as conceived by Massignon: "universalism ... is conceivable in Christianity as an incorporation into the soul of the Church through the baptism of desire."[132]

This idea of the universal finality of desire is revealed to be all the more significant as it unveils its fullness in the eschatological domain. It is doubtless on this plane, ever present in Massignon, that the accession to universality comes to light most clearly. We have already seen how Massignon's eschatology is primarily determined by a heightened sense of the thirst for Justice that torments a suffering and humiliated mankind. This eschatology with both Christian and Shī'ite undertones reconciles—the last shall be the first, *beati pauperes spiritus*—the various beams of desire forming the different communities of believers into a convergence that uncovers the hidden side of history as a real apocalypse. The impetus of the religious aspirations magnetised by this final end realises a definitive unity of faiths through the sudden eruption of the transcendent. It is the "axial divine apparition" that judges according to the truth, without mediations: this universal axis imposes itself on all, like a great sun of truth and justice, without a shadow being cast, as a "divine radiance"

---

[130] "Louis Massignon et le tawhîd shohûdî," Mémorial, 1963, p. 24.

[131] One will quite clearly grasp the terrible misunderstandings resulting from the polysemy of the term "gnosis" by being reminded that Frithjof Schuon, a gnostic if there ever was one, situates gnosis a thousand leagues away from such artificial "escapes" when repeating throughout his works *"tout ce qui est humain est nôtre"* (all that is human is ours).

[132] *Les trois prières d'Abraham*, p. 104.

which accomplishes every work of justice on earth as in heaven. The key image that accounts for the universality of this Judgement and its at once simple and complex relation with the world of confessional multiplicity is that of cleaving a diamond, as in the beautiful likeness of mankind being "cleaved" like "a crystal along its axes".[133] Thus, this final crystallisation does not really mean the abolition of confessional differences, since by virtue of the double meaning of this "cleaving", there is both separation and union. The central axis of divine fulgurating power cuts the diamond according to the axes of its desire for the truth: Massignon thus seems to introduce therein the idea of different perspectives on the same luminous and final reality. Separation is not an exclusion in the form of a preference but a sudden composition of concurrent possibilities in view of the truth. The permanent diamond thus reveals the meaning of diversity in the spirit of unity.

*

\* \*

If it is true that Massignon's life aims at the universal through the path of engagement and action, this important dimension associates the Islamicist to the figure and activity of Gandhi. The notion of *satyagrāha*, or engagement for the affirmation and defence of the truth, appears in this respect as a fruitful opening that exceeds the boundaries separating religions. Making use of the Hindu categories that define the three fundamental paths offered to the diversity of men in their quest for God, one is led to distinguish a path of knowledge, based on metaphysical discernment (*jñana*), a path of love or devotion towards a given Face of God (*bhakti*), and finally, a path of action which corresponds

---

[133] "There will be an axial divine apparition around which humanity will cleave like a crystal along its axes: that of the Guide of the fighting believers, that of the Judge of the last judgment (in Islamic terms, of the Qā'im, of the *Malik yawm al-dīn*); following the *hadīth* of Basrī and Shāfi'ī ('there is no Mahdi but Jesus'), Hallāj professes that Jesus shall also be the sovereign Judge, he who will dictate the definitive Law in a divine irradiation, with a double enthronement—terrestrial and celestial." *Parole donnée*, p. 96.

especially in Hinduism to the performance of sacrifice and rites in general, but which also extends to any form of engagement or action in view of the Good (*karma-yoga*). Now, it is very clear that what deeply attracts Massignon in the Gandhian experience of non-violent struggle for justice is the concurrence of a path of love with a path of action. For Massignon, Gandhi is *a priori* the great exception in the Hindu world, in the sense that he would have broken—at least in Massignon's eyes—with an all-inclusive metaphysical universalism to become the champion of a *bhaktic*, engaged universalism. Always profoundly reluctant vis-à-vis the synthetic character of Hindu intelligence, Massignon discovers in Gandhi an experience of love that leads to the universal through active devotion.[134] In contrast, the *jñanic* contemplative disciplines of India evoke for Massignon the negative connotations of a "spiritual egoism" on the part of the contemplative self. If he is far from following Claudel—by virtue of his instinctive respect for all forms of the Spirit—in going as far as Claudel in qualifying the soul of the *yogi* or Buddhist meditator as tinted with "Satanism" for enclosing itself in its ontological insularity, the resulting "transformation" of these techniques of meditation is nonetheless conceived by him as a "universal idea which is more virtual than alive".[135] Such positions may be read as implicitly delineating a contrast between the universality of all-encompassing inclusion—an abstract universal that he imputes to Indian metaphysics—and the universality found in the particularity of existence—a concrete universal of compassion—that runs parallel to that which distinguishes the "annihilating" contemplation of the *yogis* from the actions of the adept of *satyagrāha*, this proximate and private focus of truth as lived

---

[134] "Gandhi's singularity consists in the following: instead of explaining this global message of India through an excessive and immense mythology (or metaphysics), like many of his compatriots, he only revealed in his writings existential moral dilemmas, or his own "inconsistencies", as he says; his "regrets" a typographer would say, betray his ingenuous passion for an experimental truth ever more closely approximated." "L'exemplarité singulière de la vie de Gandhi," *Parole donnée*, p. 133.

[135] "La signification spirituelle du dernier pèlerinage de Gandhi," (1956), *OM III*, p. 345.

and witnessed. In this perspective, the illusory "immensity" of the great mythologies and metaphysics of India stands out in sharp contrast with the experimental truth more and more "closely approached".[136] In such an existential context, the universal reveals itself in the vigilant particularity of asceticism as attention to the truth. In this asceticism, grace and action are wedded: grace is manifested as love of the truth that transcends the law, whereas action is the existential evidence and test of this love. Grace "alone can deepen the return to the origin all the way to the One".[137] As for the actions of the "great souls" (*mahātma*) which are truly penetrated by grace, they untie the "psychic solutions" which resolve the crises and miseries of others. Thus, they respond to collective events as a sort of sacrificial reverse. In such a context, the message of Gandhi is universal in that it proposes a concrete response—"a path of salvation for humanity"[138]—to the two globalist temptations that have threatened and still threaten the world, that is to say capitalism in its imperialist and dehumanising excesses and Marxist socialism. But this universalism is also a religious reality: Massignon mentions the Gandhian conviction of the "profound unity of all religions" with a respect that leads one to think that therein lies the avenue through which the Catholic Islamicist could rally, albeit with some theological and existential reservations, to the idea of an intrinsic universalism. We nevertheless do not believe that this possibility can in any way be extended, in Massignon's case, to embrace a spiritual sympathy for the Hindu concept of *Sanātana Dharma*—that is, a universal and primordial tradition, but must once again be understood as an assent to the universal desire of God. This spiritual reality is therefore more subjective and "intentional" than objective and doctrinal. It can and must be accompanied by some specific external engagements, some central existential choices whose vocation is fundamentally uni-

---

[136] *Parole donnée*, p. 133.

[137] *Ibid.*

[138] "La signification spirituelle du dernier pèlerinage de Gandhi," (1956), *OM III*, p. 340.

versal in scope. In its essence, it can be simply defined as the tension of the soul towards a perfect correspondence between the witnessing word and sacrificial presence or action.[139] It is exactly the reality that Massignon suggestively defines as a "declaration of love with proofs".[140] In brotherhood with Gandhi, it is expressed through a single hope in the advent of divine Justice; however, for Massignon, it cannot unfold the fullness of its truth without opening itself to the redeeming grace of the Word made flesh.

---

[139] "Look at Gandhi. He has not been completely impeccable in this attitude of truth. Nevertheless, I believe that ninety per cent of Gandhi's actions were righteous. This has produced an effect of explosion in India, where there is no theology, no philosophy, but a desperate desire for deliverance from the forms and atrocities of this world which is all the same a divine thing. Gandhi has astounded people because he did what he said and he said what he did." Unpublished text of "Le front chrétien" conference.

[140] Unpublished text of "Le front chrétien" conference.

4

# MASSIGNON AND MODERNITY

The title of Jacques Keryell's work, *Massignon au cœur de notre temps*[1] (*Massignon at the heart of our time*) sums up beautifully the paradox of the mode of presence of Louis Massignon in the modern world. There are few French intellectuals who were as intimately engaged in the modern world and the main political and international issues of the second half of the twentieth century as he was, while being at the same time so inwardly distanced from the typically modern problems of the age. Massignon acknowledged this paradox near the end of his life when he referred to his detachment from current world issues.[2] In fact, despite the conspicuous aspect of his engagement—a major episode of which was his action in favour of the Muslim community of Algeria—his relationship with the modern world was above all inwardly driven, in the sense that he first envisaged his age from the point of view of its spiritual "heart", its eschatological significance, and its supernatural destiny. Now, this "heart" is essentially non-temporal, independent from the contingencies that shake the world and define, for most of his contemporaries, "reality". If the apotropean *compatient* witness who functions as the secret "engine" of history is the primary figure of Massignon's sacrificial universe, this is not just, as has

---

[1] Paris, 1999.

[2] Thus, in the course of his dialogue with Berque in 1960, Massignon declares: "I believe that Berque is also more in contact with the real and with the people who make history than myself, who watches from a distance, being somewhat detached...." "Dialogue sur 'les Arabes'," (1960), *OM III*, p. 622.

been rightly asserted, because his love exceeds the local milieu of his existence in order to welcome the stranger and submit to the universal, but also—and this has been less often pointed out—because this same motion of love makes him able to transcend all historical and temporal "chauvinism". If there exists in fact a geographical and ethnic "nationalism" that closes in on its illusion of self-sufficiency, there is also a contemporary "parochial mind"—if one may say—that consigns the times gone by to the outer darkness of ignorance, thus closing itself to the welcome visitation of the Stranger from the ever present past.[3] Evolutionist prejudices have indeed never been in favour with Massignon, as testified by the fact that his inner perspective was utterly founded on the perennial latency of the divine Promise that expects nothing from us, our contemporaries and generations to come, but a plenary assent. Nothing new is to be added or developed in the science of Love, except the perfecting of the lover's love. For the secretly immanent "heart" of history is nothing but an inner opening, often in the form of a wound, that makes of the man heedful of his spiritual vocation the privileged host of transcendence. His "now" is not the *modo hodierno* existence (the circumstantial, more or less arbitrary, way things are today) in its presumptuous and fleeting arrogance of being the "summit of history", but the "now and forever" of the Kingdom of heaven "which is within you".

Open through this perspective to the most profoundly sacred dimension, Massignon's mystical point of view remains essentially foreign to the totalitarian illusions that have disputed over our world, to those "little bits of (deviated) mysticism" that many intellectuals of his time believed they had to adopt as reasons for living, acting and hoping. In fact, the point of view from which Massignon envisages the problems of his time are almost never properly speaking socio-political, unless politics be defined, as it most seldom is, as the emergence in the world

---

[3] "The spiritual guides recommend to (compatient) souls ... to honour a pure spiritual motion, a call to leaving themselves to go toward the other, to love in a brotherly manner outside of their environment and their kinship of time and space in the here-below," *Parole donnée*, Paris, 1962, p. 65.

of men of a desire for truth and justice rooted in God. If there is a political thought in Massignon's opus, it lies wholly, in our opinion, in the two key concepts of justice and fidelity, to such an extent that Massignon might be defined as a legitimist of justice. Massignon does not manifest any interest in facts as mere facts; and actually, from a general point of view, it could be denied that there could ever be "facts" outside a *Weltanschauung* that determines and shapes their significance and meaning. One must also add that if there is one category of "facts" that Massignon rejects vehemently, these are the ones he readily refers to as "*faits accomplis.*" There results from this rejection an all the more rigorous appreciation of the notions of justice and legitimacy. Massignon's "legitimism" is in a certain sense the philosophical antithesis of the contemporary cult of "facts", and particularly the cynical argument of the "*fait accompli.*" Indeed, this argument is based on nothing but ignorance or disregard for the Absolute, a forgetting of the *istithnā* that teaches that "nothing is impossible for God" (Luke, 1:37). The more or less unconscious relativism resulting from this ignorance constitutes, in Massignon's perspective, the most efficacious weapon of the *princeps hujus mundi*. Its arguments neutralise every effort in view of the "incarnation" of principles by bringing the manifold aspects of reality down to the ultimate stuff of the principles of gravity and inertia. On this point, Massignon subscribes without any doubt to the principle enunciated by Simone Weil in *La pesanteur et la grace* ("Gravity and Grace"):

All the natural movements of the soul are commanded by laws that are analogous to that of gravity, the only exception being grace.[4]

Grace is the inner "lever" that Massignon defines as the *point vierge*, the "virgin heart"—virgin because it is supernatural and therefore untainted by natural flaws. Now, it is precisely by establishing and perpetuating a contact with this *point vierge* that the soul is able to "lift her head up towards heaven" and escape

---

[4] *La pesanteur et la grâce*, Paris, 1948, p. 11.

the inert gravity of the "fact".[5] Herein, we believe, is the essence of Massignonian "legitimism".

It is well-known that, historically, the notion of legitimism goes back to the political positions of the partisans of the oldest branch of the Bourbons, positions that were founded both on politico-religious principles and moral loyalty to this dynasty. The "archaism" of this position lay precisely in the principial and uncompromising intransigence to which it testified in an age—the nineteenth century—wherein economic and political upheavals fostered the emergence of a mobile and historicist concept of reality. In any case, it seems that beyond this strictly historical definition of legitimism, Massignon perceived in legitimist principles a perfect illustration of the warnings of Christ against the danger of spiritual tepidness and lukewarmness—as expressed in the ideological rallying to the values of the world—which actually means the incapacity to remain "the salt of the earth." Massignon expresses the tenets of the line of resistance to such failings in the following terms:

> Legitimists are never satisfied with themselves and they often
> end up being alone in their camp, but besides, there is an idea
> of the absolute that transports to a domain that is quasi-reli-
> gious. They do not make plebiscites, the legitimists are on their
> own and this suffices them since they represent justice, divine
> justice itself. And their testimony alone is sufficient. They even
> come to deplore that their candidate sometimes may not be-
> lieve in his own legitimacy, but for them this is essentially a
> religious thought.[6]

---

[5] This is not to say that a raw fact, including an evil fact, has no important role to play, both in Simone Weil's and Massignon's work. However, its only pertinence is its "being", which means that it cannot in any case be "justified" as such (as fact) but only accepted as a "necessity" inasmuch as it "is".

[6] "Réponse à un ami musulman," in *Massignon, mystique en dialogue*, Marc de Smedt, ed., Paris, 1992, pp. 188-89.

The rejection of all "self-satisfaction" strikes one, first of all, inasmuch as it presupposes a permanent evaluation of the subject by the yardstick of the "absolute" norm that constitutes his guiding principle of action. The "legitimist" is always in default with respect to principles, his idea of the absolute "crucifies" him in a certain way due to the imperfection of the "incarnation" of it that he presents to the world. The solitude resulting from his fidelity to the cause is the almost penitential ransom of this absolute demand. On this negative note, it is likely that Massignon refers obliquely to the ostracism and sectarian cliquishness that often characterise the concrete manifestations of legitimism. The "sectarian" phenomena of Shī'ism which held the interest of Massignon refer to the same principle: loyalty is often close to obstinacy. Nevertheless, these negative contingencies cannot devalue the intended principle and nobility of the legitimist position. In keeping with such orientations, Massignon cannot accept the idea of a plebiscitary truth, no more than he can subscribe to values that are but the expression of quantitative averages. His line of existential conduct often leads him to clash with the mainstream opinion of a given place or a given period. The essential lies, for him, in "representing justice", an expression that could sound like an obstinate or fanatical defiance to many contemporary ears, but which suggests in a powerful and distinct way the principle of a sacrificial identification with the witnessing of truth, or *martyrdom* in its most general sense.

*
* *

If Marxism and fascism have never fascinated Massignon, it is just as undeniable that, despite his engagements in favour of justice and against the oppression of colonised and "displaced" people, the author of *Parole donnée* (*The Given Word*) did not express any faith in modern humanitarianism inasmuch as the latter could be conceived as the diffuse ideology of democratic pluralism. For him, as for Simone Weil,[7] who also undertook

---

[7] The raw phenomenon, the distorted fact, is in principle the one that feeds

concrete efforts in favour of justice, the fundamental problem nesting at the heart of this purely pluralist vision of reality is that it tends to confuse fact and right, phenomenon and reality. Deprived of any principial vision and disoriented by what it perceives as the irreducible divergences and arbitrary tyrannies of religions, modern man cannot but withdraw in the reassuring—and, in his view, salutary—"objectivity" of raw sensory facts, appetites, interests and negotiated opinions. For better or worse, he is at liberty to try to set moral limits to an arbitrary entanglement of individual tendencies made legitimate by a purely negative, or empty, concept of freedom. Situated a thousand leagues away from these relativist positions that have no other horizon than that of their own precarious perpetuation, Massignon's inner stand shows him all the more indisposed towards this lowest common denominator of scepticism with humanist justifications which dominates the modern world, in its assuming the form of a global entity claiming a moral and scientific vocation. The first source of his reticence lies in an unshakable distrust of the modern myth of an indefinite and asymptomatic progress as seen in the political and religious ideologies that have gained dominion over the modern world. These visions necessarily underestimate, or ignore, even deny, the "fissure" of sin; their superficial outlook introduces a false plenitude in man's relationship with reality, deflecting and debasing his theomorphic vocation into a "theo-mimetic" intoxication. Thus, Massignon has no intellectual sympathy, to say the least, towards the various attempts at a "Christianisation" of modern paradigms, starting with that of Teilhard de Chardin. In their beautiful biography of Massignon, Jean Moncelon and Christian Destremau quote a letter to Claudel in which Massignon appears quite indignant at the blind faith of many Christians in "these hideous times of planetary suicide, wherein the modernists dance in evolutionist joy to the

---

mere opinion (the Platonic *doxa*). Knowledge is only interested in what is "right" or "conforms to the archetype": "L'âme qui a passé la tête hors du ciel mange l'être. Celle qui est à l'intérieur mange l'opinion. (The soul who has held her head above opinion feeds on being. The soul that remains within its fold feeds on opinion." *La Pesanteur et la grace*, p. 59.

flute of Father Teilhard and Emmanuel Mounier".[8] Inebriated with a desire to participate in the external realisations of modernity and converted to a cosmic and phenomenist Messainism that ignores the most elementary teachings and theological dogma, entire sections of Christianity have pledged themselves to a vision of the world that is totally divorced from the sacramental and symbolic dimension without which religion is but the vain rattle of arbitrary concepts.

There are two noticeably missing elements at the promotional market fair of this hasty progressivism: sin and the symbol. The "Original sin that has been cancelled by evolutionists' decree"[9] can be defined as the ontological gap between divine absoluteness and creaturely relativity: this is the "fissure" and the need introduced by the freedom not to "be". Neglecting or hiding this irreducible "wound" means obliterating the transcendence of God, hence gleefully adhering to a purely immanentist and pantheistic vision of the Divine that enables one to "recover" and enjoy the totality of the human experience in a desultorily optimistic cosmic scheme without any metaphysical discontinuity. In a certain sense, the modern breaking away from the symbolic vision is connected to this forgetting of sin. Indeed, the symbol is a sign of transcendence within immanence, a remembering of God within the world. As indicated by its etymology, the symbol (*symbolon*) has always two faces. The first is "limited" by its formal literality, whereas the second is "open" to the divine limitlessness to which it alludes. The symbol is a coincidence of opposites, a rational "scandal", the *barzakh* of a confluence marked by a reversal of analogy. As such, the symbol directs us beyond itself, it introduces an emptiness at the heart of presence which no evolutionist or pantheistic plenitude can ever fill. As Gilbert Durand has pointed out, in the symbol "the part of invisible and inexpressible reality that makes it a world of never inadequate indirect representations and allegorical signs constitutes

---

[8] Referring to the letter of 14th February, 1949, in Malicet, *Correspondance Claudel-Massignon*, 1973, p. 36.

[9] "L'avenir de la science," (1946), *OM III*, p. 792.

a very special kind of logic."[10] It is precisely this "inadequate adequation" of the symbol that makes it a pointer to transcendence. The same holds true for the rite. The latter is not, as many believers think it is today, a fossilised sign of arbitrariness and obscurity the value of which can only be moral and sentimental; the rite is an "exogamic intussusception",[11] a divine "springing forth" at the heart of the human being who somehow assimilates, in and through it, the alterity presented to him. Far from being a kind of magical fabrication, the rite is rather a convocation of transcendence. The disproportion separating the rite from its ultimate finality forces us to a spiritual vigilance that directs us towards transcendence from the very heart of sacred immanence.[12] In this context, Massignon does not hesitate to evoke "the solemn awkwardness" of the first kiss, precisely because the latter testifies to an, as it were, transcendent "novelty" that prepares us imperfectly for the reception and assimilation of the mystery of love; a virtual initiation into the Presence of God.

For Massignon, therefore, symbolic thinking is at the heart of the religious. There can be neither a sacred tradition nor a liturgy that does not arise essentially from the symbolic. The evolutionist, desacralised and demythologised cosmos does not affect the truth of the "liturgical cosmos"; they are two non-commensurate orders of reality. Inasmuch as progressivism is interdependent with a demythologisation founded on scientific phenomenism, it remains incapable of grasping the spiritual and qualitative reality of the objects offered to it by experience, particularly religious experience. That is why "if we know that the sun is just as ordinary a star as the others, and that it can be compared to the factories of atomic energy, the object remains incommensurable with the *image* of the unique Sun that the Creator has placed

---

[10] Gilbert Durand, *L'imagination symbolique*, Paris, 1964, p. 13.

[11] "Le rite vivant," (1951), *OM II*, p. 585.

[12] "There is not just a distinction, but a disproportion ("potential" difference at the boundaries) between the rite of reconciliation and its transcendent Object, between the witnessed Finality and its human witness who cannot but be unworthy of it, and suffer from it. To exist ritually means to "make one find". *Ibid.*, p. 585.

in the human heart and which enables us to recognise today as in the earliest times of the Church, the axial Sun of Justice that is Jesus Christ."[13] One can therefore consider this phenomenon both as a pure object devoid of all significant qualities or as an integrated element of spiritual imagination—but a completely "real" imagination—resulting from the symbolic unity of Creation.

*<br>*   *

If the modern world is for the most part founded on the negation of sin, this is precisely so because sin determines it. "The greatest of the devil's ruses is to make us think he does not exist," according to the famous expression of Baudelaire. That is why one often finds in Massignon's writings the idea according to which sin is "amalgamated" with the great aspirations and grand ventures of the contemporary world. In this perspective, modern sin is at best conceived as linked to a deviant "need for evasion" and "desire for immortality", but is also associated with technology and the prestige of its realisation.[14] The idea of an amalgam is very suggestive, in the sense that it implies both an actual admixture and the production of a seemingly homogenous substance based on such a blending. The fact is that sin—not merely nor primarily understood in its moral or even moralistic implications, but more essentially as indifference to God, or as negation of the human vocation to transcendence—is inseparably linked to most modern ventures, while being at the same time no longer perceptible in the mixture it forms with them; hence its increased degree of virulence. The dominant orientations of

---

[13] "L'avenir de la science," *OM III*, pp. 793-94.

[14] Massignon refers, as already mentioned in chapter one, to the "the hideous mechanism of our collective incarceration, where our hardened sins are amalgamated to the equipment of scientific progress and the punishment without pardon of the transgressed natural laws: annunciation of the hereafter, a Marian promise for mercy." "Notre-Dame de La Salette," (1948), *OM III*, p. 753.

modernity readily ignore sin, the forgetting of God, because it is definitely the most essential but also the most "invisible" element in the "composition of the modern place" or "non-place", to make use of Marc Augé's critique of "supermodernity" and its cultivation of transient, meaningless, quantitative and sterile places.[15] At any rate, sin is the "well-kept secret" of the closing up of intelligence and the heart to grace, and as such the only indispensable condition for the continuation of the Promethean adventure that ensures our "being fastened onto the links of a hopeless chain, from where we come out dead, ejected and emptied, like heaps of cans at the door of storehouses".[16]

If Massignon remains unswervingly faithful to the traditional Christian vision of original sin, this nevertheless does not mean that his thought can be reduced to a sentimental attachment to the past. Massignon's critique aims both at a fictitious pseudo-traditionalism and a futurist and modernist progressivism deprived of any contact with the spiritual reality of man, and is founded on his constancy to the notion of original sin.[17] It is very clear that the truth of the sacred is valid for all times and for all places; and no age could be, in this sense, privileged:

> The truly sacred makes plain the natural landscapes that are common to all times and all places, the symbolism of which is introduced to all humans by mere common sense. Taking it into account does not demonstrate an "outdated traditionalism", because a symbol is worthwhile only when actualised for oneself.[18]

---

[15] *Non-Places: Introduction to an Anthropology of Supermodernity*, Marc Augé, tr. John Howe, London and New York: Verso, 1995.

[16] *Ibid.*

[17] "Here we are neither traditionalists of the past nor modernists of the future: for men of the absolute there is, and we wish this be called our Christian existentialism, but one present, *nunc aeternitatis adhaerendo Deo*." "Un nouveau sacral," (1948), *OM III*, p. 800.

[18] "Un nouveau sacral," (1948), *OM III*, p. 798.

Therefore, the symbolism which lies at the heart of any profound religious attitude has two aspects: on the one hand it is based on natural realities and sacred institutions inherited from tradition and revelation, but it is also an actualisation—in an immanent sense—of these symbols in the present. An ossified or fossilised "traditionalism" would consist in considering symbols as *de facto* "idols", thus closing the door to any spiritual actualisation of their latent contents. A living "traditionalism", which we believe is Massignon's, consists on the contrary in linking the present to timeless truths that flow from the very elements of the religious vision. Now, in Christianity, original sin and redemption are the invariable principles of a perspective that was no more "ancient" yesterday than it is "new" today or will be either ancient or new tomorrow.

\*

\* \*

One of the fundamental principles of the modern vision that tends to foster the rejection of the traditional Christian perspective as an "outdated" residue is the claim of a specific vocation of mankind that would not be simply "submission" to the divine will, or human "powerlessness" requiring Redemption. That is why the Islamic notion of *khalīfah* and the Kabbalist notion of *tikkun* are sometimes brought in *a contrario* to buttress a humanist and progressivist interpretation of religious history. In Islam, the concept of the *khalīfah* or *khalīfatullāh* describes man as the representative of God on earth. Man is first a servant in regard to God (*'abd*), and second, by virtue of this "servitude", he is also gifted with the theomorphic privilege of assuming God's "vicegerency" in Creation. As for the Judaic *tikkun*, it appears to be a kind of spiritual "progress" incumbent upon man, particularly in Isaac Luria's esoteric thought, by virtue of the human capacity to separate the luminous from the demonic in Creation. In fact, the breaking of the Sephirotic vases of divine perfections (the containers of divine qualities, as it were) has led, according to this symbolic perspective, to a fall from the metaphysical plane which is the origin of earthly evil. The result is that the parcels of divine light are now amalgamated with demonic "shells" of opacity, the *kelippoth*. It is at this juncture that the work of mankind is needed to collect the disseminated gleams of light that have fallen in the wake of this "ontological catastrophe". "Progress" can be viewed in this sense as a human collaboration in the mending of Creation. In the context of Christian thought, one could say that the imitation of Christ, *Redemptor Hominis*, constitutes a similar "progress". Indeed, the progressivist interpretations of this "imitation" tend to see in historical changes true manifestations of this Redemption. According to this scenario, the progress of sciences and technology, parallel to a "softening of manners" in the humanitarian sense of the term, would be positive factors in the integration of mankind into the divine eschatological plan. Far from corresponding to Promethean and idolatrous tendencies, contemporary sciences and technologies would constitute a development of the human being benefitting from the support of the Holy Spirit. In the same way, the egalitarian and inclusive characteristics of modern democratic societies, as well as the march towards a wider recognition of and respect for human rights, would be the symptoms of a kind of immanent *parousia*.

It is quite evident that this type of religious interpretation reveals at the very least a fundamental ambiguity with regard to the meaning and significance that it attributes to the term "progress". To wit, the vicegerency of man in Islam cannot in any way be claimed as a form of independence from God in the affirmation of a "progress" that would lead mankind to substitute itself for the Divine as master of its own destiny. On the other hand, the *tikkun* of the Kabbalists seems to refer to an inner, spiritual *ascesis*, or a sort of progressive reduction of reality to its "essences". Ultimately, *tikkun* is nothing but the human exercise of free will, the "yes" to God and His Law. Gershom Scholem proposes the following definition:

> Every man who acts in accordance with *this law, brings home the fallen sparks* of the Shekhinah, and with it his own soul as well.

He restores the pristine perfection of his own spiritual body.[19]

And this is also, collectively, the deepest meaning of the mission of Israel in exile, for this mission amounts to a mending of the world of Creation through the peregrinating exile of worldly existence. It is therefore clear that this human "progress", and the human responsibility of vicegerency and the demands of inner reformation that it entails, are the expression of a fundamental loyalty to the divine *fiat*, and are primarily defined as spiritual work in conformity to the Law, while presupposing a terrestrial "lack" or "need" which is none other than "sin".

Massignon's thought is in complete accord with this point of view: indeed, for him, it is not a matter of defining progress as a direct and equal "collaboration" with divine work, nor that man be reduced to the status of a slave with no other choice but to obey the divine Order, far from it, but because God's immanence within the heart of the believer forbids him or her to think in separative terms that would imply a metaphysical autonomy:

> God is the root of our actions, and not an external "occupier" requiring "collaboration" from His creature.[20]

To conceive of the relation between God and man in terms of a "collaboration" means ultimately to separate God from man; it amounts to making the former a "tyrant" of the latter, hence offering mankind, now driven by a reactive revolt consciously or unconsciously expressed by his actions, to the temptations of an adventure in "progress" that flatter its ambitions as rebellious slave. In reality, Massignon conceives God as a Presence that is "more present within us than ourselves" without abolishing our liberty and the authenticity of our actions, since it is in a certain sense our own essence, that is, the *'ishq* of which one does not know whether it is God's love for man or man's love for God.

---

[19] *On The Kabbalah and Its Symbolism*, New York, 1996, p. 116.

[20] "Un nouveau sacral," (1948), *OM III*, p. 798.

Freedom is a central component of every spiritual method, since our "yes" to the vocation meant for us depends upon it. It is this same concept of freedom as theomorphic participation in divine liberty that informs what may be called—with all the precautions that this word requires—Massignon's "existentialism". The latter is based on two spiritual principles: the present moment and the choice or the consent it proposes to us. It is not a question of substituting the essence of the soul in God for a Promethean existence that would claim an illusory freedom in order to sever itself from the Principle of its existence. In reality, it is a matter of engaging oneself body and soul in bearing witness to the Truth on the basis of a total abandonment to what is enjoined to us by grace in the present moment, rather than existence "preceding" essence—for according to the stereotyped formula of Sartre's existentialism, one could argue that existence leads the essence—whose reality had been hitherto ignored, and emerging gradually. To speak of "existentialism", therefore, does not amount in any way to referring to the anxiety of a "freedom of doing" (*liberté de faire*), but rather implies an effort of spiritual realisation based on the full use of a "freedom *in order to* do" (*liberté pour faire*). It may also be said that just as the formula often cited by Massignon, *lex orandi lex credenda,* seems to subordinate theology to prayer and mysticism, doctrine to method, so Massignon's "existentialism" may be deemed to subordinate dogmatic truth to the inner engagement resulting from faith. Such is the case inasmuch as Massignon is not a theologian but a mystic, or because his "theology" is but a "theology" of witnessing in action.

This question of Massignonian existentialism leads us to specify that the concept of "anguish" (*angoisse*) of which he sometimes makes use cannot in any way be interpreted in the terms of existentialist philosophy. For Massignon, the moment of anguish is in fact synonymous to *hāl*, an inner commotion or a spiritually informed state of consciousness coloured by an emotion. More particularly, anguish refers to a *hāl* arising from an extreme contraction (*qabd*), by virtue of an instantaneous awareness of the "separation" or the "disproportion" between the servant and the Lord. This state that markedly resembles

the experience of "judgment"[21] experienced by Massignon during the "Visitation of the Stranger," constitutes a secret seed of
spiritual development, just like expansion is "contained" within
contraction:

> Thus, the instant of anguish can somehow survive, but as a seed
> of hidden immortality, buried deep inside the heart (*tadmīn*).[22]

Therefore, this "anguish" can in no way be assimilated to the
"*mal chronique*" (chronic illness) of the absurd that is so representative of the existentialist consciousness; in contrast, it is a
test and an anticipation of the judgment of human finiteness,
its most profound mystical and eschatological meaning as being
the attestation of the Unity of the Absolute.

\*

\*  \*

We have seen that Massignon's Christian witnessing is expressed first of all through the concept of substitution. The fact
is that the "substitutive" approach proposed by Massignon must
be characterised by a decentring even in relation to systems of
ideas that are most foreign. This means that we must even in a
certain way enter into the domain of the other's "error" in order

---

[21] "*Peu après le coup de couteau manqué, j'avais subi un autre: intérieur, inouï;
supplicant, surnaturel, indicible. Comme une brûlure, du cœur, au centre. Comme
un écartèlement de mes idées, l'intelligence se voyant roulée sur la roue de tous ses
propres jugements passés, frappée par chacune des condamnations qu'elle avait
si libéralement portées sur autrui; c'est vrai et juste; et pourtant, je n'avais pas
voulu cela. Non plus seul. Mais jugé. Presque une damnation.* (Following my
failure to kill myself with a knife, I had experienced another blow: inner,
unheard before, supplicant, supernatural, ineffable. As a burning of the
heart, at the centre. As a quartering of my ideas, my intelligence seeing
itself being rolled on the wheel of its own past judgments, struck by each
and every condemnation it had so liberally passed against others; it is true
and just; and still I had not wanted it. Not alone anymore. But judged.
Almost a damnation)." "Notes sur ma conversion," quoted in Destremau
and Moncelon, p. 62.

[22] "Le temps dans la pensée islamique," (1952), *OM II*, p. 611.

to restore therein a sense of integral truth. The scattered parti-
cles of desire and thought are never totally lost. Therefore, even
the "logic of error" must be penetrated, without it subjugating,
however, the truth that animates us. Nonetheless, one must recognise that the demarcation line between substitutive sympathy
and a betrayal of the Holy Spirit can be difficult to perceive all at
once and *a priori*. As Jad Hatem has shown, the substitution for
evil can be tempted, when pushed to its limits, to give the latter
every license, thereby becoming its accomplice. Herein lies the
danger of "contamination" that weighs upon the experiences of
*compatient* substitution in relation to evil, for "one thing is the
Messianic power of Jesus, the Word made flesh powerful over
evil, and another that of men, his fallible imitators in peril."[23] In
other words, only Christic impeccability guarantees the impossibility for substitutive compassion to drift into a betrayal of the
Spirit.

This matter is important with respect to the scientistic ideology of the modern world. More precisely, could we read Massignon, based upon his doctrine of decentring through substitution, as foreshadowing some of the positions of modernist
and progressive Catholics concerning science and technology?
If it is acknowledged that the attitude of the Catholic Church
towards the modern world is based primarily upon the idea
that the latter bears witness to an advance from a "static" to a
"dynamic" concept of reality—not to deplore it but to welcome
it and celebrate it—one wonders whether such an appreciation
of the pertinence of the modern world is akin to Massignon's
thought. Truth be said, it seems difficult not to perceive that
the concept of "dynamism" entails a fundamental ambiguity,
which comes to light in the fundamental difference between
the way in which it is used by Massignon on the one hand and
the upholders of progressivist ideological orientations—whether they be Christian or not—on the other hand. Massignonian
"dynamism" is a vision of reality that is at once mystical and

---

[23] *"Autre la puissance messianique de Jésus, le Verbe fait chair puissant sur le mal,
autre celle des hommes, ses sosies, faillible et risqué."* Jad Hatem, unpublished
text presented at *Colloque Massignon du Caire*, March 1999, p. 15.

eschatological. In such a view, the soul is to be understood as a "dynamic" desire for God, and history as the "dynamic" advent of Justice. But what is this force (in Greek, *dynamis*) that determines these two "tensions"? It is essentially the instinct of the Absolute or the love of God; and this is precisely why such "dynamism" cannot be completed and perfected except through the unveiling of the divine Truth. There is no doubt that, for Massignon, such dynamism, the motion of *'ishq*, has no genuine meaning independently from the End that both magnetises and consumes it. This is a unifying dynamism that integrates the faculties of the soul into an impetus of love, or, on the collective plane, sums up and transmutes mankind's secret or frustrated aspirations toward the truth. This dynamism therefore presupposes a fixing of the gaze of the heart on divine Justice and the Host who is its messenger. The convergence of the *élans* is utterly based upon each individual's inner poverty, contingent upon a posture of abandonment to the divine *fiat*. True "dynamism" presupposes a fixed point that is also the fulcrum of its *élans* and its actions. Deprived of such a backbone, as an "Invariant overhanging the flux of variations", human activity is intoxicated with a mad and directionless fervour that only keeps running on the spot at full speed.[24] Hence there is ultimately only one "dynamism", namely that of the divine Desire that animates the soul and the whole of creation. The soul submits to it in the "static" or "virgin" contemplation of the Word of God. From a certain point of view, the soul is therefore "dynamic" because it strives towards the "static" crest-line of Justice; whereas from another point of view the soul is "static" in its pure consent to the "dynamic" *fiat* of God.

In contrast, progressivist dynamism seems paradoxically connected to a remarkably static understanding of the individual. The movement of progress, a kind of collective march towards a greater exterior, an apparent control over phenomena

---

[24] "For those of us who know that there is a Holy of Holies, who is alive, an Absolute who must be worshipped, an Invariant overhanging the flux of variations, it is in his call that we seek the fulcrum that makes the salvation of mankind possible until the celestial Zion." "Un nouveau sacral," p. 800.

and, as a consequence, a greater well-being, does not presuppose any transcending of oneself, nor any enthusiastic desire for transcendence. In fact, the very notion of transcendence or inner surpassing is, in this context, affected by non-sense. Being virtually no more than bundles of tendencies determined by their interactions with the environment, individuals cannot find in themselves any other "dynamism" than that of the intensity of their reactions to the stimuli that shapes them. The attendant dynamics is often described by Massignon in terms of an agitated, wrecked and impotent agony. The motions and actions of modern man arise, on the one hand, from the mechanical chain of what may be called the manufactures of the indefinite production of the world of consumption, and on the other hand from our magnetisation by industrial and technological centres that confine us in a more or less comfortable prison, unless it reflects the horrible and desperate concentration camps of misery in contemporary slums. This movement then is no longer a movement, since the different techniques of distance communication carry out an alienation that in fact takes place "in place".[25] Thus, technology tends to despatialise human existence by taking it back to a kind of "abstract point", a "non-place". Far from liberating the dynamism of a genuine *élan*, modern movement definitely leads to a collective "incarnation" which Massignon sees as the antithesis of the liberating flux of pilgrimage to sacred places. In Massignon's thought, modern mankind appears like cattle penned into a wild universe of hardening and opacity. Although there is movement in this modern "debacle", it can

---

[25] "'Presse' et 'traite des esclaves' depuis le XVI<sup>e</sup> siècle, empilés méthodiquement dans les mines, plantations et usines, encasernement pénitentiaire des militaires et des écoliers, camps hitlériens du travail force, font entrevoir, avec les progrès de l'action à distance et des robots, radio, télévision, télédirection, notre incarcération intégrale, sur place. (The capture and trade of slaves since the 16th century, methodically crammed in mines, plantations and factories, the penitentiary corralling of soldiers and schoolboys into barracks, hitlerian forced labour camps, all give us an insight into the progress of remote control, robots, radio, television, teledirection, our integral incarceration on site." *Notre-Dame de La Salette*, (1948), *OM III*, p. 753.

be more adequately described as a fragmentation, a decomposition, or even a dissolution, by virtue of the principle of individual separateness and the illusion of "spiritual exterritoriality" to use the expression with which Frithjof Schuon has characterised the induced drowsiness and metaphysical indifference of most contemporaries who picture themselves as having been promoted to the status of lord and master of their destiny. The Massignonian image of humans "ejected and emptied" like "food cans" expresses in a very suggestive manner this mechanical agony that nevertheless continues to be taken for "life".

Faced with this "apocalyptic" situation resulting, to a great extent, from the influence of technology on modern man's modes of being, what should be the function and the modes of substitutive compassion? It seems that Massignon's thought shows us two different paths. Firstly, there is the path of the Church, of the Magisterium as well as the men and women who belong to it; and secondly, there is the path of scientists and, in general, of all those of us, a multitude, who feel more or less constrained by circumstances to "ride the tiger" of modernity. As for the first path, the attitude of Massignon is extremely clear: the Church cannot in any way whatsoever compromise with a science that lies at the foundation of the modern *Weltanschauung* at the expense of the "Good News" of the Gospel. Massignon's positions on this point seem significantly different from those that emerged from the Second Vatican Council:

> The Church, insofar as it is the voice of God and carries out his Promises, cannot compromise. It is said that it is about to lose the world. She has to adapt to it, but the world in question is the industrialised world; now, nothing would be more seriously wrong than a situation in which, under the guise of improving its preaching technique, the Church were to disfigure and even destroy the "Good News". It must, first of all, preserve the affinity of the souls with the Mysteries—for, despite scientism, there are still *souls*—and it does not have to pay lip service to the factors of disintegration. The "Truth" must

not be compromised with a science that, itself, does not create truths that take flesh and blood.[26]

The two keywords of the critique of this may be deemed to be "Mystery" and "Incarnation". The Mysteries refer to the spiritual depths of dogmas that can only be approached from the point of view of the soul, that is to say, from the perspective of a mystical interiorisation which presupposes that human destiny is fulfilled beyond pure materiality, in transcendence. Therefore, it is also a matter of "incarnated" truth, that is, of transformative, life-nourishing truth, and not a simple abstraction or theoretical postulation having no direct grip and spiritual or moral consequences on the immediate experience of consciousness. Modern science is by definition incapable of offering such an "incarnated" truth since it is but a detached, fragmentary knowledge that cannot by itself determine inner orientations, let alone merely moral rules of behaviour.

However, the scientific and technological world exists, and its *de facto* reality raises a circumstantial problem for all those whose inner lives are determined by spiritual principles. First of all, it is appropriate to note that although modern science is incapable of uncovering a positive spirituality and a foundational ethics, this does not mean that it is not capable of corroding or destroying the spiritual and moral economy of religions and the world of faith. On the one hand, it presupposes a point of view that excludes or neutralises any consequent consideration of God, and on the other, its effects and by-products contribute to the formation of a psychological, social and aesthetic ambience in which God can appear only as a comforting myth or a useless luxury. Scientistic science works toward the creation, "on the margin of the 'liturgical cosmos', of a dark underground into which (men) are banished".[27] It is in this underground that Christians, particularly the scientists among them, must work in "a situation of excruciating struggle and experiencing expiat-

---

[26] "L'avenir de la science," (1946), *OM III*, p. 795.

[27] *Ibid.*, p. 796.

ing anguish".[28] They cannot escape the structures that modernity imposes upon them, being just as powerless in this respect as "a Christian worker who would like to escape working at a factory today". Their presence in the world will nevertheless have two spiritual dimensions, one sacrificial and the other sacralising, the first being the reverse of the other. Thus, a man of science must consider his relation with the modern world as a sacrifice that is the "ransom of original sin": "He must be incarcerated in it (science) just like the voluntary slave descends into the dark well to send the water up: this is his way of paying the ransom for original sin."[29] In doing so, he must nonetheless never lose sight of the theophanic character of Creation, and he must always remain aware of the fact that the world is not just a set of quantitative data about which he may advance hypotheses, but beyond and above all, the temple of divine Presence.[30]

*
* *

Considering its main area of development in the West, the cradle of the modern world, Christianity has found itself in a noticeably different situation than Islam and other religions with regard to the questions of modern sciences, scientism and technology. For better or, also sometimes secondarily, for worse, the world of Islam can in fact be envisaged as a religious universe which has not yet been quite "integrated" into the modern enterprise; hence no doubt some of the tensions by which it is shaken, and which often situate it, at least on the surface, in an antagonist relationship regarding the Western world. In order to understand Massignon's view of technology in this context, one can benefit from his conversation

---

[28] *Ibid.*, p. 794.

[29] *Ibid.*

[30] "*Et surtout qu'il tremble d'oublier, dans le dangereux suspens des hypothèses de travail, que le monde créé est une théophanie* (And above all let him tremble from fear of forgetting, in the dangerous suspense of theories of work, that the created world is a theophany)." *Ibid.*

with Jacques Berque entitled *Les Arabes d'hier à demain* (The Arabs of yesterday until tomorrow), while keeping in mind that the positions expressed by Massignon date back to almost fifty years ago and that, consequently, the recent evolution of Arab societies and mentalities would have probably led Massignon to modify, or at least qualify, his views, had he lived till this day. The exchange between the two great Islamicists is most interesting in that it reveals two fundamentally different understandings of Islam in its relationship with the modern world and its main orientations. We will therefore ponder and analyse this exchange in some detail in order to delineate Massgnon's positions in sharp contrast with those of an apologist for the modernisation of Islam. Indeed, Islam has been in many ways the catalyst of a reflection on the overpowering orientations of Western societies inasmuch as it has often remained, at least in the civilisationist imagery of Europe and America, as well as in the eyes of its own Westernised economic and cultural élites, synonymous with a "civilisation of the goat" desperately closed to the prodigies of scientific ventures and modern technology. It is in this context of Islam's relationship with modernity that the dialogue between Berque and Massignon is placed. To the "axial" approach of Massignon, which consists in entering immediately into the "vertical" logic of the Muslim vision of divine transcendence and its moral and social consequences, Berque opposes a dialectical vision of Islam, which is based on a synthetic integration of modernity into Islam. Beyond the imperatives of academic courtesy and the reciprocated sentiments of high personal esteem, this conversation consists essentially in a juxtaposition of ardent monologues from which merely emerge, here and there, points of mostly secondary agreement on contingent aspects of the question. Now, the main catalyst of the divergence between the two discourses lies precisely in the interpretation of technology. In answer to the question of Jean-Marie Domenach, who was then the editor-in-chief of the journal *Esprit*, concerning the possibility of a "reconciliation of Islam with technology", Berque's response is quite revealing as to his understanding of Islam:

238

I hope that they (Muslims) will ... become not just the clients
but also the actors of the industrial civilisation. In the absence
of which, it would be a terrible thing for them and for us: they
would remain eternally opposed to the Other and, by refusing
to accept the Other, they will refuse to accept themselves.[31]

The necessity, as Berque perceives it, of an integration of Islam into the industrial enterprise is defined, in a rather interesting way, in terms of identity and otherness. To refuse this integration amounts to refusing the Other, which, in this case, is the
modern Western world. Berque's position presupposes two elements: the necessity of otherness, and a need to accept the Other. It is to be presumed that this acceptance is not synonymous
with identification or assimilation, without which the very notion of otherness would be invalidated. The fundamental question, therefore, in the last analysis goes back to determining how
Islam can integrate this otherness without denying itself. It has
to be noted in passing that, according to this vision of things,
emphasis is rarely made on the fact that the modern West must
also integrate otherness, and not reject it. Although Berque does
not follow this aspect of the question, and the range of issues
that it raises, in the context of the dialogue at hand, one must
also suppose that another duty vis-à-vis the Other falls on Islam:
that of preserving its own difference in order that the Other may
be enriched thereby.

A central question to be raised by an analyst sharing Berque's point of view is, of course, that of defining this Other that
has to be integrated. If the Other, for Islam, is the West, the
latter is primarily defined by Berque in terms of a pre-eminence
in the nature of a mastery and promotion of technology; a reference that is certainly not without ambiguities. In his question,
Domenach moreover makes use of the term "technique", which
refers directly to the Greek *techne*: nevertheless, it is likely that
what is meant by this term is actually "technology" in the modern sense, otherwise it would be clearly incorrect to declare that

___
[31] "Dialogue sur 'les Arabes'," 1960, *OM III*, p. 610.

239

Islam allowed itself to ignore "technique". As Seyyed Hossein Nasr has richly demonstrated, contrary to those who tend to make of Islam a rationalistic religion for it to be more palatable to the modernist psyche, the majority of Islamic sciences and techniques have been developed in the context of spirituality and gnosis.[32] Be that as it may, it can be considered that, between technique and technology, there lies all the distance that separates a skill from an ideology, or still more that which distinguishes a use of nature based on a kind of crafty ruse with its laws from the *Weltanschauung* of mechanistic materialism.

It is therefore significant that while Massignon more or less identifies technology, mechanisation and technocracy with considerations regarding their common ends and consequences, Berque maintains a firm distinction between "technical civilisation" (*civilisation technique*) and "technocracy" (*technocratie*).[33] For Berque, the crux of the matter lies in the idea that the technological orientation is not situated on the same plane as the content or substance of Islam; hence it cannot be incompatible with Islam: technology is a form, not a content, a means, not an end. Such a presupposition may be due either to the fact that Berque does not conceive of technology as a phenomenon of metaphysical and spiritual proportions, or that there may on his part be a more or less unconscious reduction of Islam to a mode of being and thinking of a strictly social, moral and psychological character. And yet, there is no intellectual "form", method or approach independent of a certain perception of reality: which is to say that there is no intellectual form that is metaphysically neutral. As for the second supposition, it is appropriate to point out that reducing Islam to a purely moral, psychological, or even sociological phenomenon, empties it of its very *raison d'être* as a "warning" of transcendence.

---

[32] Seyyed Hossein Nasr, *Science and Civilization in Islam*, Cambridge 2003, 2nd edition.

[33] "*Mais, Monsieur, il ne s'agit pas de technocratie, il s'agit de civilization technique et c'est fort différent* (But, sir, the matter is not one of technocracy, the matter is one of technical civilisation, and that is quite different)." "Dialogue sur 'les Arabes'," *OM III*, p. 618.

It is remarkable to note that, in his response to Berque concerning the evaluation of the situation of Islam with regard to technology, Massignon seems vigorously determined to circumvent the question. Asked about the future of Islam in relation to technology, Massignon responds by referring to the Semitic spiritual roots of the Arabs: "*Je pense que, pour le problème de l'avenir des Arabes, il faut le situer dans le sémitisme* (I think that the problem of the future of the Arabs needs to be situated in Semitism)."[34] In other words, Massignon refuses to envisage the question in the perspective which has been imposed upon him as a normative point of view, namely that of technological ideology as a directing principle. His perspective does not arise from the categorical imperative of developing a dialectic of Islam and modernity, but opens from an axial definition of "Semitism" as determined by divine transcendence and expressed in the relationship of mankind with the language of revelation, election and justice. In this respect, Israel constitutes for Massignon the symbol of two diverging definitions of reality and history— *L'Israël veritable est fils du sacrifice d'Isaac* (The true Israel is the son of the sacrifice of Isaac):[35] on the one hand the power of technology as finalised by production and consumption, and on the other, the "inner witnessing" as rooted in the Semitic spiritual etymon that is subservient to divine Justice, that is, to the discernment between absolute Reality and relative realities. The ambivalence of Israel lies in its freedom to choose one way or the other, so that, according to Massignon, the role of Islam— through its exclusive affirmation of transcendence—may be that

---

[34] *Ibid.*, p. 610.

[35] "Isaac was given back to his father forever only because his father had offered him, and Isaac had a posterity only because he had silently accepted to be sacrificed. In the same way, his descendants were slowly trained to return to the Holy Land in the spirit of penitence and tears of their liturgy, in the spirit of Abraham ... but during the nineteenth century, European influence made its appearance among the Jews returning to Palestine, in order to "de-messianise" their hope, to secularise it, and to base it on 'economical means'." "La Palestine et la paix dans la justice," (1948), *OM III*, pp. 464-65.

of a catalyst in view of a renewed manifestation of the genuine Israel.

For Berque, in contrast, Massignon's way of understanding history is flawed with serious limitations insofar as it ignores the universality of that which Berque calls the modern "anthropological variation". In such a view, Massignon's spiritual archaeology amounts to a negation of modernity and a refusal to surpass Biblical anthropology. For his part, Massignon does not conceive the latter as a kind of provincial specialisation, as shown by the fact that this anthropology opens out on two universal principles: hospitality and justice. These notions are neither simply social nor strictly moral; for Massignon, they arise essentially from the mystical domain and from the eschatological dimension. As we have seen earlier in this book, hospitality is a kind of retreat of the ego thanks to which the Other, or the transcendent, is welcome within oneself. Its essence is prayer, worship, invocation, and for Massignon and the whole Abrahamic lineage in which he situates himself, is the only unconditional imperative of human destiny, as it lets itself be defined as a witnessing to transcendence from within immanence. It is in the wake of this spiritual hospitality that all the other modes and attitudes of receptivity become fully real and fruitful. This explains why Massignon sometimes defines hospitality—quite surprisingly, knowing his scarce affinity with any emphasis on formal spiritual methods—as a "spiritual technique",[36] which could sound ill-sounding, or perhaps even shocking, if one were to think of religion simply in terms of "doing good", in whichever way this "doing" and this "good" might be understood.

Berque does not reject this notion of hospitality, but he understands it in purely social and psychological terms, in the perspective of a representative French intellectual whom several centuries of secularisation have contributed to alienate from the vertical dimension. More interestingly perhaps, he perceives Muslim hospitality as the consequence of a greater proximity

---

[36] "But we will be saved only through this, through a certain spiritual technique of the right of sanctuary, *Salam Allāh*, the hospitality that is given." "Dialogue sur 'les Arabes'," p. 614.

of Islam to the cosmic order. On some level, the paradox of this position lies in the fact that theological Islam tends to emphasise the *tanzīh*—abstraction or discontinuity—that is, the transcendence of God with respect to His Creation. Despite this Islamic concern with keeping God's pure Being "removed from" terrestrial analogies, Islam as a lived faith seems, in Berque's eyes, to have been on average more familiar with the cosmic order than Christianity.[37] Although Berque does not pursue this paradox in its theological or mystical implications, it is permitted to think that the situation it plausibly describes results from the fact that Muslim "transcendentism" has been harmoniously conjoined to a traditional cosmology based on the Qur'anic notion of *āyāt*, in the sense of divine "signs" on the macrocosmic and microcosmic horizons that are the natural and cosmic theophanies through which Muslims have traditionally gained intimation of divine Intelligence and the omnipotence of *Allāh*. In contrast, Christianity absorbs, so to speak, the cosmos into Christ who constitutes its divine Prototype, but it also tends by so doing to lose interest in, or even distrust, the natural order that it perceives as bearing the mark of the Fall. Be that as it may, the understanding of this paradox is without any doubt linked, in Berque's thought, to his highly problematic argument according to which Islam could not be legitimately considered as a religion of the sacred. This surprising, quasi-provocative assertion can only begin to sound meaningful if one situates it within the non-incarnationist and non-sacramental context of Islam. In this sense, to say that Islam ignores the sacred ultimately amounts to affirming that it considers the totality of creatures and beings as sacred. If Christianity distinguishes so clearly the sacred from the profane, and tends to include nature in the domain of the latter, Islam smooths the distinction between these domains. Paradoxically, it is the Islamic insistence on transcendence which is at the heart of this

---

[37] "In reality, what you and I here sense the most among Arabs is this participation in great values, their participating humanity, full of transcendence and 'adherence' to the divine. This attitude differs from that of Christians because it is much more distant from the cosmic order and much more familiar with it at the same time." *Ibid.*, p. 614.

indistinction, since it contributes, unlike the doctrine of Incarnation, to not drawing a demarcation line, within the terrestrial experience, between that which comes from the flesh and that which comes from the Spirit. From this closeness to the cosmic and the natural, which Berque defines as "participating humanity", there follows a "warmth" of behaviour that epitomises Arab hospitality. It is very significant that Berque understands this aspect of Islamic identity, on the importance of which Massignon is in perfect agreement with him, in terms of social psychology. In other words, hospitality is, for him, a mode of participation in the cosmic and natural richness of an environment, whereas for Massignon it amounts to a state of spiritual poverty *vis-à-vis* the divine *kun*.

Berque's one-sided insistence on psycho-social immanence is one of the keys enabling us to understand his vision of Islam, a vision that may be deemed to underestimate, unlike Massignon's, the dimension of transcendence that is foremost in Islamic *tawhīd*. This is not to say that Berque denies the transcendent dimension; in fact, his concept of Islam is neither capable of reaching a spiritual archetype nor reducible to a mere set of sociological data; it is rather a dialectical interplay between the two:

> The ideal does not consist in breaking away from the real, which would tend to destroy the organic fullness of life and disperse it in painful oppositions, but in a perpetual effort to seize the real so as to absorb it if possible. Behind any religion, and Islam in particular, there is not just metaphysics, there is not just sociology. There is a relation between one and the other.[38]

This passage is of capital importance for grasping the contrast between the positions of Berque and Massignon concerning the relation between Islam—and religions in general—and the modern world. Therein are proposed two visions of the religious ideal, one presented in terms that denote a striving and suffering affirmation, the other involving by contrast a sort of

---

[38] *L'islam au temps du monde*, Paris, 1984, p. 240.

pleasure in and through the process of social and historical integration. There is no doubt that Berque's point of view can capitalise on Islam's ability to function as a religion of integration and even, in certain respects, "easiness". Berque sets out to highlight this dimension of equilibrium that Massignon's Christian and mystical sensibility would be prone, not without justification in some contexts, to interpret as mediocrity. There nonetheless remains the question of defining the status of this "real" that Berque welcomes as having to be "seized" —as one "seizes" a moment—by Islam. Is he referring thereby to the "human reality" in its physical, psychological and social concomitances, or in other terms, the very wide range of possibilities, vocations, and even weaknesses which, aside from any historical or ideological specificity, characterise—without defining them—human beings as human? Or is Berque alluding to a *de facto* ideological and social posture resulting from specific metaphysical choices that have determined a historical and ideological evolution in the very definition and perception of reality? In other words, the expression "the real" can refer to a more or less permanent share of human and natural possibilities—which can moreover be "integrated", or at least accounted for, historically and circumstantially in a variety of religious institutions and practices—just as it can also refer to the reality of the historical *fact* of the modern world as a specific model of development based on a radical ideological and moral rupture away from metaphysics as the chief principle of affirmation of divine transcendence. Depending on whether "reality" is understood in the one sense or in the other, one will be led to formulate a different diagnosis concerning the perceived need of Islam to "seize the real". As for Massignon, it is clear that his understanding of the "real" is primarily akin to the first sense of the term: man's poverty before God constitutes the *alpha* and *omega* of all spiritual anthropology, and this spiritual poverty conditions in return the vocation and the finality of the religious domain. Religion, therefore, can only integrate this "reality", all the rest must in a certain way be burnt in the fire of divine Justice. And it follows that all that is not "real" cannot therefore be "seized" in any way. It is also clear that

Berque understands as "reality" a certain moment in the evolution of Western mankind, a moment primarily characterised by the acquisition of an unmatched quantity of observations and deductions concerning phenomena by way of modern scientific investigation, and by an unimaginable proliferation of technological applications that modify not only our everyday environment, but above all our inner "reflexes" and the style of our psychic, not to say physical, life. It is with this state of affairs that religions—and Islam in particular—are confronted. Now, inasmuch as this "reality" constitutes a set of more or less unavoidable facts, religion cannot, according to Berque, but integrate it at the risk of seeing itself excluded from the real, or giving rise to the irreconcilable "painful oppositions" mentioned above.

If one returns, on this basis, to the central question of the dialectics proposed by Berque, the fundamental question to be raised is that of the essence of the "metaphysics" and "sociology" that are to be reconciled amidst a complex blend of harmonies and tensions. Now, the metaphysics of transcendence, which cannot be dispensed with in Islam, is akin to a mystical theology and its cosmological and psychological prolongations that do not coincide with the modern definitions of cosmology and psychology. In other words, Islam, in this sense, is inherently wedded to a hierarchic and qualitative cosmology and a spirituality based on self-transcendence. It is certainly in this way that Massignon wishes Islam to be understood, even if the cosmological dimensions of traditional Islam may have betrayed at times, in his view, some Hellenic "interferences". But the notion of a "metaphysical foundation" could also be associated, as is the case in most sectors of contemporary Islam, to a kind of transcendentalist rationalism impervious to the supernatural, and fully capable of accommodating itself—most often with a hasty enthusiasm that betrays its lack of spiritual grounding—with many questionable options of modernity, especially in the scientific and technological realms.

As for the "sociology" that constitutes the other pole of the dialectic proposed by Berque, it too can give rise to very diverse definitions. In the case of Berque, it appears to consist essentially in the pressure of the *"fait accompli"*, especially in all that touches upon the psychological and social mutations that have issued from Western influences and postulates. It presupposes, in particular, the all-embracing dynamics of modern economy, the technological forces of which are endowed with an unquestioned and quasi-totalitarian ineluctability. In sharp contrast to these modern axioms, Massignon's "sociology" amounts to a set of psychological, cultural and social data informed by religious reflexes that are determined by a collective "instinct" of the Divine. In this sense, sociology is already, inherently, engaged in a "dialectical" relationship with metaphysics; and there is indeed no sociological fact, in Islam as in other religions, that is not metaphysically informed in its very "texture". It goes without saying, therefore, that these two types of understanding of the sociological pole cannot but lead to diverging conclusions concerning the problem of Islam's relationship with modernity.

Berque proposes to discover the key of a harmonious relationship between the metaphysical "ideal" and the sociological "reality" in Islam in the concept of "authenticity", a concept that he derives from the Arabic notion of *asl*, that denotes root and "originality". Although authenticity implies a mode of faithfulness to the origin, Berque insists that it is also diverse and mobile by definition, allowing the integration of intellectual and cultural elements that are not directly articulated with the divine Mystery (*ghayb*) or with the Qur'ān. In fact, Berque's *asl* "authenticates" the most diverse human experiences by marking them with a seal of religious and cultural identity. In other words, what is essential according to this vision is neither the creed nor the circumstantial cultural practices, but the mobile relationship between the two, which oscillates like a "water dancer". For the French sociologist, it is actually this very relationship that defines Islam, and opens Islam to change by defining it. It goes without saying that this scheme of an ever-moving "authentic" dialectics is in complete contrast with the essence of Massignonian spiritual authenticity, or *ihsān*, which presupposes on the contrary the heroic "fixity" of a vow and an oath that leave no room for any "dance".

\*

\*  \*

In Massignon's work, scientific and technological modernity appears as one of the final consequences in the unfolding of the Fall. In following the gradually accelerated development of the fragmentation that ensues from the latter, Massignon's analysis of the modern world unveils an ontological and epistemological "schizophrenia" that characterises the "post-Christian" West:

> To the Promethean spirit giving rise to *a separated and separat-ing science* there corresponds the birth of a modern economy which is about to conquer the world through the disintegrat-ing abstraction of money.[39]

Since the end of the Middle Ages and the beginning of the Renaissance, a new understanding and practice of science has been separated from the spiritual vision which heretofore had been a product of the intellective realisation of the message of Revelation. Science built up more and more as a self-enclosed, independent domain, a kind of seed of alienation within the Christian world. Separated from the homogeneous world of the traditional Christian vision, it is also "separating" in the sense that it isolates the phenomena it studies from the universal reality within which they derive meaning, that is a *cosmos* filled with divine intelligibility, and cut them asunder from the single Reality that constitutes their principle of conception and existentiation. The shaping of *homo oeconomicus*, or in fact the *homo aequalis* studied by Louis Dumont,[40] is based on a similar schizoid departure. Economics becomes a separate, independent and all-powerful domain, as though endowed with a kind of extra-territoriality; it also stands as the basis of a new vision of reality which isolates the interests of finance and banking from the spiritual and moral principles which should normally contain and

---

[39] 'L'avenir de la science," (1946), *OM III*, p. 792.

[40] *Homo aequalis: genèse et épanouissement de l'idéologie économique*, Paris, 1977.

constrain them. For Massignon, it is the great merit of Islam to have embodied a religious resistance to the idea of the "intrinsic fecundity of money".[41] In this context, Massignon sees in the last Crusades the manifestation of a clear tendency toward religious compartmentalisation that would but lead to an asphyxiation of the spiritual conscience that had animated the original venture.[42] Henceforth, modern times can only be conceived as the "precipitation" of these centrifugal tendencies. Massignon highlights four moments in this fall: the Reformation, Cartesianism, Kantism, and the historical dialectics of Hegel, soon followed by that of Marx. Let us note that the terms used by Massignon to describe the effects of this quadruple rupture that demonstrate an exponential intensification all suggest a separation between man and God: "digging a ditch", "dissociating", "separating", "delimited subject". The first moment of this involution, the Reformation—as well as its effects upon the spiritual climate of the Roman Church—contributed to "digging a first ditch between man and the incarnated and glorious Word".[43] It is probable that Massignon allusively aims at two concomitant phenomena, in other words, a relative dilution of the sacramental economy and a "privatisation" of piety. The reference to the mystery of the glory of Christ suggests that Massignon understands the Reformation as having fostered a sense of distance from the triumphant Presence of Christ, thus opening the way to a kind of Jansenist withdrawal from within a world deprived of the sacramental light of the Kingdom. On the epistemological plane, this separation is confirmed and amplified by the Cartesian di-

---

[41] "Islam has always condemned interest and usury and, in the code of corporations, it is clearly specified that it is the right price and not the spirit of competition that must rule." "Les corps de métiers et la cité islamique," (1920), *OM I*, p. 378.

[42] "Parallel to this, in the order of facts, following the profane crusade that destroyed Constantinople, the crusade of Frederic II in the first half of the thirteenth century, in contrast to the pure enthusiasm of popular faith that characterised the first crusade, degenerated into an equivocal enterprise ... And it only took a century and a half to transform the Order of the Templars into an association of bankers." *Ibid.*, p. 791.

[43] *Ibid.*, p. 792.

chotomy between *res extensa* and *res cogitans*. On this point, Massignon takes up the Pascalian argument concerning the "useless and uncertain" character of Descartes, his surreptitious substitution of the God of Abraham and Isaac with a rationally-founded Deity whose function is reduced to that of the famous "flick". The God of Massignon is a "Living God" and not a "mathematician Creator". The ethical consequences of the Cartesian divorce between matter and spirit—an ontological scission which makes out of man a mysteriously two-fold creature whose unity hangs on a hypothetical "pineal gland"—come out more clearly in Kantian criticism and the principles of his practical reason. Kant's "delimited subject", deprived of any intellective opening onto the God of the prophets and mystics can only envisage moral life as being suspended by the categorical imperatives of a reason that makes itself autonomous, distinct from any revealed source. Thus, Kant's practical reason functions on its own level as Descartes' "mathematician God". Such rational abstractions—under the pretext of basing all metaphysics and ethics on pure reason—end up secularising and "naturalising" the principles of people's lives, thus laying the ground—without ever suspecting it, since they still postulate the universality of reason—for the individualist relativism of the twentieth century. Kant's "autonomised" subject then goes through the "grinding" of the Hegelian Absolute Spirit, "then through Marx's 'social Man', the latter being a pure object of economic determinism". An illusory individual autonomy founded on a reason truncated from its "supernaturally natural"[44] intellective dimension is succeeded by an illusory universalism of the Spirit, and then of matter. This historical devolution contributes, according to Massignon's analysis, to a double alienation: separated from God and from his natural vocation, man is also "uprooted from the earth" since he no longer realises his function but in the artificial and abstract world of sciences and technologies, as well as their innumerable and spiritually vain products. This historical drama reproduces indeed the transgression illustrated by the myth of the "old tree from Paradise"; not only as an excessive

---

[44] The expression is Frithjof Schuon's.

and displaced curiosity for knowledge, but also as a dualist and fragmentary apprehension of the real, a preference for phenomenal limitation over noumenal totality. This choice then gives rise to the creation of an "underground of darkness ... on the margin of the 'liturgical cosmos'".

If one keeps to his analyses of the symptoms of the "*mal contemporain*" (contemporary malaise), Massignon's thought is likely to be branded with a label of "apocalyptic" pessimism. Massignon was quite aware of it, and he actually made explicit note of it on the occasion of a speech by Emmanuel Mounier[45] given at the inaugurating conference of UNESCO at the University of Paris-Sorbonne. Mounier's critique, which was aimed at Massignon among others, amounted to warning Christians against what he conceived as the dangers of a prophetic exclusivism closed to the half-divine half-natural evolutionist providence revealing itself in the ascending trajectory of the sciences and technology "*en plein mouvement linéaire à travers l'espace d'un destin indéfiniment ouvert* (in full linear motion through the space of an indefinitely open destiny)".[46] Mounier seems to suggest that Massignon's "traditional" vision is paradoxically at odds with the Christian concept by reproducing the self-enclosure of the cyclical model of Greek thought.[47] In parallel to Teilhard de Chardin's evolutionist concepts, Mounier highlights the primacy of the "dynamic" concept of reality that the Second Vatican Council would place at the centre of its apostolic philosophy. To these critiques originating in ideological perspectives that interpret Christianity in terms of a modern vision, Massignon's responses are two. They come down to two lapidary formulae: death is needed for life, and salvation comes from within. Mas-

---

[45] Mounier (1905-1950) was a Catholic philosopher and the main figure of the so-called French Personalist movement. He argued for a Catholic engagement in politico-social life, and his work was one of the main inspirations in the Catholic Worker movement.

[46] "Un nouveau sacral," *OM III*, p. 798.

[47] "Et il suppose que notre primat de la revelation, de l'absolu, du transcendant, nous emprisonne dans l'universe sphérique de la science antique." *Ibid.*

signon calls for "apocalyptic" suffering insofar as the latter is a condition *sine qua non* for resurrection. Any religious perspective worthy of this name always ends up treating human realisations—however noble they may be—"*ut palea*".[48] But this aspect is ultimately only extrinsic, marked as it is by inherent limitations, the scar of relativity: the essential is that "the Kingdom of God is within you,"[49] thus rendering futile and dangerous the temptations of a global, externalised realisation of the Good through the inextricable—and intrinsically tyrannical—engineering web of metaphysical illusion.

---

[48] "Like chaff", to make use of Aquinas' reported evaluation of his own theological writings in the light of what must have been a very deep spiritual experience. "As for the misguided experiences, if we are reproached for our "apocalyptic" pessimism with respect to their cosmic consequences, we suffer them, and want to suffer them with their responsible authors, in order that they uncover in solidarity with us, the secret vice, and the means to cure it, intellectually and morally, before the present world dies, for one must be dead to be resurrected, and we are all condemned to death, and the "chaff" of our systems will burn, once the good wheat has been harvested and stored up by Angels on high." *Ibid.*, p. 802.

[49] "Et cet appel de Dieu ne retentit pas dans ce dirigisme humaniste opérant du dehors, mais dans le silence de l'âme qui souffre de compassion; cette voix surintelligible ne viole pas la conscience, elle s'y introduit 'januis clausis', comme le Verbe dans la Vierge, comme la resurrection dans le tombeau (And this call from God does not echo in a humanistic dirigism operating from outside, but in the silence of a soul suffering from compassion; this superintelligible voice does not do violence to one's conscience, where it introduces itself *januis clausis* [behind closed doors], as the Word in the Virgin, as the resurrection within the tomb)." *Ibid.*, p. 800.

# CONCLUSION

Massignon's work does not flow as much from thought as it does from experience, or from an array of converging experiences, the result of a "breakthrough" or "springing forth", to use two key terms of his vocabulary. For him, academic research and findings can never be separated from existential orientations that give them a new life, a new height. Furthermore, this is also why Massignon's work has remained somewhat unsettling in the academic world: he is readily suspected of transforming and finally betraying the objects of his study by turning them covertly into objects of his desire, or a mirror of himself. His mystical "subjectivism" cannot but "disturb" and "puzzle" the illusions of scientific objectivity of many, because his critical approach grasps the forms of the spirit from the point of view of the experience which has placed them in his way and which, therefore, guided him towards an intimate goal. From this point of view the criticisms levelled at him often result from an incapacity to intimate the gap between a conscientious analyst and a spiritual "visionary". In his case, there are, properly speaking, not objects as such, but rather encounters of a subject and an object, welcoming postures, de-centring self-abandonment, desires, commotions, consents.

Given its dependence on personal experience—and on the collective experience with which it converges—Massignon's thought tends towards universality by integrating the various aspects of the desire for God, but it remains basically incapable of—and basically little concerned with—resolving theological dilemmas and oppositions on a doctrinal and intellectual plane, inasmuch as it tends to "outclass" them by a *lex orandi*, a contemplative, inner way. Thus, it reaches universality in spiritual action, rather than in conceptual crystallisation. It always testifies to an effort to remain within its own religious and dogmatic fold while striving towards a mystical inclusion of otherness within the dynamics of a desire for God. Only this desire universalises and immortalises; it is a fire burning under the glow of a secret vow, when it is not, in addition, the crackling fire of martyrdom.

Fire is not just a metaphor of mystical passion; it is in a sense the very "reality" of the Absolute, the language of witnessing to It, and that of Justice that draws its paths. There is actually nothing, for Massignon, but the *hic et nunc* of the divine Fire which consumes all that is not "harvested and stored up by the Angels", everything in us that is not immortalised in the acceptance of inner poverty and prayer. Every instant is a judgment by fire, the metaphysical and mystical ordeal of a Presence that alone *is*, truly.

# SELECTED BIBLIOGRAPHY

## WORKS BY LOUIS MASSIGNON

*Passion of Al-Hallaj: Mystic and Martyr of Islam* (Bollingen Series, 98), Princeton: Princeton University Press, 1986.

*Essay on the Origins of the Technical Language of Islamic Mysticism*, Notre Dame, IN: University of Notre Dame Press, 1997.

*Kitāb al Tawwasin*, Albany, NY: Bibliolife, 2009.

*Akhbār al-Hallāj*, Paris: Librairie Philosophique J. Vrin, 1957.

*Ecrits Mémorables, tome 1*, Robert Laffont, Paris, 2009.

*Ecrits Mémorables, tome 2*, Robert Laffont, Paris 2009.

*Essays on the Origins of the Technical Language of Islamic Mysticism*, translated by Benjamin Clark, Notre Dame, IN: University of Notre Dame Press, 1994.

*Hallaj: Mystic and Martyr*, translated, edited and abridged by H. Mason, Princeton, NJ: Princeton University Press, 1994.

*La guerre sainte suprême de l'islam arabe*, Paris: Fata Morgana, 1998.

*La Passion de Hallaj: Martyr Mystique de L'Islam*, Paris: Gallimard, 1975.

*Le Diwan D'Al-Hallaj*, Paris: Librairie Orientaliste Paul Geuthner, 1955.

*Les allusions instigatrices—Les méthodes de réalisation artistique des peuples de l'Islam—Introspection et retrospection—Sur l'origine de la miniature persane*, Paris: Fata Morgana, 2000.

*Les Sept Dormants d'Ephèse en Islam et en Chrétienté*, Paris: Librairie Orientaliste Paul Geuthner, 1955.

*Les trois prières d'Abraham*, Paris: Le Cerf, 1997.

*Opera Minora, 4 vols.*, Collected texts presented by Y. Moubaraq, Beirut: Dar Al-Maaref, 1963.

*Parole donnée*, Paris: Le Seuil, 1983.

*Sur L'Islam*, Paris: L'Herne, 1995.

*The Passion of al-Hallaj: Mystic and Martyr*, translated by H. Mason, Princeton, NJ: Princeton University Press, 1983.

*Testimonies and Reflections: Essays of Louis Massignon*, Selected and Introduced by H. Mason, Notre Dame, IN: University of Notre Dame Press, 1989.

## SELECTED BIBLIOGRAPHY

Augé, Marc, *Non-Places: Introduction to an Anthropology of Supermodernity*, tr. John Howe, London and New York: Verso, 1995.

Armstrong, R.J., Hellman, J.A.W., and Short, W.J., eds., *Francis of Assisi: Early Documents, Volume I: The Saint*, Hyde Park, NY: New City Press, 1999, p. 395.

Basetti-Sani, Giulio, *Louis Massignon orientalista cristiano*, Milano, 1971.

Bloy, Leon, *Celle Qui Pleure: Notre Dame De La Salette* (1908) (French Edition), New York: Kessinger Publishing, 2010.

Buck, Dorothy C., *Dialogues With Saints and Mystics: In the Spirit of Louis Massignon*. New York: Khaniqahi Nimatullahi Publications, 2002.

Cleef, Jabez L. Van, *The Tawasin of Mansur al-Hallaj: A Mystical Sufi Treatise Interpreted in Poetry (Voices of World Religions)*, 1st ed. MP3: Spirit Song Text Publications, 2008.

Destremau, Christian & Jean Moncelon, *Louis Massignon*, Paris: Plon, 1994.

Deutsch, Bernard Francis, *Our Lady of Ephesus*, 1st ed., New York: Bruce Publishing Company, 1965.

Drevet, Camille, (ed.), *Massignon et Gandhi, la contagion de la vérité*, Paris: Le Cerf, 1967.

Ellsberg, Robert & Charles De Foucauld, *Charles De Foucauld: Writings (Modern Spiritual Masters Series)*, Maryknoll, New York: Orbis Books, 1999.

Foucauld, Charles de & Jean-Francois Six, *The Spiritual Autobiography of Charles De Foucauld*, 1st ed., Santa Fe: Word Among Us Press, 2003.

Fraser, Antonia, *Marie Antoinette: The Journey*, New York: Anchor, 2002.

Gardet, Louis & G. Anawati, *Mystique musulmane*, Paris: Vrin, 1961.

Gude, Mary Louise, *Louis Massignon: The Crucible of Compassion*, Notre Dame, IN: University of Notre Dame Press, 1997.

Harpigny, Guy, *Islam et Chritianisme selon Louis Massignon*, Louvain-la-Neuve: L'Université Catholique de Louvain-la-Neuve, 1981.

Keryell, Jacques, *L'Hospitalité sacré*, Paris: Nouvelle Cité, 1987.

_____, *Jardin donné*, Paris: St. Paul, 1993.

_____, *Louis Massignon et ses contemporains*, Paris: Karthala, 1997.

_____, *Louis Massignon au cœur de notre temps*, Paris: Karthala, 1999.

Laude, Patrick, *Pathways to an Inner Islam: Massignon, Corbin, Guénon, and Schuon.* Albany, New York: SUNY Press, 2010.

Mason, Herbert, *Death of Al Hallaj: Theology*, Notre Dame, IN: University of Notre Dame Press, 1991.

_____, *Memoir of a Friend: Louis Massignon*, Notre Dame, IN: University of Notre Dame Press, 1988.

_____, (tr.), *The Passion of al-Hallaj*, Princeton: Princeton University Press, 1982.

_____, (tr.), *Testimonies and Reflections: Essays of Louis Massignon*, Notre Dame, IN: University of Notre Dame Press, 1989.

Nasr, Seyyed Hossein, *Traditional Islam in the Modern World*, Albany: SUNY Press, 1990.

Rials, Stephane, *Le legitimisme (Que sais-je?)*, 1st ed., Paris: Presses Universitaires de France, 1983.

Rocalve, Pierre, *Louis Massignon et l'islam*, Damascus: Institut Français de Damas, 1993.

Schuon, Frithjof, *The Transcendent Unity of Religions*, Wheaton, IL: Quest Books, 1984.

Six, Jean-François, (ed.), *Louis Massignon*, Paris: Cahiers de l'Herne n. 13, 1972.

Smedt, Marc de, (ed.), *Louis Massignon: Mystique en dialogue*, Paris: Albin Michel, 1992.

Stétié, Salah & Gabriel Bounoure, *Louis Massignon*, Paris: Fata Morgana, 2008.

Watanabe, Yasutada, *Shinto art: Ise and Izumo shrines (The Heibonsha survey of Japanese art)*, 1st English ed., New York: Weatherhill/Heibonsha, 1974.

Yonge, Charles Duke, *The Life of Marie Antoinette, Queen of France*, Fq Books, 2010.

# TITLES IN THE MATHESON MONOGRAPHS